SICILIA NUTRIX PLEBIS ROMANAE

BULLETIN OF THE INSTITUTE OF CLASSICAL STUDIES SUPPLEMENT 97

GENERAL EDITOR: MIKE EDWARDS

MANAGING EDITOR: RICHARD SIMPSON

SICILIA NUTRIX PLEBIS ROMANAE

RHETORIC, LAW, AND TAXATION IN CICERO'S *VERRINES*

EDITED BY
J. R. W. PRAG

INSTITUTE OF CLASSICAL STUDIES
SCHOOL OF ADVANCED STUDY
UNIVERSITY OF LONDON

2007

The front cover image shows the reverse of a denarius of 71 BC: see note on p. vi.

BICS SUPPLEMENT 97

ISBN 978-1-905670-11-6

First published in 2007 by the Institute of Classical Studies,
School of Advanced Study, University of London,
Senate House, Malet Street, London WC1E 7HU.

Designed and computer typeset at the Institute of Classical Studies.

Printed by Short Run Press Limited, Bittern Road, Exeter EX2 7LW.

TABLE OF CONTENTS

THE COVER IMAGE: A NOTE ON THE *DENARIUS* OF 71 BC (*RRC* 401/1)

Full discussion of this coin (and the Aquilii) must be reserved for another place, but its potential relevance to Cicero's *Verrines* deserves comment. The exact date of issue is uncertain, but 71 or 70 BC seems most likely (see *RRC*, pp. 83, 86, preferring 71 BC; dates between 72 and 54 have previously been suggested). The exact relationship of the moneyer (*RE* 9), who is not otherwise known, to the other known Aquilii is also not certain; he may be the grandson of the M'. Aquilius (cos. 101, *RE* 11) alluded to on the coin. Both obverse (bust of *Virtus*) and reverse (Roman soldier raising *Sicilia* from the ground) refer to the ending of the Second Slave War by M'. Aquilius in 100/99 BC (DS 36.10; Liv. *Per.* 69; Flor. *Epit.* 2.7). Only two previous writers have suggested a connection with the trial: H. Zehnacker, *Moneta* (BEFAR 222, Rome 1973), I, 591-92 and W. Hollstein, *Die stadtrömische Münzprägung der Jahre 78-50 v. Chr.* (Munich 1993), 110-11. Both note that there is a clear message of Roman solicitude for the provinces, and one which stands in stark contrast to the actions of Verres. Such solicitude was itself highly self-interested, as Cicero's praise of Sicily in the *Verrines* makes clear (Cic. *Ver.* 2.5: *Itaque ille M. Cato Sapiens cellam penariam rei publicae nostrae, nutricem plebis Romanae Siciliam nominabat* – 'Cato Sapiens called Sicily in consequence the nation's storehouse, the nurse at whose breast the Roman people is fed' – whence our title).

However, an alternative reading is also possible. Cicero himself refers at length to the prosecution of M'. Aquilius in 98/97 BC in the final *Verrine* (Cic. *Ver.* 5.3-14; M. C. Alexander, *Trials in the Late Roman Republic* (Toronto 1990), no. 84). His reason for doing so is to subvert the notional defence of Verres by Hortensius. M. Antonius famously won Aquilius's acquital on the grounds of his brave defence of the *imperium Romanum* in Sicily (Cic. *de Orat.* 2.194-96; *Flac.* 98) – he defeated the slave leader Athenion in single combat, Antonius displaying his wounds at the trial, whence the bust of *Virtus* on the coin. Cicero scornfully asks Verres (*Ver.* 5.5), *Quid dicis? an bello fugitiuorum Siciliam uirtute tua liberatam?* – 'What are you going to say? That Sicily was liberated from a slave war by your *uirtus*?' The coin may simply show Aquilius's family stressing 'his earlier *aristeia* in view of his disastrous failure in the first war of the Romans against King Mithradates VI of Pontus' (in 88 BC; so E. W. Gray in *The Proceedings of the Xth International Congress of Classical Archaeology* (Ankara 1978), II, 965). But, it is perhaps not wholly fanciful to suggest, especially if the coin were minted in 71, when, as Hollstein noted, the first skirmishes of the future trial of Verres were already underway, that the coin represents not the Ciceronian attack, but the intended Hortensian defence – Verres as the new Aquilius, alongside Pompey and Crassus. Cicero can scoff at the idea (*Ver.* 5.5), but he does so in victory, and we should not presume that it was so one-sided before the *Verrines* were composed and published.

JRWP

ABBREVIATIONS

References to Greek and Latin texts in general follow the abbreviations of the *Oxford Latin Dictionary* (ed. P. G. W. Glare, Oxford 1982) and the *Greek-English lexicon* (ed. H. G. Liddell and R. Scott, revised H. S. Jones, 9th edn, Oxford 1940).

Note in particular that references to Cicero's *Verrines* follow the practice of the *OLD*, viz. the *Actio prima* is referred to in the form Cic. *Ver.* 00, where the numeral is the chapter number, while speeches of the *Actio secunda* are referred to in the form Cic. *Ver.* 0.00, where the first numeral is the number of the speech within the *Actio secunda*, the second the chapter number within the speech.

Journals are referred to in the bibliography after the fashion of *L'Année philologique*.

The following abbreviations are also employed:

ANRW	Temporini, H. (ed.). 1972-. *Aufstieg und Niedergang der römischen Welt* (Berlin)
FGrHist	Jacoby, F. 1923-. *Die Fragmente der griechischen Historiker* (Berlin)
*FIRA*²	Riccobono, S. 1940-41 (2nd edn). *Fontes Iuris Romani Anteiustiniani*, 2 vols (Florence)
IGDS	Dubois, L. 1989. *Inscriptions grecques dialectales de Sicile, CEFR* 119 (Rome)
IGSI	Arangio-Ruiz, V. & A. Olivieri. 1925. *Inscriptiones graecae Siciliae et infimae Italiae ad ius pertinentes* (Milan)
MRR	Broughton, T. R. S. 1951-86. *The magistrates of the Roman Republic*, 3 vols (New York, Atlanta)
*ORF*³	Malcovati, H. 1953 (3rd edn). *Oratorum Romanorum Fragmenta liberae rei publicae* (Turin)
RE	Pauly, A. F., G. Wissowa, W. Kroll, *et al.* (eds). 1894-. *Paulys Real-Encyclopädie der classischen Altertumswissenschaft* (Stuttgart)
RRC	Crawford, M. H. 1974. *Roman Republican coinage*, 2 vols (Cambridge)
RS	Crawford, M. H. (ed.). 1996. *Roman Statutes*, 2 vols, BICS Suppl. 64 (London)
SB	Shackleton Bailey, *i.e.* Cicero letters in the reordered sequence of the editions published by D. R. Shacketon Bailey.

Map of Sicily

The map indicates the locations of a) places referred to in the *de Frumento* (Cic. *Ver.* 3), and b) other places in Sicily referred to in the course of this volume. Place names are normally given in their Latin form. Note that some of the identifications remain disputed.

For a detailed map of ancient Sicily, including physical geography and an accompanying gazzette, see Map 47 (R. J. A. Wilson), in the *Barrington atlas of the Greek and Roman world* (ed. R. J. A. Talbert, Princeton NJ, 2000).

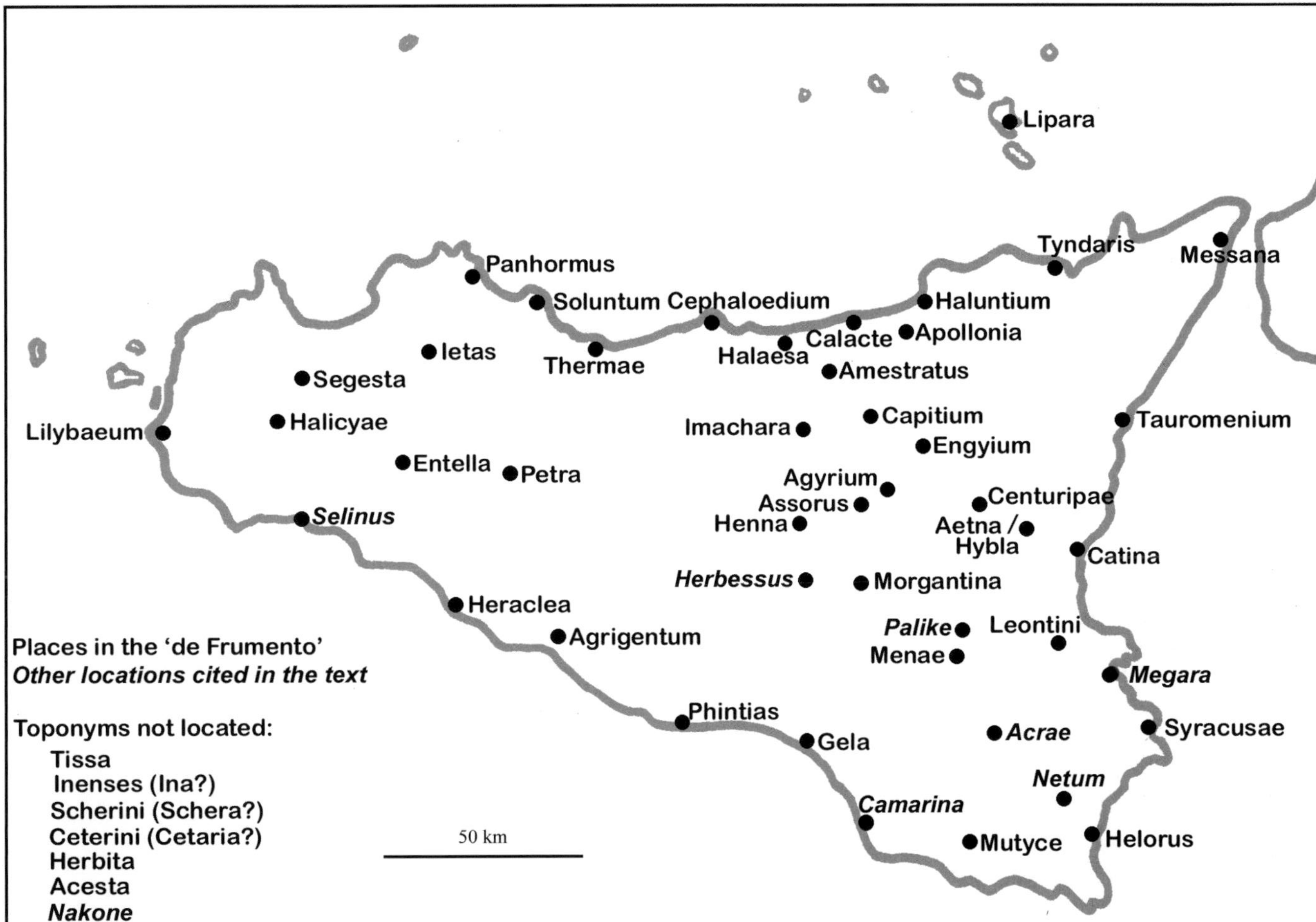
Lipara
Tyndaris
Messana
Panhormus
Soluntum
Cephaloedium
Haluntium
Calacte
Apollonia
Halaesa
Amestratus
Ietas
Thermae
Segesta
Halicyae
Lilybaeum
Imachara
Capitium
Engyium
Tauromenium
Entella
Petra
Agyrium
Assorus
Henna
Centuripae
Aetna / Hybla
Catina
Selinus
Herbessus
Morgantina
Heraclea
Agrigentum
Palike
Menae
Leontini
Megara
Phintias
Gela
Acrae
Syracusae
Netum
Camarina
Mutyce
Helorus
50 km
Places in the 'de Frumento'
Other locations cited in the text
Toponyms not located:
Tissa
Inenses (Ina?)
Scherini (Schera?)
Ceterini (Cetaria?)
Herbita
Acesta
Nakone

INTRODUCTION

The *Verrines* present a peculiar challenge to the ancient historian. The seven speeches (including the *Diuinatio in Caecilium*) constitute almost a quarter of all surviving Ciceronian oratory, some 400 pages in the *Oxford Classical Text.* Yet the majority of the speeches, the entire *Actio secunda*, were never delivered in court.[1] Furthermore, the *Verrines* are the only surviving example of a prosecution speech (from either Cicero, or the Republic as a whole) and, by virture of their non-delivery, we lack any clear indication of the response which the defence might have offered. Reading the *Verrines* as a historical source is therefore an activity fraught with difficulty. At the same time, the *Verrines* are a uniquely rich source of information on Republican provincial administration.[2] The challenge, which the papers in this volume confront, is how to read these speeches and to use them as evidence for matters of law, taxation, or provincial government.

The *Verrines* themselves are remarkably understudied. The relatively few modern commentaries are aimed at school or university students, although a full historical and archaeological commentary of the *de Signis* has recently appeared.[3] They are not of course unstudied, but much of the best recent work on the *Verrines* has focused either upon rhetoric, or upon the information which they purport to offer on Sicily, provincial government, and the *repetundae* process. The majority of the papers presented here bridge the gap between rhetoric and history, meeting head-on the question of the extent to which Cicero's rhetoric enables, or confounds our ability to extract 'historical fact' from the speeches. Indeed, it is a recurring theme across these papers that Cicero's tactics and rhetoric all too often confuse the issue, instead of clarifying.

The rhetorical strategies and devices of the *Verrines* have come in for considerable study in recent years, often alongside the various defence speeches in cases *de repetundis* published by Cicero: Ann Vasaly, Rita Scuderi, and Catherine Steel, among others, have illuminated the

1 See most recently Frazel (2004). The best general introduction is Vasaly (2002), with Marinone (1949), (1950).

2 *Cf.* Brunt (1980) 287: 'the *Verrines* are of great value to us as a source of information on Roman provincial government, and for their incidental allusions to the political issues at stake in 70.' The word 'incidental' should be stressed.

3 To the best of my knowledge, the complete commentary of George Long (1862), now severely outdated, remains the only significant modern commentary on the *de Frumento* (*Ver.* 3). Commentaries on individual speeches of the *Verrines* include Levens (1946) on *Ver.* 5, Mitchell (1986) on *Ver.* 1, and Dickison (1992) on *Ver.* 4. On the *de Signis* (*Ver.* 4), see now Lazzeretti (2006).

ways in which Cicero presents Verres, and the Sicilians, to his own advantage;[4] detailed studies of specific episodes also exist.[5]

The first three papers presented here are all concerned with the question of Cicero's rhetorical strategy. Andrew Lintott's paper combines a survey of the chronology of the trial with Cicero's overall strategy, before moving on to Cicero's specific tactics. In doing so, he elucidates the role of Cicero's many witnesses, something which has not previously been the focus of attention. Lintott's paper opens the way to Kathryn Tempest's evaluation of Cicero's rhetorical strategy from the perspective of rhetorical technique. Tempest makes a virtue of the speeches' lack of comparability, emphasizing their purpose of prosecution. In doing so, she adds an important further element to the existing studies, elucidating the clear Attic antecedents to Cicero's oratory.

Catherine Steel then focuses specifically on the 'boringly repetitive' *de Frumento*, which lies at the heart of the *Actio secunda*, and of this volume. The *de Frumento*, longest of the speeches, is devoted entirely to Verres' activites in relation to the Sicilian grain harvest and the associated exactions by the Roman state. The speech is central to much of the study of both Republican Sicily's organization and Republican *frumentatio*,[6] as well as being important for the light which it sheds on the provincial governor's edict, and legal administration in the provinces.[7] The modern starting point, and the closest thing to a commentary on the speech, is Jérôme Carcopino's *La loi de Hiéron et les Romains* (1919). However, that study, like most of those which have followed, pays much less heed to the rhetoric, and much more to points of law and taxation. Steel's paper offers the first rhetorical analysis of the speech. Like Tempest, Steel never lets us forget that Cicero's purpose was condemnation, and she brings out sharply the way in which Cicero overcomes the problem that Verres' own defence would have lain in an appeal to the interests of the *populus Romanus*. To do this, Steel argues, Cicero creates an image of lucidity – but an image alone. Cicero's object is to render it difficult to explain what occurred in Sicily in any way other than his own. It is precisely that rhetorical strategy which makes our own task as historians that much more difficult.

This evaluation is complemented and developed in detail by Sylvie Pittia, in a paper which examines the numerical data which Cicero presents, in particular in the *de Frumento*. Pittia's comprehensive study tackles the philological and palaeographical difficulties which numerals present, as well as the common modern responses to this data, such as its inventorizing, or its use in attempts at economic or cliometric history.[8] Steel's paper has already suggested why such number-games might be risky; Pittia, adopting a cautiously agnostic stance on the numerals' inherent validity, takes us a step farther, challenging us to consider why a number (inherently problematic as any numeral in the manuscript tradition may be) is included by

4 Vasaly (1993), Scuderi (1994), (1996), Steel (2001); see also Fuhrmann (1980), Ochs (1982), Innocenti (1994).

5 Recent examples: Nisbet (1992), Steel (2004).

6 See, *e.g.*, Calderone (1964-65), Pritchard (1969), (1970), (1971), (1972), (1975), Rickman (1980), Pinzone (1999), and Soraci (2003).

7 Mellano (1977), Genovese (1999); also the classic article by S. Mazzarino (1961).

8 Inventorized by Scramuzza (1937); cliometric use, *e.g.*, Brunt (1987) 376-82, Pritchard (1972), Garnsey & Saller (1987) 80.

Cicero in the first place. The very use of numbers is, she suggests, a rhetorical strategy, and she explores the range of tactics employed in this specific aspect of rhetoric. Not only does this study bring out an important dimension of Cicero's skill; it also casts serious doubt on earlier attempts to infer land-holding patterns in Republican Sicily.[9]

Jean Andreau confronts another aspect of the *Verrines*, and the *de Frumento* in particular, namely the use of documentary evidence, which has recently been the subject of an extended study, within a broader Ciceronian context, by Shane Butler.[10] Steel's observation regarding Ciceronian obfuscation is echoed once again: Andreau shows that Cicero capitalizes on the lack of a rich technical vocabulary to describe multiple categories of documents, while Cicero's rhetorical object of prosecution means that he has little interest in the niceties of Sicilian ethnographic detail (*e.g.* the non-descript *Siculus magistratus*, for which see Bell's paper also). While putting flesh upon the bare bones of Cicero's allusions to the falsification of documents, Andreau also brings out what such material reveals about Cicero's rhetorical method.

Moving to the specifically legal sphere, Julien Dubouloz, in a careful analysis of Verres' behaviour in granting *iudices* and *recuperatores* in the course of his legal administration of Sicily, neatly demonstrates that we learn more about the importance of the inclusion of material concerning judicial practice in the construction of an accusation than we do about Verres' actual judicial actions. A great many of the legal scenarios which Cicero presents are in fact heavily coloured by moral and political elements: Verres' violence and intimidation mean that all too rarely do matters reach the point where Verres might actually transgress the letter of the law. Cicero can, and does make considerable capital out of the very ambiguous position of the lone provincial governor with *imperium*. As in the preceding papers, Dubouloz has a clear methodological message of warning for those seeking, in this instance, to write strict legal history from a text like the *Verrines*. Numbers, documents, legal cases, all are present in the *Verrines* first and foremost for their rhetorical value; statistical accuracy, lucid explanation, ethnographic detail all take second place to the strategy of the accusation.

The limitations of mining the *Verrines* for historical material on Republican Sicily are given a different twist in Malcolm Bell III's suggestive presentation of the physical reality behind Cicero's vignettes of extortion in the *ciuitates* of Sicily. Accounts of the Republican province are few, and accounts of life in the province even fewer, and often driven by, or limited to the material in the *Verrines*.[11] Bell's picture of Ciceronian Morgantina is a stimulating dialogue between archaeology and literature, which complements very effectively the recent archaeological survey of Ciceronian Sicily by Roger Wilson.[12] Neither archaeology, nor Cicero can be expected to act as direct controls upon each other, but a richer picture emerges from the use of the two together.

9 Coarelli (1981) is merely one recent example of a tendency which goes back to Carcopino (1919) and beyond. See also Manganaro (1972), Vergbrugghe (1972), Mazza (1980-81).

10 Butler (2002) esp. 35-60.

11 A lucid account of the modern historiography of Republican Sicily, with bibliography, can be found in Campagna (2003). Note in particular Manganaro (1980) and Mazza (1980-81).

12 Wilson (2000).

Finally, Jérôme France explores what led our predecessor Jérôme Carcopino to produce the book which has so dominated study of Republican Sicily and in particular the *de Frumento* in the last century. This paper is an important addition to the growing body of material on the historiography of ancient Sicily.[13] At the same time, France paints a rich and illuminating picture of turn-of-the-century French scholarship, as well as the early stages of Carcopino's illustrious career. He concludes on a poignant note: the impact of the Great War upon a generation of French scholarship.

The papers in this volume represent all but one of those delivered at a two-day colloquium, held at the Institute of Classical Studies, 6-7 February 2004.[14] The meeting is one of several offshoots of a French, *CNRS*-sponsored commentary project, initiated by Jean Andreau, under the overall direction of Jean-Louis Ferrary, and of which the members are Jean Andreau, Julien Dubouloz, Jérôme France, Sylvie Pittia, and Jonathan Prag. The project will result in a new French translation of the *de Frumento*, with extensive commentary and a moderately revised text. The focus of this first conference, as will be apparent, was directed towards rhetorical aspects of the *Verrines*, and in particular the *de Frumento*, and how these affected various diverse aspects of our study. A second conference, 'La Sicile de Cicéron: regards croisés sur les *Verrines*', was held in Paris, 19-20 May 2006, at the Centre Glotz. This meeting tackled the subject of Sicily, in the light of the *Verrines*, and the resulting volume (J. Dubouloz and S. Pittia (eds), *La Sicile de Cicéron: lectures des Verrines* (Besançon 2007)) forms a larger companion piece to this one.

It is a pleasant duty to thank Michael Crawford and the Institute of Classical Studies for their support of the original conference; the Jowett Copyright Trustees for financial support of the conference itself; the Society for the Promotion of Roman Studies for financial support of the publication; Mike Leach for the index; and Richard Simpson for his assistance with and production of the publication itself. Finally, I must beg the forgiveness of all those whose work is presented here, since their own efforts in producing so promptly the research which is this volume's *raison d'être* have been very poorly rewarded by my own indolence. The papers published here were almost all submitted by early 2005, and the authors have been unable to incorporate more recent scholarship.

Jonathan R. W. Prag
Merton College, Oxford

13 See Momigliano (1984), La Rosa (1987), Salmeri (1992), de Angelis (1998), Ceserani (2000), Pinzone (2000), Giammellaro (2005).

14 The other paper, 'Political self-representation in the *Verrines*', was given by Ann Vasaly; for a flavour, readers are warmly recommended to her overview piece on the *Verrines* (2002) and her stimulating rhetorical study (1993).

THE CITADEL OF THE ALLIES

ANDREW LINTOTT

Cicero suggested in the speech with which he claimed the right to prosecute Verres (*Diuinatio in Caecilium*) that it was beyond doubt that the whole statute concerning the recovery of money (*de pecuniis repetundis*) was established for the sake of the allies: when money was seized from Roman citizens, this was generally pursued by civil action and private law (17-18). This somewhat misrepresents the legal position. It is true that a simplified private law action was available in the Gracchan statute – known to us from the fragments of the 'Tabula Bembina' – and we know of one private action in the 70s BC,[1] but this was not apparently confined to Roman citizen prosecutors. In fact even in the Gracchan statute, where prosecution was a matter for the injured parties or their delegated representatives, it appears that Roman citizens could prosecute under the main provisions of the law.[2] In the accusation of Verres, the complaints of Roman citizens in Sicily and elsewhere formed an important part of the prosecution case. Nevertheless, even if his premiss is dubious, Cicero's conclusion that 'this is the statute for the allies, this is the law of foreign nations, they have this as a citadel [...]' – a point reiterated in the later *Verrine* speeches – remains true. The court was the chief countervailing force against the all-powerful Roman magistrate and his companions in the military field and provincial government.[3]

I. The mounting of the prosecution

Cicero's involvement in the opposition to Verres began before the latter left his governorship. In 72 BC Sthenius of Thermae, a former guest-friend of Verres, became his enemy when he resisted the removal of bronze statues from his city and was consequently indicted, at Verres' instigation, for the corruption of public documents at Thermae. Verres decided to judge the case himself and Sthenius fled to Rome. The case was now made capital by Verres; the legitimacy of Sthenius being tried in his absence was discussed in the senate, but in the end Sthenius was condemned in his absence by Verres on 1 December of that year. His case was taken up by Lollius Palicanus, one of the tribunes who entered office on 10 December 72 BC. Subsequently, probably early in 71 BC, Cicero himself successfully defended Sthenius before this college of tribunes, who had to decide whether to apply to Sthenius their edict forbidding

1 *Lex rep.* (*RS* I no. 1) ll. 7-8; Asc. 84C.

2 This is implied in *lex rep.* ll. 22 and 76; l. 87 is best interpreted as providing rewards for Roman citizen prosecutors, as does the later statute partially preserved on the *fragmentum Tarentinum* (*RS* I no. 8 ll. 7-12).

3 Cic. *Diu. Caec.* 18; *cf. Ver.* 2.15, 3.218, 4.17.

anyone condemned on a capital charge residing in Rome.[4] Sthenius was to be one of Cicero's chief assistants from the province (*Ver.* 2.83) and it is clear that from this time onwards the orator was well briefed on Verres' offences.

Among Sthenius's former guests were Pompey and C. Marcellus, praetor in 80 BC and afterwards governor of Sicily.[5] Cicero never ascribes any direct interest in the case to Pompey and, whatever the great man's concern for his Sicilian clients – such as Sex. Pompeius Chlorus and Cn. Pompeius Theodorus (*Ver.* 2.23, 2.102) – he may not have wanted to involve himself openly in the controversy over Verres. It was different with the Claudii Marcelli, traditional patrons of Sicily. In the *Diuinatio in Caecilium* Cicero appeals to C. Marcellus and Cn. Cornelius Lentulus Marcellinus as witnesses to the pressure brought to bear on him by the injured Sicilians – the former was actually on the jury for the *diuinatio*, the latter is claimed by Cicero to be present (13-14). In the published second action of the main trial C. Marcellus is again invoked as a juror and Cicero appeals to him about the appropriate procedure for governors of the province (*Ver.* 4.90, 3.42, 3.212). As for Lentulus Marcellinus, he was a witness for Cicero in the first action (*Ver.* 2.103). The elder M. Marcellus (*aed.* 91 BC) had been himself treated unjustly by Verres as urban praetor in 74 BC, but was apparently not available as a witness. By contrast, Verres had sought to involve in his defence about a certain charge the young M. Marcellus Aeserninus – described by Cicero as 'a young man born to that (high) station, a patron of Sicily' – but the attempt had been futile.[6]

We have no reason to reject Cicero's picture of himself as the preferred accuser of Verres for a number of Sicilians and their patrons, one who had been sought after for some time before proceedings actually started.[7] This could not take place until Verres' return to Rome. The chronology of the early stages of the accusation cannot be fixed with complete precision, but, in the light of Cicero's comments on the chronology of the later procedure (see below), the first move can hardly be later than the middle of January 70 BC, the year when Pompey and Marcus Crassus had their first consulships and the praetor Manius Acilius Glabrio had been allotted the presidency of the *quaestio de repetundis* (*Ver.* 4, 51).

Under the procedure laid down in the Gracchan law, an accuser used to proceed immediately to formal denunciation (*nominis delatio*), whereupon, if the charge was accepted, he was offered a *patronus*, if he wished, and facilities to collect evidence in Italy. It seems to have been assumed that any witnesses from abroad had already arrived. Meanwhile, a process was set in motion for selecting the jury that involved a delay of over seventy days.[8] By the 90s BC a new form of procedure had been introduced that was still in force in the post-Sullan period. The prosecutor was selected by *diuinatio*. This meant that the summons (*postulare*) of the accused by an accuser was in a sense provisional, since he might not in fact be assigned the task of prosecution. Moreover, the usually Roman accuser was afforded, once selected,

4 Cic. *Ver.* 2.86-101 (Cicero's defence, 100).

5 Cic. *Ver.* 2.110; also C. Marius and L. Cornelius Sisenna.

6 Cic. *Ver.* 1.135, 1.143, 1.153; contrast 4.91.

7 The scepticism of Stroh (1975) 181ff. goes too far.

8 *Lex rep.* ll. 9-12, 19-24, 31.

an opportunity to conduct an *inquisitio*, that is an investigatory tour to collect evidence, abroad as well as in Italy.[9]

Cicero had a rival – Q. Caecilius Niger, a former quaestor of Verres, probably at Lilybaeum. He had been educated in Sicily and is alleged by Plutarch to have been a freedman and a judaizer.[10] He claimed to have been treated unjustly by Verres, but his quaestorship had involved a degree of cooperation with the governor and complicity in his acts, which provided Cicero with a useful argument against his being permitted to accuse.[11] Cicero could also argue that there was a quasi-parental connection between a governor and his quaestor, which made such an accusation an impiety: former quaestors had tried to accuse their governors but their claims had been rejected.[12] In fact we do not know of a case where a quaestor obtained the right to prosecute his governor under the Republic. The first, ill-omened example we have is that of Granius Marcellus by Caepio Crispinus under Tiberius.[13]

If we combine in a calculation first Cicero's statement that the trial had been postponed for three months, secondly the period allotted for his *inquisitio* (*Ver.* 1.30), and thirdly the actual trial date, 5 August 70 BC (*Ver.* 31), the *diuinatio* should have been over by the beginning of February. February was traditionally the climax of the period in which foreign embassies petitioned the senate, and some of the communities who later supported Cicero at the trial may have already sent delegations to Rome.[14] After success in the *diuinatio*, Cicero denounced Verres and asked for a period of 110 days for *inquisitio* (*Ver.* 1.30). At about the same time another prosecutor going to Achaea was awarded 108 days and was placed higher in the order of cases.

Cicero claims to have spent in fact only fifty days on his tour of Sicily (*Ver.* 6), where he was supported by his cousin Lucius, who was probably his *subscriptor*.[15] He also relates that he had made a hasty and dangerous return journey from Vibo Valentia up the toe of Italy to Velia, through the midst of the pirates (*Ver.* 2.99). Vibo was not a necessary stopping-place on his route back to Rome, but he must have gone there to collect evidence about P. Gavius of Consa whom Verres executed (*Ver.* 5.158ff.). The tour of Sicily and southern Italy provided him with a mass of documentary evidence and a great number of witnesses. Some of these were not used in the first action in August but deliberately deferred. In particular, he was supported by embassies from most of Sicily and from Vibo, Consa, and Regium in Italy (see below). Cicero also seems to have investigated at least one house of Verres in Italy, in search of the looted works of art and in order to collect witness statements. He claimed that he saw the pictures and statues taken from the Greek cities of the Aegean and Asia Minor in

9 Cic. *Scaur.* 23ff.; Asc. 19C, *cf.* Lintott (1992) 28-29.

10 Cic. *Diu. Caec.* 4, 39, 56; Plut. *Cic.* 7.6.

11 Cic. *Diu. Caec.* 29ff.; *cf. Ver.* 15.

12 Cic. *Diu. Caec.* 60-63 (impiety: 62; precedents: 63); on the dates of these precedents (and a problem of nomenclature) see Badian (1984).

13 Tac. *Ann.* 1.74. For an investigation of this quasi-parental relationship see Thompson (1962).

14 By a later *lex Gabinia* the senate's agenda in February was confined to hearing embassies until they had all been sent home (Cic. *Fam.* 1.4.1 = SB 14; *Q. fr.* 2.12(11).3 = SB 16).

15 Cic. *Ver.* 4.145; Ps. Asc. 213 St.

Verres' porticoes and in his ornamental grove: after the first part of the trial all but two were no longer there, but he planned to use the testimony of Verres' household about them.[16]

If we allow time for Cicero's journeys to and from Sicily, including the visit to Vibo, and for his pursuit of evidence in the neighbourhood of Rome, from Verres' house and from Romans wronged by Verres as urban praetor in 74 BC, then the total time he spent collecting evidence will not have been so far short of the 110 days he was granted. He would not have been ready to proceed to jury selection before early May – that is, assuming his Sicilian witnesses had arrived – and, had he then prosecuted, the trial would have coincided with the last two months of his candidature for the aedileship, which, as he admits, in the event considerably distracted him from preparing the case (*Ver.* 24). The problems he had in the management of the prosecution to a great extent resulted from the complexity of the case and his own pursuit of a magistracy.

Before Cicero's election as aedile in late July, probably earlier that month, the jury was selected.[17] Jury-panels under Sulla's *lex Cornelia* were no longer created according to the prescriptions of the Gracchan law, where the prosecutor, after being informed by the defendant of any members of the (non-senatorial) album who were connected with him, offered a hundred names of those unconnected by kinship or association with himself, which were in turn reduced to fifty by the defendant. The jurors now were allotted from the album, which consisted entirely of senators, and then subject to a process of rejection, probably alternately between prosecution and defence.[18] Cicero took the opportunity to make forensic capital out of this process, by alluding to Verres' bribery and suggesting that foreign embassies should go to the senate requesting the repeal of the *lex de repetundis*, since then Roman magistrates would only take what they needed for themselves and their families: at present they extorted extra money to pay their defence counsel and legal advisers and to bribe the presiding praetor and the jury.[19]

We have the names of a number of the jury: Q. Manlius, Q. Cornificius, P. Sulpicius, M. Crepereius, L. Cassius, Cn. Tremellius, M. Metellus (*Ver.* 30); M. Lucretius (*Ver.* 1.18); C. Marcellus (*Ver.* 4.90); and the consulars, Q. Lutatius Catulus (*Ver.* 4.69) and P. Servilius Isauricus (*Ver.* 4.82). An almost certain addition, although the text may be thought ambiguous, is L. Octavius Balbus.[20] Among the names rejected we have: P. Galba,

16 Cic. *Ver.* 1.50-51. For the phrase *obsignandi gratia*, referring to witness statements, see *Flac.* 21 (there the seals of the jury were required by the later *lex Iulia*); for the collection of evidence in Italy, see *lex rep.* l. 31.

17 Cic. *Ver.* 1.18-19; *cf. Ver.* 29-31.

18 See esp. Cic. *Ver.* 10, 16, 41, 1.17ff. For procedure under the Gracchan law, see *lex rep.* ll. 19-27.

19 Cic. *Ver.* 41, *cf.* 40 where he rehearses an alleged dictum of Verres, that he had allocated the profits of one year for himself, one for his *patroni* and defence counsel, and the third most profitable year for the jury.

20 Cic. *Ver.* 2.31. Here Balbus is referred to as a *iudex*, a learned and high-principled one, in a context where he is being also imagined as the judge appointed under one of Verres' tendentious formulae. Since the two other men named in the legal formula, Q. Catulus and P. Servilius, are also on the trial-jury, Cicero is clearly using three members of the jury as his examples. McDermott (1977) correctly counts the names mentioned in the text (eighteen), but develops a strained argument from a comparison with the trial of Oppianicus – where the voting jury numbered thirty-two (Cic. *Clu.* 74) – to the effect

Sex. Peducaeus, Q. Considius, Q. Iunius, P. Cervius, and the consular C. Cassius Longinus.[21] Cicero's statement that almost the whole jury would be changed the following year through the enforced resignation of seven members is an obvious exaggeration (*Ver.* 30), but it must be allowed vestigial plausibility. It is possible that the final panel contained no more than the twelve names we know and it is unlikely to have exceeded fifteen members. The jurors originally allotted to the panel were no less than eighteen and may have numbered considerably more.[22]

II. Strategy and timing

The trial proper began on 5 *Sextilis* (August), at the eighth hour – with most of that day already lost. As Cicero explains, there were then ten clear days before Pompey's votive games on 16 August, which effectively postponed further proceedings till 2 September. The *ludi Romani* followed, from 4 to 19 September. Verres, Cicero claims, did not expect to have to reply to the charge until after these games, after an interval of almost forty days.[23] After 19 September there were thirty-five days available (which, according to Cicero, Verres would have liked to eliminate) before the *ludi victoriae Sullae* on 26 October. These constituted the chief period remaining for the trial before the end of the year, since the *ludi victoriae Sullae* ended on 1 November and the *ludi plebeii* then followed from 4 to 17 November.[24]

Cicero accelerated the trial by using a brief speech in the first action and then calling his witnesses (*Ver.* 55, 1.25). After three days of hearing witnesses, he later alleged, their cumulative effect was so overwhelming that Verres effected an adjournment by pleading illness – probably a form of *intertium* adjournment to the third day, that is the day after next, since otherwise the first action would not have finished before Pompey's games.[25] We are in

that a *repetundae* trial required a greater number of jurors because of the greater *dignitas* of the defendants: he opts eventually for fifty. I would suggest that in the thinking of Sulla a senator would be better tried by a small jury of high calibre (including former curule magistrates) than by a large jury dominated by *parui senatores*.

21 Cic. *Ver.* 1.18, 3.97, 5.114. Cicero talks of a restriction of rejection (presumably for either side) to three potential jurors under the *leges Corneliae* (*Ver.* 2.77), but in the context this applies only to trials of non-senators. Senators, it is implied, were allowed more.

22 For the reduction by rejection of a panel of *recuperatores*, from forty-five to fifteen, see *lex prou. praet.* (*RS* I no. 12) Cnidos V ll. 6-22.

23 Cic. *Ver.* 31. The 'almost forty days' must be counted from 16 August onwards. Under the Republic *Sextilis* had twenty-nine days. I have counted the fifteen days eliminated by Pompey's games inclusively from 16 August.

24 Cic. *Ver.* 2.130, *Ver.* 31. In *Ver.* 2.130 I read 'XXXV', the reading of the fragments of the *uetus Cluniacensis*, which is an approximately accurate rendering of the time available. 'XXXXV' or 'XLV' in other manuscripts seems to be a repetition of the number of days in the extended intercalary month of Cephaloedium, mentioned in the previous sentence. There is no point in retaining this reading as a deliberate echo by Cicero as he would then be echoing an increase in time, not a subtraction.

25 Cic. *Ver.* 1.20; *cf. lex Irnitana* cc. 90-92; *cf. TPSulp*. 32-33 (Camodeca (1999) I 100-02 with earlier bibliography); Metzger (1997) 9ff.; Rodger (1996); Wolff (1997). Alexander (1976) 47 also interprets Cicero to mean a one-day interval.

fact told elsewhere that the first part of the trial before the *comperendinatio* was over in nine days (*Ver.* 1.156).

Hortensius contributed to the speed of the process by refraining for the most part from questioning Cicero's witnesses (*Ver.* 1.71, 3.41). We hear of only a few interventions. Hortensius interrupted Tettius's evidence about the trial of Philodamus of Lampsacus, pointing out that Philodamus and his son had been condemned; he also complained about Cicero's production of the boy Iunius in court during the evidence of his uncle and guardian M. Iunius: it was directed merely towards creating odium for Verres (*Ver.* 1.71, 1.151). In addition there was an exchange between the orators recorded by Quintilian (*Inst.* 6.3.98): while Cicero was examining a witness, Hortensius said to him, 'I do not understand these riddles'; 'You should do,' Cicero retorted, 'as you have a Sphinx at home' (a bronze Sphinx, a present from Verres). However, in general there is no reason to disbelieve Cicero that Hortensius, on the whole, gave his opponent's witnesses a clear run. Moreover, if he did not on the whole cross-examine, as Cicero alleges, it is hard to see how he could have argued at length in an *altercatio*. He did, nevertheless, have witnesses of his own, such as the embassy from Messana (*Ver.* 5.47; *cf.* 4.15), and he did deliver at the beginning of the trial an oration: a published version of Hortensius's speech for Verres was still available in Quintilian's time.[26]

After the first action Verres does not seem to have abandoned the case immediately. Cicero in fact portrays him as still in Rome, *comperendinatus*, that is with an adjourned trial hanging over him, on the morning of the circus day of the *ludi Romani* – the last day (19 September). He is said to have showed excessive interest in the silver displayed by his friend, the historian Sisenna, on that occasion.[27] Although the interpretation of the event may be Cicero's and only Cicero's, it is hard to imagine Cicero gratuitously inventing Verres' presence at Sisenna's home on that day. We must conclude that it only became clear that Verres had abandoned the case when the trial was due to restart at some point after 19 September.[28] Even in Verres' absence, it was not all over. The second action would have been a formality, but it would still have been necessary for the praetor presiding to pronounce a verdict of 'guilty', probably after consulting the jury. Moreover, the third part of the trial, the *litis aestimatio*, would still have been required to assess the damages due to the various plaintiffs.[29] The large number of these would have necessitated a long and complex process and it is easy to imagine the *litis aestimatio* lasting as many days as the first action.

26 Quint. *Inst.* 10.1.23; *cf.* Alexander (1976). Gelzer (1962-64) II 169 thought his speech might have occurred during the *litis aestimatio*, but we know nothing of formal speeches by advocates being held on this occasion. Note that Quintilian (*Inst.* 5.7.6) advised against cross-examining solid witnesses and Cicero himself admitted the dangers of cross-examination (*Font.* 22).

27 Cic. *Ver.* 4.33; *cf.* 1.20 for Verres being *comperendinatus* during 'these intervening days of games'. The chronology is correctly set out by Gelzer (1962-64) II 168-70; *cf.* Alexander (1976) 51-52.

28 His departure into exile is noted but not dated in the scholia to the speeches, Ps. Asc. 205, 223 St. See Gelzer (1962-64) II 168 n. 124 for a refutation of the view that the second action actually took place.

29 *Cf. lex rep.* l. 29 for the pursuit of charges when a man had gone into exile or (probably) died before the end of a trial. Mommsen, followed by Lintott (1992) 124, took the fragmentary text ([*ea*]*m rem ab eis item quaerito*[...]) to refer to the pursuit of money from connections of the accused; *RS* I 103 prefers investigation of the matter with the jury. Both would have in fact been necessary.

III. Tactics

The first *Verrine* is not so much a prosecution speech as an extended *prooemium*. The orator seeks to win sympathy for himself in the battle he is having with the money of Verres (*Ver.* 3-17, 22-23) and the authority of Hortensius and the Metelli (*Ver.* 18-37), and to secure in advance the support of both jury and presiding magistrate. The meat of the action was to be in the evidence. However, this must have been a feature of most prosecutions *de repetundis*, whose function was to bring forward the pleas of the plaintiffs and whose strength lay more in the clear delineation of the crimes committed than in any refined argument about whether the actions constituted a crime in law. One important function of the *quaestio* was to give the provincials their day in court and thus provide a safety-valve for the inevitably numerous complaints about Roman oppression. As for Cicero, he needed to make enough of his evidence stick as to render acquittal impossible. Condemnation was not itemized under particular counts in a *quaestio* under the Republic: the defendant was either guilty under the law or not. Once Verres was condemned, the validity of the particular charges could be re-examined in the *litis aestimatio*.

Cicero says in his introductory speech that his policy of moving immediately to his witnesses is not a new one, but one used by many who were now leaders in the community (*Ver.* 55). Such people, now in their forties or older, would have prosecuted as young men before the Social War. It is likely that the impetus towards this practice was provided by Glaucia's introduction of *comperendinatio* shortly before 100 BC.[30] With the certainty of another action to follow, in which he could display his oratorical skills, a prosecutor might well judge it best to get the bulk of his evidence heard first and reserve a long oration until he had discovered the line of defence that would be pursued against it.

Thanks to the evidence from the texts of the second action we are well informed about Cicero's witnesses. Moreover, Cicero usually indicates whether these had been already heard in the first action or were yet to be called in the second action, should it have occurred (they might well have also had a part to play in the *litis aestimatio*). The sheer number of these was formidable. Thirty-two Roman citizens can be counted (including one anonymous Roman *eques* from Messana and the wife and mother of the dead quaestor C. Malleolus).[31] Of these, twenty-six certainly gave evidence in the first action, while three were to give evidence in the second, and there are a further three men who probably either gave evidence or were about to give it.[32] At least thirteen embassies gave evidence for the prosecution in the first action,

30 Cic. *Ver.* 1.26. On the dispute over the precise date, see Lintott (1981) 189; Gruen (1968) 85ff.; Sumner (1973) 101.

31 Butler (2002) 27ff. correctly stresses the importance of written testimony but seems misguidedly to minimize the amount of oral testimony actually given in court. What is especially relevant in the second *Actio* is not calls for new testimony but references to testimony given earlier in the first *Actio*.

32 Cic. *Ver.* 1.14, 1.71, 1.93, 1.139, 1.151, 2.23, 2.69, 2.80, 2.102-03, 2.119, 3.36-37, 3.61, 3.97, 3.148, 3.166-67, 4.62, 4.70, 5.15, 5.73-74, 5.147, 5.154-56, 5.158, 5.163, 5.165. I take it that when Cicero refers in the second action to someone 'having spoken', this is evidence that the person concerned was actually a witness, as are references to someone as a past or future *testis*. When he claims that someone 'says' in the present tense, this may be simply a reference to written testimony which may or may not be supported in person in court. On this basis, we find that L. Suettius, L. Flavius, M. Annius, C. Matrinius, P. Tettius, P. Titius, M. Iunius, L. Domitius (Ahenobarbus), L. Caecilius, L. (Octavius)

eleven from Sicily and two from Italy. Seventeen more were to follow in the second action.[33] Fifteen individual *peregrini* (non-Romans) are named and one mentioned anonymously, who certainly spoke in Cicero's interest in the first action; three more are attested as being ready to speak in the second action. In addition three named citizens from Centuripae are likely to have spoken with their embassy in the first action.[34] We should also allow for a contribution from Sthenius of Thermae, who was seeking to overturn his condemnation and assisting Cicero with the case (*Ver.* 2.83; 5.128), but whose own evidence is not specifically mentioned by Cicero.

Of the named non-Roman witnesses who spoke for Cicero in the first action, eleven can be associated with embassies who appeared then; Posides Macro from Soluntum spoke, although the Soluntine embassy was reserved for the second action (*Ver.* 2.102, 3.103); Diodorus of Melita spoke on his own behalf (*Ver.* 4.38); Heius of Messana was persuaded to give evidence against Verres, although the Messanan embassy had officially been sent to support him (*Ver.* 2.13, 5.47).[35] There were also documents other than witness-statements, taken from the records of an earlier prosecution, from the *publicani*, and from various Greek cities. Cicero imagines these being read during his speech in the second action.[36] He never refers in the second action to the previous recitation of documents in the first action, but it is possible that some of these needed to be read to elucidate the evidence of witnesses.

All the non-Roman witnesses gave evidence about injuries to themselves or their own communities. As for the Romans, two testified to Verres' early misconduct at Lampsacus (*Ver.* 1.71), two about the estate of Malleolus (*Ver.* 1.93), three about Verres' treatment of

Ligus, T. Manilius, L. (Fufius) Calenus, M. (Terentius Varro) Lucullus, Q. Minucius, Sex. Pompeius Chlorus, Cn. Pompeius Theodorus, Cn. Cornelius Lentulus Marcellinus, Q. Varius, C. Licinius Sacerdos, Cn. Sertius, M. Modius, M. Lollius (on behalf of his infirm father Q. Lollius), C. Numitorius, the mother and grandmother of the boy Malleolus, and an anonymous *eques* from Messana spoke in the first action. C. Cassius Longinus, P. Vettius Chilo, and P. Granius were expected to speak in the second action. To these we may add M. and P. Cottius and Q. Lucceius, who also seem to be described as *testes* (*Ver.* 5.165). As for C. (Visellius) Varro (*Ver.* 1.71) and Cn. Cornelius Lentulus Clodianus, censor in 70 BC, (*Ver.* 5.15), it seems to me that *dicit* leaves it uncertain whether they appeared in court. Alexander (2002) 26-28, *cf.* Appendix 2 253-62, has rightly argued that we should take seriously Cicero's representation of his witnesses and documents. Our calculations about who actually appeared and when differ slightly.

33 Cic. *Ver.* 2.120, 2.123, 2.128, 2.156, 3.103, 3.120, 4.84, 4.91, 4.113-14, 5.108, 5.158, 5.164.

34 First action: Dio of Halaesa (*Ver.* 2.23-24); Heraclius of Centuripae (*Ver.* 2.66); Posides Macro of Soluntum (*Ver.* 2.102); Artemon, Andron, and Nympho of Centuripae (*Ver.* 2.156, 3.53, 3.114); Eubulidas Grospus of Centuripae (*Ver.* 3.56, 5.128); Apollodorus Pyragrus of Agyrium (*Ver.* 3.74); Mnesistratus of Leontini (*Ver.* 3.109); Heius of Messana (*Ver.* 4.15, 5.47); Phylarchus of Centuripae (*Ver.* 4.29, 4.50); Diodorus of Melita (*Ver.* 4.38); Poleas and Demetrius the gymnasiarch of Tyndaris (*Ver.* 4.92); Theodorus, Numerius, and Nicasio of Henna (*Ver.* 4.113); an anonymous Syracusan (*Ver.* 4.125); Onasius of Segesta (*Ver.* 5.120). Second action: Sositheus of Entella (*Ver.* 3.200); Phylarchus of Haluntium and Phalacrus of Centuripae (*Ver.* 5.122) – said to be present and speaking in the present, not past tense.

35 Heraclius of Syracuse gave written testimony against Verres, allegedly because he had been prevented from obeying Cicero's summons, although the city council had under pressure given written testimony for Verres (*Ver.* 2.15, 2.65, 4.125, 4.141-44).

36 Cic. *Ver.* 1.96, 1.99, 2.182-83, 3.83, 3.85, 3.87, 3.89, 3.99-100, 4.92, 4.140, 5.148, 5.164; *cf.* 5.10.

the ward Iunius during his praetorship (*Ver.* 1.139, 1.151), the rest about Verres' conduct in Sicily. Many of these were Roman citizens resident in Sicily. However, we also find two consular witnesses, C. Cassius Longinus and M. Terentius Varro Lucullus, and one who submitted evidence, Cn. Cornelius Lentulus Clodianus, currently censor, as well as the former praetor and governor of Sicily, C. Licinius Sacerdos.[37] The young aristocracy were represented by L. Domitius Ahenobarbus and one of the patrons of Sicily, Cn. Cornelius Lentulus Marcellinus (*Ver.* 1.139, 2.103).

Any attempt to gauge the time occupied by Cicero's witnesses must be speculative. We do not necessarily know all of them. If the non-Roman witnesses knew little Latin, no more might be expected of them than to give brief verbal confirmation to previously provided written testimony. However, given the richness of the available resources and the powerful Roman influence in Sicily, it is likely that Cicero could deliberately choose witnesses who spoke Latin effectively. For each Roman witness a minimum average of half an hour seems reasonable, hence a minimum of thirteen hours in the first action. Where witnesses formed part of an embassy, it is perhaps better to calculate from the time occupied by that group. Here a minimum of one hour for each embassy seems reasonable, hence a minimum of thirteen hours in the first action. To this we must add time for allied witnesses not belonging to embassies – another four hours. In total this makes a minimum of thirty hours for hearing witnesses against Verres. Compared with this, any other element in the first part of the trial was small.

IV. The rhetoric of the second action

The published second action was not needed to convict Verres. However, it was not merely an oratorical exercise *in uacuo*. It must have been in part intended to be read by Cicero's Sicilian clients, to acknowledge their contribution to the case, and to publicize their complaints. A Roman reader would also recognize a political argument that was forward-looking but would not have been inappropriate in the actual trial.

After an *exordium*, in which the orator expresses surprise that Verres has in fact reappeared (*Ver.* 1.1-3, 1.7-9) and justifies his compression of the first part of the trial against potential criticisms by Hortensius, perhaps actually made in the first action, that he had provided no case to answer (24-32), Cicero proceeds to a systematic catalogue of Verres' offences – from his quaestorship under Cn. Carbo in 84 BC onwards – and this dominates the rest of the corpus of the oration. The quaestorship does not detain Cicero long (34-40): he moves on to the proquaestorship in Cilicia (41-102) and the urban praetorship (103-58). The case is put by pointed narrative. The condemnation by C. Claudius Nero of Verres' enemies, Philodamus of Lampsacus and his son – Hortensius's one strong point (71) – is explained by the corruption of Dolabella and Verres. Only at one point does Cicero develop an elaborate argument when he asks why, if the Lampsacenes had really raised an unjustified riot, there were no reprisals against the city as a whole (78-85).

This is the pattern for the subsequent orations. Essentially they are a parade of witnesses, with Cicero retelling or occasionally anticipating their stories in a way that was most likely to engage the sympathies of a reader or juror. Sometimes he needs to set some background. Sicily is praised at the outset of the Sicilian narrative, its importance to Rome, its loyalty, its

37 Cic. *Ver.* 2.23, 2.119, 3.97, 5.15.

unhellenic character resembling traditional Roman virtue (*Ver.* 2.2-11). Cicero explains the Sicilian judicial system under the decree of P. Rupilius, but briefly (*Ver.* 2.32). He would have needed to do no less in the first action to give point to the evidence of some of his witnesses. A rather longer explanation is given of Sicilian taxation under the *lex Hieronica* and its retention by the consuls of 75 BC when they let the contracts, which has the additional function of stressing the part played by Sthenius in resisting alterations.[38] Later in the same oration Cicero has a brief introduction to the terms under which Verres was required to buy grain under the *lex Terentia Cassia* (*Ver.* 3.163). Regarding the thefts of works of art, Cicero carefully distinguishes this from the borrowings made by other Roman magistrates (*Ver.* 4.6) and notes that an ancient law forbad purchases by magistrates in provinces absolutely (*Ver.* 4.9-10), but his chief point is to demonstrate in the narratives that Verres' acquisitions never came about in fact with the consent of the previous owners.

We may reasonably wonder whether Cicero would have dwelt so long on these stories in court, when the evidence had already been given or was about to be given, especially as the account of Verres' manipulations of grain-taxation was boringly repetitive, as Cicero himself admitted (*Ver.* 3.10). What may be more illuminating about the speech that Cicero actually would have given is to notice special pieces of argumentation. Four items seem of interest here. Firstly, appeals to the text of the relevant law; secondly, financial calculations; thirdly, anticipations of Hortensius's defence; fourthly, general arguments about the nature of Roman provincial government.

Cicero does not cite formally the text of the current *lex de repetundis*, as he cites, for example, the *lex Cornelia de ueneficiis* when defending Cluentius (*Clu.* 148). Arguably, a jury familar with trials in this court would not need citations of those parts of the law that were most relevant for them, those that defined the crime and the classes of persons liable to be charged. However, Cicero does allude to the language of the law when he wants to make a point. In the middle of the section on the tithe-collection he exclaims, 'quid est aliud capere et conciliare pecunias, in quo te lex tenet, si hoc non est, ui atque imperio cogere inuitos lucrum dare alteri, hoc est pecuniam dare?'.[39] In *capere et conciliare* we have clear reference to the phraseology known to us through the epigraphic *lex repetundarum* (ll. 3, 59). Cicero returns to this allusion at the end of the oration, when he asks the jury whether, seeing that they are a jury *de pecunia capta conciliata*, they can overlook so much money taken (*Ver.* 3.218). Interestingly, the one occasion when we know that Cicero did read out the law was not in court but when he was seeking to compel the governor of Sicily, L. Metellus, to lift his veto on the supply to Cicero of a decree of the Syracusan senate: at this point he read out the *sanctio* (enforcement clause) of the law and its penalty.[40]

38 Cic. *Ver.* 3.12-20 (on Sthenius see above with nn. 4-5). Sthenius would surely have been called to bear witness to this, unless he was regarded as disabled from giving evidence.

39 'What else is stealing and procuring money, the act in which the law holds you liable, if it is not this, to compel people by the force of *imperium* to give a profit to another against their will, that is, to give money?' (*Ver.* 3.71).

40 Cic. *Ver.* 4.149. A further possible reference is in *Ver.* 5.126: 'non argentum, non aurum, non uestem, non mancipia repetunt, non ornamenta [...]' ('They do not claim back their gold, their silver, their tapestries, their slaves, nor the works of art [...]'). The catalogue of objects of theft may have formed part of the current law.

Cicero had plentiful evidence of Verres' extortionate practices in relation to Sicilian grain, but largely from one side, that of the Sicilian complainants. He had apparently no access to Verres' accounts before or during the first part of the trial.[41] Apronius, Verres' agent, refused to produce any accounts when formally requested to do so before the magistrate, on the ground that he had kept none (*Ver.* 3.112). In order to make plain Verres' excessive profits, Cicero calculates the maximum product of the *ager Leontinus*, in the light of the quantity of land (in *iugera*) declared under seed, and compares this with the quantity of *medimna* for which the contractor had bought the right to collect the tithe. This last sum was vastly more than a tenth of the maximum possible harvest in an excellent year.[42] Verres had also made money out of the sums assigned him to buy grain for the *res publica*. He had not only been mean about his payments to the cities but had profited from the interest accruing to the money while it was deposited with the *publicani* at Syracuse. The relevant documentation had largely disappeared, deliberately weeded, Cicero claims, following a decree of the tax-collectors. Nevertheless, Cicero found two copies of a letter from the *magistri* of the company to their colleague L. Carpinatius in Sicily, saying that they were going to see whether Verres was going to declare this profit in his accounts and return it to the public treasury: if he did not so return it, they were intending to claim it for the company.[43]

There are two main lines of defence that Cicero anticipates, apart from the demand that he should back his claims with evidence.[44] First, that Verres' behaviour was not unusual, secondly, that any harsh actions could be ascribed to the needs of the *res publica*. Early in the account of the thefts of works of art, Cicero mentions that a marble Eros stolen by Verres from Messana had previously been loaned for exhibition in the forum to C. Claudius Pulcher during his aedileship, but the latter had duly returned it. Other nobles had adorned the forum and the basilicas with similar works of art – temporarily (*Ver.* 4.5-6). Verres, by contrast, had taken and kept. But Verres had bought his pieces, so Cicero imagines the counter-argument. There was in fact an old law forbidding purchases by a Roman magistrate abroad, that seems, at least in part, to have been in force at the time of the *lex agraria* of 111 BC.[45] However, Cicero accepts the objection that this is now outmoded. He will cease to question Verres' intentions in the purchase, if he can show that he bought the statues at the vendor's price (*Ver.* 4.10).

At the beginning of the fifth *Verrine* Cicero assumes that Verres' wholesale depredations are manifest, but he may be still defended as a man who saved Sicily in a military crisis (*Ver.* 5.1). The volume that follows is thus presented not only as a denunciation of Verres' corruption and cruelty as evils in themselves, but as a move to subvert the defence that he was

41 Cic. *Ver.* 1.98-99, 4.36. Verres apparently stated in the senate that he was waiting on the accounts of his quaestor.

42 Cic. *Ver.* 3.112-13, rightly highlighted by Butler (2002) 44.

43 Cic. *Ver.* 3.165-68, esp. 167; *cf.* 2.177; Butler (2002) 47-48.

44 This is explicit at Cic. *Ver.* 2.177-78. The weak argument that Verres was not responsible for what his subordinates did is put forward more cautiously at *Ver.* 2.27 – to be dismissed. On this see Alexander (2002) 69-70, in relation to *Font.* 19.

45 Cic. *Ver.* 4.9-10; *cf. lex agraria* (*RS* I no. 2) ll. 54-55; *Dig.* 49.16.9; Lintott (1981) 176; Crawford (1977) 51 n. 4.

a good governor in the respect that concerned Romans most, military effectiveness. Cicero goes on:

> I know the *topos* (*locus*); I see where Hortensius is likely to make an exhibition of himself. He will recall the perils of war, the political situation, the shortage of commanders; at one moment he will seek your indulgence, at another he will even argue from his own legal standpoint (*pro suo iure*) that you should not allow such a commander to be snatched from the Roman people by the testimonies of Sicilians, that you should not consent to the lustre of a commander's glory being rubbed away by charges of greed (*Ver.* 5.2).

Later, when dealing with the case of Apollonius of Panhormus, he anticipates a response by the defence to his charges: 'I am not going to act so roughly, I will not follow that tradition among accusers of denouncing any act of clemency as lax, of extracting the odium of cruelty from any strict punishment.' His point is that Verres had acted arbitrarily: the defendant should have been tried by a jury under oath.[46] There follows an emotional appeal by *praeteritio* to the misery of Apollonius. This Cicero swiftly leaves aside:

> I foresee the line of defence Hortensius will take; he will admit that neither the age of the father, nor the youth of the son, nor the tears of both were more important to Verres than the interests and survival of the province; he will say that public affairs cannot be managed without the threat of stern punishment; he will ask why the rods are carried before praetors, why axes are given them, why the prison was built, why so many penalties have been established by our ancestors for bad men (*Ver.* 5.21-22).

Cicero has of course an answer. After this stern and impressive diatribe, he will ask why Verres suddenly let Apollonius out of gaol.

The sentiments Cicero ascribed to the defence seem in context a pastiche of rhetorical commonplaces, but the point was surely that, however trite, they were used to good effect in other cases. Cicero had no doubt heard them used in the *repetundae* court before. He used a similar argument from public interest in the *pro Fonteio*, which, on its likely date of 69 BC, was delivered when the written *Verrines* were circulating. Fonteius is portrayed there as a defender of the province, supported by the most reliable elements in it – the colony of Narbo Martius, the allied city of Massilia, the mass of resident Romans – and attacked by the Gauls whom he had forced to pay their proper dues to the Roman people.[47] The important difference between him and Verres was that the Roman citizens were on his side and the threat to Gaul was more serious than that to Sicily.

Cicero also portrays Hortensius resorting to the argument that Verres was no different from the average provincial governor. This comes after the elaborate *exposé* of his profiteering over the grain (*Ver.* 3.205-06). Cicero's response is to pick up this very point and dilate on the misery of allies everywhere: 'the provinces are all in mourning, the free peoples are all crying in distress, to cap it all, even the kings are protesting about our greed and injuries' (*Ver.* 3.207). This distress, Cicero maintains, is worse than armed rebellion and the Roman people cannot stand against it. The same theme recurs in an appeal to the jury during the

46 Cic. *Ver.* 5.19; *cf.* 5.18 (*indicta causa*).

47 Cic. *Font.* 11-15, 21, 26, 32, 46. On the Fonteius case see Alexander (2002) 59-77.

examination of Verres' military conduct in the fifth *Verrine*. Where, asks Cicero, can the allies find help? This is no longer the practice of the senate. The people have provided this court, the citadel of the allies. The allies no longer resort to it as they used to. They assume that the Roman people expect them to be robbed of their gold, silver, clothing, slaves, and the works of art from their shrines.

> For it is for many years now we have been tolerating it in silence, when we see the wealth of all nations has passed into the hands of a few men [...]. Where do you think the wealth of the foreign nations is, who are all now in poverty, when you see Athens, Pergamum, Cyzicus, Miletus, Chios, Samos, in short the whole of Asia, Achaia, Greece, and Sicily behind the doors of so few villas? (*Ver.* 5.126-27).

As a depiction of the iniquities of the Roman empire, these passages are more powerful than the much quoted passage from *de imperio Cn. Pompeii* (68), when Cicero tells the people that it is hard to describe how much the Roman people are hated.

What we cannot tell, of course, is how far such expostulations were the stock-in-trade of representatives of allies in the *quaestio de repetundis*. We have no parallel in the speeches of other Roman orators of the time. However, other material suggests that Cicero may be part of a long tradition. Before the era of the *quaestio*, Cato the Censor made a practice of denouncing the greed and corruption of his contemporaries in the courts and on other public platforms.[48] A further parallel is the words put in the mouths of foreigners by Roman historians. The letter of Mithridates inserted by Sallust in his *Histories*, set in the same period as Cicero's *Verrines*, is a reprise of Cicero's sentiments, and from this we can look onwards to the famous speech given by Tacitus to Calgacus.[49] We should therefore be cautious about ascribing to Cicero a heartfelt identification with the allies. Such passages were demanded by his duty to his clients – and this would have been a convenient excuse, should anyone have suggested that he was being excessively *popularis* and subversive.

The same defence was available if anyone suggested that his passionate appeal to the *prouocatio* laws (*Ver.* 5.163ff.) was demagogic to excess: it was the appropriate argument for this part of the case. What Cicero's real sentiments were in this period can at best be roughly gauged by considering a great deal of other evidence. The important thing was that he could appear *popularis* in a text like this, while having a retreat ready prepared from this position. At the same time he could appear deferential to the senatorial order, as in earlier speeches in the corpus (*Ver.* 43-50. *cf. Ver.* 1.21-23).

Caution is therefore required in using the *Verrines* as evidence for Cicero's politics. With later speeches the evidence of the *Letters* is often a useful corrective. The texts are, nonetheless, better evidence than might be thought for the conduct of a *repetundae* prosecution. Curiously enough, the mass of published rhetoric demonstrates clearly the paramount importance of witnesses and evidence. This is reflected by Cicero's later defence speeches in this court: most of what we possess, apart from the perorations, is concerned with the demolition of prosecution witnesses. The 'defence of good men', to which Cicero promised

48 *ORF*[3] no. 8 frr. 58-61, 69-71, 132, 154, 173-74 (204), 177, 224.

49 Sal. *Hist.* 4.69.5-9, 17 (M); Tac. *Ag.* 30.4-31.2.

he would turn at the end of the *Verrines*, largely depended on destroying the character and reliability of those who suggested in their testimony that his clients were not good.

Worcester College, Oxford

SAINTS AND SINNERS: SOME THOUGHTS ON THE PRESENTATION OF CHARACTER IN ATTIC ORATORY AND CICERO'S *VERRINES* [1]

KATHRYN TEMPEST

> For if you can reply to me and to what I am saying today, if in one single expression you manage to depart from that book composed out of other people's speeches that some schoolmaster has given to you, then I shall grant that you might not be a failure in the trial too and that you can do justice to the case and your duty.[2]

The imitation of example was an integral part of the trainee orator's education and in the above passage Cicero mocks Caecilius for his dependency upon model speeches. However, this paper will argue that while Cicero is critical of those who transfer argumentative moves from one speech to another with little or no creative imitation, he still knew that valuable lessons could be learned by reading other people's speeches. Indeed, in the *Brutus*, Cicero refers to Crassus's speech against the law of Caepio as a 'sort of textbook' from his boyhood, and George Kennedy has even noted imitations of Crassus in some of Cicero's earlier works.[3] But how much he owes to his Roman contemporaries and predecessors remains a fairly moot point: there are simply not enough of their speeches extant to provide the basis for any firm conclusions.

The lack of comparative material by which to assess Cicero's originality consequently set in motion what has been a long standing tradition of comparing Cicero's speeches to the precepts laid out in the rhetorical treatises. This approach doubtless has its merits, but its problems have not gone unnoticed: ultimately, such an approach discourages the reader from interpreting the speeches as documents of persuasion intended for an audience of listeners. Instead, a number of scholars have offered some convincing arguments as to why one ought to read the speeches as examples of practical oratory in their historical context,[4] and in recent

1 I am very grateful to Jonathan Powell and Lene Rubinstein who have read and improved various drafts of this paper, as well as to Jonathan Prag for his helpful and detailed suggestions in the editorial process. I would also like to acknowledge the financial support of the AHRC.

2 Cic. *Diu. Caec.* 47: 'si enim mihi hodie respondere ad haec quae dico potueris, si ab isto libro, quem tibi magister ludi nescio qui ex alienis orationibus compositum dedit, uerbo uno discesseris, posse te et illi quoque iudicio non deesse et causae atque officio tuo satisfacere arbitrabor.'

3 Cic. *Brut.* 164: 'a pueritia quasi magistra fuit'; Kennedy (1972) 147.

4 There is not space to argue for this in detail now; I broadly follow Stroh (1975), Classen (1985), and more recently Vasaly (1993). This does, of course, raise the question of the reality of the *Verrines* but this problem has, I believe, been fully addressed by Frazel (2004), who has argued against the tendency to read the second *actio* of the *Verrines* as a 'literary fiction'.

years it has become more fashionable to examine Cicero's use of persuasive techniques and manipulation in his speeches.

What should be noted here, however, is that while the move to understand Cicero's practical concerns in his deployment of rhetorical strategies and arguments has excited much valuable scholarship, the study of prosecution oratory has undoubtedly remained dependent on a comparison with the strategies used in the defence speeches. Apart from some fragmentary evidence, the *Verrines* are our only surviving example of a prosecution case and so a far more fruitful approach might be to compare Cicero with a set of orators whom we do happen to know: the Attic orators. Cicero's familiarity and admiration for Attic oratory looms large in his rhetorical works and it is telling that, in his quest for the ideal orator, Cicero concludes that Demosthenes comes closest to that ideal.[5] But Demosthenes was not the only model promoted by Cicero, who considered Hyperides as second only to Demosthenes,[6] appreciated Lysias as the perfect example of Atticism,[7] and considered Aeschines as one of the two most eloquent speakers, the other, of course, being Demosthenes.[8] That Cicero knew a wide range of Attic oratory is thus beyond doubt, but how much it influenced him as he composed his own speeches, and at what stage in his career it did so, remains to be fully explored. It is these issues that I wish to address in this paper.

It has long been observed that Cicero was influenced by Demosthenes and one work in particular points the way to further study. In a short article, Lionel Pearson attempted to survey the kind of debt Cicero's *Verrines* may have owed to Demosthenes, concluding only:

> I hesitate to use the word 'borrowing' or 'imitation' in speaking of the kind of lesson that Cicero may have learnt from these speeches of Demosthenes. The only way to build up any real case is by multiplying instances, and for that there is no time today. What I wanted to do was to show the kind of debt that an intelligent and widely read man like Cicero would be only too willing to acknowledge, the kind of profit that he enjoyed from his intimate knowledge of Demosthenes, without perhaps always being conscious exactly what it was that he found so useful.[9]

It should be clear that the kind of study I propose is essentially a development and extension of what Pearson started: first, by building up the case for Cicero's debt to Demosthenes with multiple instances of imitation, and second, by widening the scope of the discussion to examine Cicero's debt to a larger number of the Attic orators than has been appreciated before now.[10] With the exception of Alfons Weische's work, little has been produced that fully

5 For example, Cic. *Brut.* 35; *Orat.* 6, 23; although even Demosthenes is not perfect (*Orat.* 104).

6 For example, Cic. *Brut.* 138; *de Orat.* 1.58.

7 For example, Cic. *Orat.* 29.

8 For example, Cic. *Opt. Gen.* 14.

9 Pearson (1968) 54.

10 For a different view see Wooten (1983) *passim*, but especially chap. 3. In my opinion, he has underplayed the evidence for Demosthenic influence in Cicero's earlier speeches, and especially the *Verrines*, by admitting only that there may have been some 'occasional imitations' (47 n. 3). For the same argument elsewhere, see Wooten (1977).

appreciates the extent of Cicero's debt to the wider spectrum of Attic oratory.[11] Imitations of the Attic orators' works are, according to Weische's study, present in even Cicero's earliest speeches, and he uses this evidence, alongside papyri, quotations in the rhetorical handbooks, and imitations in Sallust to gauge an idea of the Attic speeches that were used in the rhetorical instruction of Cicero's time. Weische's aim was to learn more about the rhetorical education of an aspiring orator, and the kind of education that Cicero would have received; his secondary goal was to examine the difference between the Attic orators and Cicero, to understand more about the influence of Hellenistic and early Roman rhetoric, for which our evidence is otherwise scanty. My aim is different: I believe that the presence of Greek techniques in the *Verrines* can further our understanding of Roman prosecution oratory, by informing us about what kind of arguments could feasibly be admitted.

Indeed, it is the comparative evidence offered by the Attic orations that makes a new approach to the *Verrines* possible. As mentioned above, a very large part of the study of the *Verrines* has been heavily dependent upon comparison with Cicero's surviving defence *repetundae* speeches and surprisingly little has been produced examining the *Verrines* for what they really are: a prosecution. They are, after all, our only extant prosecution speech and it seems to me that the only way we can ever wholly appreciate the mechanisms of Roman oratory, and the somewhat larger collection of defence speeches, is by enhancing our knowledge of what was expected of a prosecutor and the techniques he was most likely to use. A recent study by Michael Alexander has also seen the merit such an approach holds. In his *Case for the Prosecution* (2002), Alexander has attempted to recreate some of the arguments of our lost prosecution speeches by analysing Cicero's extant speeches for the defence. Furthermore, in his examination of the defence speeches in extortion trials he has used the *Verrines* as a tool in the process of reconstruction.[12] The results of this approach are valuable, but, as Alexander admits, they are also relatively limited and methodologically problematic: it is difficult to reconstruct the prosecution's speech on the basis of the defence speech because Cicero may well be misrepresenting his opponent's arguments.[13]

In what follows I shall be focusing upon the practicalities of making a speech for the prosecution and the strategies that Cicero employed. The discussion will be concerned with proving, first, that Cicero was influenced by Demosthenes at an earlier stage in his career than scholarship has often allowed and, second, that discussions about Cicero's indebtedness to Attic oratory should embrace a larger number of the Attic orators, whom Cicero also admired. To do so I shall examine the techniques, *topoi*, and argumentative moves that Cicero adopts, or rather adapts, from his Greek predecessors, whilst asking how it was that techniques and *topoi*, originally formulated for a Greek audience, were able to find their way into Roman litigation and, indeed, to work so well in it. This paper forms part of a broader investigation into the presence of Greek oratorical techniques in the *Verrines*, which may tell us more about prosecution techniques in general: as one step towards understanding Cicero's use of Greek

11 Weische (1972).

12 Alexander (2002) 59-118.

13 Alexander (2002) 29: 'Relying on what the defence says about the prosecution is a third choice at best. The Roman forensic speaker did not have as his primary aim the transmission of facts.'

oratory, it will concentrate on how Cicero presents his own character and the character of his opponent, Verres.

I. Self-representation in the 'Diuinatio'

It is not an exaggeration to claim that, from the moment a speaker stands up, his own character will play a central role in the proceedings. A prosecutor in particular needs to establish from the outset that he is a good man, whose motives are honourable. Cicero's recognition of the need to establish his own moral character, as he makes his first appearance as a potential prosecutor in the *Diuinatio*, follows a long rhetorical tradition: according to Aristotle, the ethos of the speaker was one of the most effective means of persuasion (*Rhet.* 1356a). In the *Diuinatio in Caecilium*, however, Cicero faced the even more difficult task of presenting himself as more suited to undertake the prosecution of Verres than Caecilius, whilst eliminating any of the hostility a case of this sort might generate in the audience.

The theoretical tradition could only take Cicero so far in his quest to succeed in both the *Diuinatio* and the subsequent prosecution of Verres. Further, practical assistance was required and the published speeches of the Attic orators allow us to see the kind of argumentative moves Cicero could draw upon in order to gain his audience's goodwill. And so, Cicero's first move is to cast himself in the role of the reluctant prosecutor. He tells us that he was, in a way, forced into the prosecution, because the people of Sicily had begged him to do so: 'They all approached me often and publicly so that I might undertake the cause of defending their common fortunes.'[14]

The *topos* of the reluctant prosecutor, deployed here by Cicero, had its roots firmly in the ideology of the Athenian democracy: in what John Crook calls their 'populist ideal of law', the Athenians regarded professionalism, coupled with the 'seductive power of rhetoric', with suspicion.[15] Intrinsically linked with this suspicion were the frequent allegations by defendants that their opponent was a *sykophant*, a man who made a practice of prosecuting for gain. The *topos* of the reluctant prosecutor thus arose from a system in which the prosecutor needed to guard himself against such attacks. Yet in Athenian oratory the *topos* was conventionally employed to argue that, although the prosecutor had been personally harmed by his opponent, he was forced into court because he could also see that this man was harming others, and that he could not stand back and let this happen. Demosthenes begins his speech *Against Meidias* with this conventional plea: he had been personally harmed by Meidias, who had punched him, but he could see that Meidias's brutality was directed at everyone. Similarly, Aeschines takes care to claim that he only initiated his prosecution of Timarchus when he saw that the latter was harming the city. Having prostituted himself as a youth, Timarchus was automatically disqualified from speaking before the people (*atimia*) – a disqualification he continually ignored.[16]

14 *Diu. Caec.* 2: 'quare nunc populati atque uexati cuncti ad me publice saepe uenerunt, ut suarum fortunarum omnium causam defensionemque susciperem.'

15 Crook (1995) 39, 33.

16 Dem. 21.1, Aeschin. 1.1, 3. For other expressions of reluctance, see: Lys. 12.3, Dem. 24.1, 58.2, 59.12.

Yet Cicero alleges that he had been forced into the prosecution by the Sicilians, rather than by his opponent directly, and a striking precedent can be found in the speech *Against Meidias,* where Demosthenes is keen to stress the public dimension of his prosecution: he claims that, following his success in an initial *probole*, many citizens approached him and even begged him to take the further step of bringing Meidias into court.[17] The legal procedure of *probole* was used in cases of prosecution for offences at festivals and, as part of that procedure, the would-be prosecutor was required to present his case to the assembly.[18] Here both he and the defendant would put their respective arguments forward and those citizens present would cast their votes as to whether or not they thought the case should proceed. If the assembly voted in favour of the defence then the case would be automatically dropped, but if it went against the defendant the decision to convict lay with the prosecutor. If he then decided to proceed, the trial would take place, as normal, before a jury in the lawcourt. Demosthenes won this initial vote of the people and it was thereafter that he claims to have been approached by many who asked and urged him to take the further step of actually prosecuting Meidias in court, just as the Sicilians would later approach Cicero.[19]

What makes the similarity of the introductions to Cicero's speech in the *Diuinatio* and Demosthenes' speech *Against Meidias* really striking, however, is that the *topos* of the reluctant prosecutor is coupled with the technique of role reversal: that is, the claim that this prosecution is really a defence. Cicero argues that he is actually the defender of Sicily (*Diu. Caec.* 5), and thus it is that he justifies his position as prosecutor. He is not so much the accuser of Verres, as the champion of Sicily. Cicero steps into the role of defending the oppressed: a role with which he is much more at ease. Demosthenes too claims that he is more like a defendant, for he is the victim of *hubris* (Dem. 21.6), but also that he is not just defending himself, because Meidias's brutality is directed at the laws and everyone alike (Dem. 21.7).

Lionel Pearson also notes how Demosthenes' speech *Against Meidias* serves as a literary precedent for Cicero's claim that he is acting as the defender of Sicily.[20] However, Pearson ignores examples of the role reversal technique in the speeches of other Attic orators and the context in which they use it: there it is normally the defendants who reverse the roles and the prosecutors who say that it should not be done. It is thus only when we realize that Demosthenes is himself twisting a tradition that we can fully appreciate Cicero's specific 'debt to Demosthenes' here.

17 Dem. 21.2. According to Athenian expectations of 'decent conduct', private matters should be settled out of court, if possible, but where the interests of the collectivity were at stake, the situation was exactly the opposite: the man who behaved counter to the public good should be reprimanded accordingly. This explains why Demosthenes is keen to stress the public dimension of Meidias's offence: if looked at as a private matter, between Demosthenes and Meidias, then the decent thing for Demosthenes to have done would have been to reach a compromise with Meidias. For more on the public nature of this case see Wilson (1991).

18 For a fuller explanation of the *probole* procedure see MacDowell (1978) 194-97.

19 This should not be taken to suggest that Cicero was lying when he said that the Sicilians had approached him in the first instance, but it is important to note that Cicero may not have been as passive in affairs as he makes out: he is, after all, competing for the right to prosecute Verres.

20 Pearson (1968) 50.

The technique of role reversal can be seen as early as the *Tetralogies* – the rhetorical exercises commonly believed to be the work of Antiphon. As in the other *Tetralogies*, the case under dispute is divided into four speeches: two for the prosecutor and two for the defendant, with the prosecutor speaking first. The *Second Tetralogy* concerns a dispute over a javelin-thrower's share of the guilt in an accident whereby he struck and killed a young man who was running onto the field to collect the javelins. The prosecutor charges the javelin-thrower with unintentional homicide, the penalty for which was temporary exile. However, believing that the verdict was a foregone conclusion, the prosecutor declines to make a full opening speech and, later, in his second prosecution speech, complains that he would never have done so had he known that the defendant would have had the two-fold advantage of 'making one speech in defence of himself against my one speech and making his accusations when they could not be answered'.[21]

I follow Gagarin's interpretation here that 'the defendant's first speech was, in effect, a prosecution speech accusing the boy of killing himself'.[22] The father of the javelin-thrower, speaking on his son's behalf, had claimed that, since the boy struck by the javelin had run onto the field when he should not have done, he was guilty of killing himself. In sum, it is the defendant who has reversed the roles here by speaking more like a prosecutor, and it is the prosecutor who is voicing criticism at his opponent's strategy.

Indeed this example is very much in line with what we see in later oratorical practice, where the technique of role reversal became the object of the prosecutor's attack on the defendant's strategy. At Lysias [6].42, the speaker anticipates a move that he thinks the defendant, Andocides, will make: that 'perhaps he will bring a counter accusation against Cephisius' (ἴσως οὖν καὶ Κηφισίου ἀντικατηγορήσει), the main prosecutor in the trial. Rather clumsily, the speaker actually claims that some of the accusations the defence might throw back at the prosecutor are likely to be true, but his main point is that this is what the defence are likely to do. In fact, by far the most frequent tactic we encounter of this type is the prosecution's anticipation and deflection of the arguments the defendant will use. Two further examples from Aeschines can be adduced to illustrate this point.

The first example appears in Aeschines' speech *Against Timarchus*. Timarchus was expected to call upon Demosthenes as a *sunegoros*, a co-speaker. Aeschines tells his audience to imagine what will happen if Timarchus is acquitted. He presents the hypothetical situation of Demosthenes later boasting of his success to his pupils, claiming that he had managed to divert the jurors' attention away from the charge against Timarchus by reversing the roles of prosecutor and defendant:

> For I led them away from the charges against Timarchus, and I carried them off and led them towards the prosecutor and Philip and the Phocians, and I hung such fear above those listening that the defendant began to be the prosecutor and the prosecutor to be on

21 Antiph. *Second Tetralogy* 3.2: ἕνα μὲν πρὸς ἕνα λόγον ἀπολογηθείς, ἃ δὲ κατηγόρησεν ἀναποκρίτως εἰπών.

22 Gagarin and MacDowell (1998) 35 n. 1.

trial, and the jurors forgot what they were judges of and they listened to those [charges] that they were not judges of.[23]

Aeschines repeats this same charge against Demosthenes' rhetorical strategy in his speech *Against Ctesiphon*. This time Aeschines is attacking Ctesiphon for proposing that Demosthenes should be presented with a crown for his services to the state. Whilst Ctesiphon is the ostensible defendant in the trial, the real object of Aeschines' attack is Demosthenes, whom Aeschines charges is unworthy to receive the crown. Once more Aeschines complains that legal procedure has been confounded by Demosthenes, so that now 'while the prosecutor defends himself, the defendant of an indictment plays the part of the prosecutor'.[24]

What these examples show is that to play with the boundaries of prosecution and defence is an old technique, but that it is a technique conventionally employed by the defence: either the defendant acts more like a prosecutor, but he does not claim to be one, or the prosecutor anticipates that this is how the defence will behave. One example that appears to run counter to this suggestion may be found in Dinarchus's prosecution speech *Against Demosthenes*. Here the prosecutor seems to be behaving like a defendant, even to the point of adducing witnesses in order to clear his name (Din. 1.52), but closer inspection reveals that he, too, is in fact making an elaborate anticipation of the defendant's strategy: that the defence will accuse him of having been condemned by the Areopagus.

And so, returning to Demosthenes' claim, in the speech *Against Meidias*, of being more like a defendant than a prosecutor, it does not seem quite so conventional. In fact, it is the only example of which I know where the prosecutor chooses to change roles and put himself into that of the defendant. As far as our extant corpus suggests, what Demosthenes has done here is unique. When Cicero cast himself as a reluctant prosecutor or a defence advocate he was not just rehashing a worn *topos*, but he was picking up on an adaptation that Demosthenes had made long before him. To argue that Cicero made this exact same twist on a familiar motif by chance and independent of direct Attic influence would surely be to trust in coincidence too far. It is certainly not implausible that Cicero would have been familiar enough with the speech *Against Meidias* to reproduce some of its strategies, consciously or not, in his own preparations for the trial against Verres.[25]

It may now be asked how these techniques, which were suited to the context of Athenian litigation, were able to be adapted to Roman proceedings, and how much cultural adaptation was required. While it has long been observed that Roman rhetorical theory owed a heavy debt to its Greek predecessor, there have been relatively few comparative studies of the actual oratory of Athenian and Roman litigation. This reluctance, it seems, stems from a deeply embedded belief in the radically different approaches of self representation in the Athenian

23 Aeschin. 1.175: ἀπαγαγὼν γὰρ αὐτοὺς ἀπὸ τῶν περὶ Τίμαρχον αἰτιῶν, ἐπέστησα φέρων ἐπὶ τὸν κατήγορον καὶ Φίλιππον καὶ Φωκέας, καὶ φόβους ἐπήρτησα τοῖς ἀκροωμένοις, ὥσθ' ὁ μὲν φεύγων κατηγόρει, ὁ δὲ κατηγορῶν ἐκρίνετο, οἱ δὲ δικασταί, ὧν μὲν ἦσαν κριταί, ἐπελάθοντο, ὧν δ' οὐκ ἦσαν, περὶ τούτων ἤκουον.

24 Aeschin. 3.193: ὁ μὲν γὰρ κατήγορος ἀπολογεῖται, ὁ δὲ φεύγων τὴν γραφὴν κατηγορεῖ.

25 Weische (1972) 139 suggests that the speech *Against Meidias* played a role in the rhetorical education of the first century BC: he adduces this conclusion from the very presence of Demosthenic imitations in Cicero's speeches.

court compared to the advocacy of its Roman counterpart. Whilst it cannot be denied that advocacy altered the rhetorical situation of the courts,[26] it must be noted that the situations of Greek and Roman volunteer prosecutors were, in fact, very similar. Rewards for prosecutors in both systems meant that their motives were questioned, and a similar hostility was attached to the vexatious prosecutor who sought to further his own career on the back of other people's misfortunes. It was for these reasons, among others, that Cicero was able to fit the *topos* of the reluctant prosecutor and the technique of role reversal into a Roman context with remarkable ease.

In Cicero's case, the hostilities that could potentially mount against him were many. First, added to the general antipathy towards the act of prosecution was Cicero's age: he was thirty-six and comparatively old for a debut prosecution. Generally speaking, social convention conceded young men at the beginning of their public careers the privilege of prosecuting a senior opponent without incurring too much criticism; thus Cicero grants the excuse of youth to Atratinus for undertaking the prosecution of Caelius when he was only seventeen years old (Cic. *Cael.* 2). Secondly, there were the rewards for prosecutors and Cicero may well have been open to the charge that he was after the *spolia*, the spoils, of Verres. Indeed, Cicero appears eager to dismiss such a charge when he defends his decision to prosecute by claiming 'for it was not the spoils of Gaius Verres but the good opinion of the Roman people that I desired most'.[27] It has been argued that advancement in rank was one of the benefits a successful prosecutor could expect to gain and that Verres' place in the Senate was available to Cicero if he did indeed defeat his opponent. Whilst it is not within the scope of this paper to examine the evidence for this argument, it is clear that some kind of incentive for *repetundae* cases may have prompted some to prosecute.[28] To eschew this suspicion, and the attendant hostility, Cicero could introduce the *topos* of the reluctant prosecutor and the technique of role reversal, both originally Greek, with minimum cultural adaptation: for years Greek and Roman volunteer prosecutors alike had had to establish that their motives were not selfish.

Furthermore, just as the procedure of *probole* had allowed Demosthenes to stress that his trial was the result of the people's vote, so the traditions of the *repetundae* court enabled Cicero to stress his relationship with the provincials. Earlier in the history of the *lex repetundarum*, the provincials could ask for a *patronus* to take up their case and the *patroni* hence assumed a somewhat different position to other prosecutors. In the previous paper, Andrew Lintott notes how this procedure had changed by the 90s BC and that the new procedure – the *diuinatio* – was still being used in the post-Sullan period, that is, when Cicero undertook the prosecution of Verres. Despite this new procedure, we can confidently assume that it would have remained conventional, and indeed necessary, for a prosecutor in an extortion trial to state that their prosecution was the will of the provincials.[29] This tradition would have enabled

26 Kennedy (1968).

27 Cic. *Ver.* 1.21: 'non enim spolia C. Verris sed existimationem populi Romani concupiui.'

28 For the view that there was such a system of rewards see: Mommsen (1899) 504-11; Taylor (1949) 112-16; Russell (1950) 54-84. For a different view see Alexander (1985).

29 See Cic. *Scaur.* 23-30 where the prosecutor failed to demonstrate that he had the support of the provincials behind his prosecution: this well illustrates that if a prosecutor did not put forward a convincing display of provincial support at the trial he could hardly hope to get a conviction.

Cicero to make that same claim and it illustrates well how he could have adapted Demosthenes' argumentative move, to assert popular support, into an entirely different cultural and procedural context.

II. The characterization of Verres

The ethos of the speaker, coupled with his *auctoritas*, were undoubtedly key components in winning the jury's favour. However, gaining the conviction of one's opponent required more: the jury had to believe that the defendant was guilty as charged.[30] To the modern eye, the insurmountable evidence against Verres was, of course, sufficient to prove his guilt, but, as Harold Gotoff says, 'logical and legal arguments, even when favourable, can get complicated, facts and figures confusing; and his [Cicero's] listeners are neither logicians nor computers'.[31] Catherine Steel argues in the following paper that Cicero purposely obfuscates the facts in the trial, to mislead the audience and even misrepresent the evidence. Her approach illustrates one of the chief ways in which Cicero was able to convince the jury of Verres' guilt; the second part of this paper will hopefully illustrate another way: it will examine how Cicero goes about proving that Verres is the sort of man who could be guilty.

From the onset of the *Diuinatio*, Cicero is working to generate his audience's hostility towards Verres and, indeed, the first mention of his opponent corroborates the main charge against him. The Sicilians have been telling Cicero that:

> [...] Now they do not even have the gods left in their cities in whom they might take refuge, because Verres has carried off their most holy images from their most sacred shrines; that whatever luxury had been able to accomplish in the way of vice, or cruelty in the way of punishment, or greed in the way of thefts, arrogance in the way of outrage, all these they bore during the three years that this one man was praetor.[32]

Not only is Cicero whetting his audience's appetite for what he might have to say, if he wins the right to prosecute Verres, but he also uses the *Diuinatio* as a platform from which to launch his attack on Verres. What he effectively does here is start with the conclusion: in the remaining speeches he will proceed to answer the questions that lead us there. Moreover, this introduction is shortly followed by a strong condemnation of Verres' character, as Cicero describes his opponent as 'a man endowed with unparalleled greed, impudence, and wickedness'. Enlisting the knowledge of his audience, Cicero continues, claiming that 'we know the great disgrace of his thefts and outrages not only in Sicily, but even in Achaia, Asia, Cilicia, Pamphylia, and even at Rome before the eyes of us all'.[33]

30 As suggested by Riggsby (1997).

31 Gotoff (1986) 123.

32 Cic. *Diu. Caec.* 3: '[...] sese iam ne deos quidem in suis urbibus ad quos confugerent habere, quod eorum simulacra sanctissima C. Verres ex delubris religiosissimis sustulisset; quas res luxuries in flagitiis, crudelitas in suppliciis, auaritia in rapinis, superbia in contumeliis efficere potuisset, eas omnes sese hoc uno praetore per triennium pertulisse.'

33 Cic. *Diu. Caec.* 6: '[...] ut homo singulari cupiditate, audacia, scelere praeditus, cuius furta atque flagitia non in Sicilia solum, sed in Achaia, Asia, Cilicia, Pamphylia, Romae denique ante oculos omnium maxima turpissimaque nossemus [...] .'

Cicero works on two levels here and he has a Greek precedent for each. First is his use of Verres' behaviour at Rome as indicative of his behaviour across the water, where he was out of public view. An obvious precedent for this can be found at Aeschin. 1.108, where Aeschines asks whether the people can really expect a man, who has shown himself licentious in Athens, to place any limit on his license when he receives a magistracy abroad. Second, Cicero adopts the *topos* of 'everyone knows', which is used here to shame men into agreement with him by working on the assumption that no one would dare admit their ignorance of an allegedly notorious fact. If no one dares admit that they do not actually know of Verres having ever acted in this way, the foil works: for everyone presumes the person next to them must know and something which may never even have happened is taken as fact.

Indeed, in this latter respect, the whole tone of the passage bears resemblance to the opening of Demosthenes' speech *Against Meidias*. Cicero's introduction of Verres in the opening lines of the *Diuinatio* exemplifies a well-worn technique of building prejudice against one's opponent. As Pearson also notes of Demosthenes' oratory:

> [He] often begins with a strong complaint about the character of the opposing party, so that the jury will be prejudiced against him from the start. The narrative will then appear to illustrate his character and show him behaving as such a man might be expected to behave.[34]

In the current examples, however, the fact that Cicero and Demosthenes both introduce their villains with strong complaints about their behaviour, and that they both couple this with the claim that their opponent's behaviour is notorious, is inescapably obvious. Thus it is that Demosthenes introduces his speech *Against Meidias* with the powerful remark that: 'The brutality, gentlemen of the jury, and the insolence, with which Meidias always treats everyone alike are, I suppose, as well known to you as to all other citizens.'[35]

This said, it now remains to explain how the orators succeed in unfolding their opponent's character, via the narrative, to support the initial presentation they have made. One method is to establish the *uita ante acta* of the opponent and elaborate on how his earlier life renders plausible the crimes with which he is now being charged. The strategy was undoubtedly a persuasive one; so much can be inferred from the unsuccessful prosecution of Flaccus, which had failed to establish his *uita ante acta*. Flaccus was, like Verres, being prosecuted under the *lex repetundarum*, but this time Cicero was speaking for the defence. When therefore the prosecutors in the trial of Flaccus focused their arguments on his offences as a governor, Cicero responded that even if Flaccus were guilty of the allegations being made against him, the prosecutors should not pass over the rest of his career in silence.[36]

On the other hand, Cicero states that he will set out Verres' whole career in detail, by dividing his speech into the four main periods of activity:

34 Pearson (1976) 76.

35 Dem. 21.1: τὴν μὲν ἀσέλγειαν, ὦ ἄνδρες δικασταί, καὶ τὴν ὕβριν, ᾗ πρὸς ἅπαντας ἀεὶ χρῆται Μειδίας, οὐδέν' οὔθ' ὑμῶν οὔτε τῶν ἄλλων πολιτῶν ἀγνοεῖν οἴομαι.

36 *Cf.* Alexander (2002) 79.

> These years were spent by him in the quaestorship, as a legate in Asia, as urban praetor, and as the governor of Sicily; on which account the division of my whole accusation will be according to these same four parts.[37]

It is surely not a coincidence that Aeschines does precisely this in his speech *Against Ctesiphon*. Aeschines is here attacking Ctesiphon's proposal of the crown and thus needs to undermine Demosthenes' career to show that he does not deserve it. Aeschines tells us that he will speak explicitly concerning the crimes of Demosthenes' public life, for it is his understanding that Demosthenes, speaking for the defence, will enumerate the four periods in the history of the city as the periods of his own political activity (Aeschin. 3.54-55). In fact, Demosthenes' defence of Ctesiphon, his speech *On the Crown*, makes no such division. But this is not important to Aeschines' speech, for he continues to tell us how he will structure his prosecution: 'I shall speak firstly concerning the first period, secondly concerning the second, thirdly concerning the next one, and fourthly concerning the present situation.'[38]

It is beyond doubt that this four-way division of Demosthenes' career in Aeschines' speech readily suggested itself as a structural model for Cicero's speech against Verres. The similarity speaks for itself, but Alfons Weische has also suggested that the two speeches, for and against Ctesiphon, were of primary importance in the rhetorical education of Cicero's day, thus accounting for his familiarity with them. His conclusion is drawn from both the physical evidence and the rational assumption that the unusual privilege of having, in full, the two speeches from a single and highly acclaimed trial would make them very appealing for instructive purposes.[39] In addition to Weische's suggestions, it should also be remembered that these two speeches had made such an impression on Cicero that later in his life he translated them both into Latin: the extant *de Optimo Genere Oratorum* purports to be the introduction to these, now lost, translations (Cic. *Opt. Gen.* 14).

Returning to the speeches themselves, however, it is worth mentioning that while Aeschines' focus here is to deflate the success of Demosthenes' career, Cicero's object is to show that Verres' track record proves that he already has certain tendencies in his system and, as a leopard does not change its spots, neither does Verres change his ways. The argument is one from probability: if the defendant has acted in such a way before, it is likely that he is also guilty of the current charge of which he is accused.[40] The more time Cicero devotes to building such prejudice against Verres at the onset of the trial, the less he will have to convince the jury of Verres' guilt later on: he has already prepared the way for these accusations to carry weight.

37 Cic. *Ver.* 1.34: 'hi sunt anni consumpti in quaestura et legatione Asiatica et praetura urbana et praetura Siciliensi; quare haec eadem erit quadripertita distributio totius accusationis meae.'

38 Aeschin. 3.57: λέξω δὲ πρῶτον περὶ τοῦ πρώτου καιροῦ, καὶ δεύτερον περὶ τοῦ δευτέρου, καὶ τρίτον περὶ τοῦ ἐφεξῆς, καὶ τέταρτον περὶ τῶν νυνὶ καθεστηκότων πραγμάτων.

39 In our extant corpus these are Aeschin. 3 (*Against Ctesiphon*) and Dem. 18 (*On the Crown*). See Weische (1972) 136-38, 189, as well as 130-33 (evidence from papyri), 125-27 (the frequency of citations in the rhetorical handbooks), 127-30 (imitations in Sallust's work, although pertaining to the Demosthenic speech only).

40 *Cf.* Riggsby (2004).

The first questions to be asked, then, are how can Cicero build upon this initial presentation to prove that Verres is the sort of man who could be guilty? What sort of character could be driven to commit the tax frauds of the *de Frumento*, the plunder of public, private, and sacred artefacts in *de Signis*, and to treat provincials and fellow Romans as atrociously as the *de Suppliciis* reports? And what would be the drives and aims of that character? The answer must have been screaming out at Cicero from the centuries of literature that had produced the fully delineated prototype of the tyrant.[41] Furthermore, the catalogue of tyrants produced by the Sicilians' stormy history made the choice an altogether obvious one: Cicero himself makes his aim explicitly clear when he asks his audience to 'observe how much more a hateful tyrant of Syracuse he [Verres] had been than any of his predecessors'.[42]

The role of the Greek tyrant in Roman rhetorical invective generally, and in the *Verrines* specifically, has long been observed.[43] Indeed, the numerous examples of tyrants found in all genres confirm that rhetorical precedents for the tyrant were not lacking, but what has not been appreciated is how Cicero fitted this prototypical tyrant to serve his oratorical needs, or the role of Attic oratory as his precedent for doing so.

Returning to the questions posited above, the first of these has been answered: only a man with tyrannical aspirations could commit the atrocities with which Verres is charged. But, to make his listeners believe that Verres has these tyrannical aspirations, Cicero needs to paint him in the colours of a tyrant and herein lies the answer to what drives a man in his quest for such power: wealth and the love of luxury. Once in power, the behaviour of the tyrannical man typically culminates in the actions summarized by Herodotus, who, in the words of Otanes in the constitutional debate, describes him as the kind of man who 'turns the laws of the land upside down, who rapes women and kills men without judgement'.[44] One need only think of how Verres overturned the Sicilian corn tithe laws (*Ver.* 3), his attempts on the virtue of Philodamus's daughter (*Ver.* 1), and the endless accounts of the alleged tortures and executions he committed to see that Cicero has not deviated far from this model. Indeed, much more could be said about Cicero's presentation of Verres as a formidable tyrant; however, the following discussion will concentrate on the parallels which may be found in the Attic orators. These parallels reveal how Cicero and the Attic orators prepare their audiences to accept the picture of their opponent as a tyrant, by first presenting them as guilty of the kind of behaviour one can expect an aspiring tyrant to exhibit.

The overwhelming factor contributing to the make-up of the tyrant is his wealth and how he uses, or rather abuses it. Let us first consider how men spend their wealth and the sort of behaviour those driven by wealth exhibit. Naturally, the speaker's opinion of such people is expressed in accordance with the assumed voice of the citizen body. This technique of argumentation, commonly used by the Attic orators and Cicero alike, has nothing to do with proving the so-called facts of the case, but it has everything to do with making the jury believe

41 For a survey of the antipathy towards the tyrant in Greek literature, see Parker (1998).

42 Cic. *Ver.* 4.123: 'ac uidete quanto taetrior hic tyrannus Syracusanis fuerit quam quisquam superiorum.'

43 In general: Dunkle (1967) and Erskine (1991); in the *Verrines*: Steel (2001) 30-31, 34-35 and Vasaly (1993) esp. 122-24, 213-15.

44 Hdt. 3.80.5: νόμαιά τε κινέει πάτρια καὶ βιᾶται γυναῖκας κτείνει τε ἀκρίτους.

that his opponent is the sort of man who would commit the crimes with which he is being charged.

It will be seen that the real object of the attack against the wealthy man is actually not his wealth *per se*, but how he spends it. Thinking back to some of Cicero's earlier character creations, it is clear that the *topos* of luxury was already part of his armoury. Naevius in *pro Quinctio* and Chrysogonus in *pro Roscio Amerino*, for instance, well illustrate that nothing gets in the way of the man who wants to indulge his lust for money, or how that man spends his ill-gotten gains in an extravagance beyond comparison. Cicero draws upon these same weapons of attack in the *Verrines*, but the edge needed to be that bit sharper: Cicero needed to prove that Verres' character was filled with such arrogance that he believed that the laws did not apply to him, and with such greed that he would act, as charged, to get his hands on whatever he desired.

A passage from Aristotle (*Rhet.* 1391a) neatly summarizes the kind of prejudices that the image of the wealthy man could excite. Once in possession of wealth, he says, men become 'insolent' (ὑβρισταὶ) and 'arrogant' (ὑπερήφανοι), believing that it is 'a sort of measure of other things, so that everything seems purchasable by it' (ὁ δὲ πλοῦτος οἷον τιμή τις τῆς ἀξίας τῶν ἄλλων, διὸ φαίνεται ὤνια ἅπαντα εἶναι αὐτοῦ). As for their characteristic behaviour, rich men are 'both luxurious and ostentatious' (καὶ τρυφεροὶ καὶ σαλάκωνες): 'luxurious because of their life-style and the display of their prosperity' (τρυφεροὶ μὲν διὰ τὴν τροφὴν καὶ τὴν ἔνδειξιν τῆς εὐδαιμονίας) and ostentatious and ill-bred because all men are accustomed to spend their time upon what they love and admire, and because 'they think that everybody else emulates the same things as they do' (καὶ τὸ οἴεσθαι ζηλοῦν τοὺς ἄλλους ἃ καὶ αὐτοί).

These characteristics should be borne in mind when assessing the character of Verres, for he certainly fits this image. In a memorable anecdote, Cicero emphasizes the luxury of Verres' lifestyle and the display he makes of his prosperity, as he reports:

> Just as the custom had been for the old Bithynian kings, he [Verres] travelled on a litter carried by eight bearers, in which there was a gleaming Maltese cushion stuffed with rose petals; whilst he himself had one garland on his head and another round his neck, and he used to put to his nose a little net-bag of the finest linen, its delicate mesh full of rose petals.[45]

The move to present one's opponent travelling in the height of luxury is a strategy that aims at denigrating his character in the light of both Athenian and Roman attitudes towards such behaviour. Catherine Steel notes that it is 'a cliché of inappropriate luxury' for a Roman magistrate to travel on a litter, and for the Athenian such luxury runs counter to democratic ideals of egalitarianism.[46] Thus it is that, in his prosecution of Meidias, Demosthenes could mock his opponent for 'riding on a silver mule chair, which was from Euboea, carrying his

45 Cic. *Ver.* 5.27: 'ut mos fuit Bithyniae regibus, lectica octaphoro ferebatur, in qua puluinus erat perlucidus Melitensis rosa fartus; ipse autem coronam habebat unam in capite, alteram in collo, reticulumque ad naris sibi admouebat tenuissimo lino, minutis maculis, plenum rosae.'

46 Steel (2001) 26 n. 14.

fine cloaks, his cups, and wine jars'.[47] This same charge was later made against Demosthenes himself, whom the speaker of Dinarchus 1 accuses of 'living in luxury in the midst of the city's hardships, and travelling down the road to the Piraeus in a litter'.[48]

Returning to the characteristics of the wealthy man, it should be remembered that he is not just ostentatious but, in his belief that all men are emulous of the same things as he is, he likes to boast, show off, and play the connoisseur. According to Cicero, this is precisely the way in which Verres behaves:

> He is so eager of that distinguished reputation, to be thought of as having good taste in such matters, that just the other day – mark the madness of the man: after his case had been adjourned, when he was already as good as condemned and (judicially) dead, early on one of the days of the games in the circus, when the couches had been spread and the silver plate all set out in the house of Lucius Sisenna, a man of the first rank, and when, as was suited to the dignity of Lucius Sisenna, the house was full of the most honourable of men, he went up to the silver and began in a leisurely way to examine and consider every single piece.[49]

At this point attention should be drawn to another passage from Demosthenes' speech *Against Meidias*, in which Demosthenes charges his opponent firstly with his excessive ostentation and secondly with aspiring to the reputation of being a connoisseur:

> He has built a house at Eleusis so big that it overshadows everyone in that place; and he drives his wife to the Mysteries, or anywhere else she wishes, with a pair of white horses from Sicyon, and he pushes his way through the agora, with three or four attendants by his side, describing beakers and drinking cups and vessels so loudly that the passers-by hear him.[50]

We may well ask what the purpose in all of this is. Pearson says of Demosthenes' presentation of Meidias that, when the monstrous side of his character has been built up in the speech, it only remains to add the finishing touch that will make the portrait more credible. Meidias, he says, has some lesser faults which make him at the same time human and ridiculous.[51] Cicero

47 Dem 21.133: ἐπ' ἀστράβης δ' ὀχούμενος ἀργυρᾶς τῆς ἐξ Εὐβοίας, χλανίδας δὲ καὶ κυμβία καὶ κάδους ἔχων.

48 Din. 1.36: τρυφῶν ἐν τοῖς τῆς πόλεως κακοῖς, καὶ ἐπὶ φορείου κατακομιζόμενος τὴν εἰς Πειραιᾶ ὁδόν.

49 Cic. *Ver.* 4.33: 'at ita studiosus est huius praeclarae existimationis, ut putetur in hisce rebus intellegens esse, ut nuper – uidete hominis amentiam: posteaquam est comperendinatus, cum iam pro damnato mortuoque esset, ludis circensibus mane apud L. Sisennam, uirum primarium, cum essent triclinia strata argentumque expositum in aedibus, cum pro dignitate L. Sisennae domus esset plena hominum honestissimorum, accessit ad argentum, contemplari unum quidque otiose et considerare coepit.'

50 Dem. 21.158: οἰκίαν ᾠκοδόμηκεν Ἐλευσῖνι τοσαύτην ὥστε πᾶσιν ἐπισκοτεῖν τοῖς ἐν τῷ τόπῳ, καὶ εἰς μυστήρια τὴν γυναῖκ' ἄγει, κἂν ἄλλοσέ ποι βούληται, ἐπὶ τοῦ λευκοῦ ζεύγους τοῦ ἐκ Σικυῶνος, καὶ τρεῖς ἀκολούθους ἢ τέτταρας αὐτὸς ἔχων διὰ τῆς ἀγορᾶς σοβεῖ, κυμβία καὶ ῥυτὰ καὶ φιάλας ὀνομάζων οὕτως ὥστε τοὺς παριόντας ἀκούειν.

51 Pearson (1976) 110.

certainly used the rhetorical gain that laughter provided him in his speeches, and it is highly probable that he sought to inject his presentation of Verres with a similar element of the ridiculous here.[52] However, I have tried to show that Cicero and Demosthenes are aiming at something else as well: to present their opponents as aspirant tyrants.

Of course, Meidias is never charged with tyranny itself. The charge against him was to prove that he was arrogant enough to deserve the punishment meted out to those who commit *hubris* and *asebeia*:[53] the arrogant brutality he demonstrated in his attack on Demosthenes and his impiety, exhibited in the fact that the offence took place at a religious festival. As such, the comparison with Verres ends here: both men were unparalleled in their excessive arrogance and their impiety, and the actions of both men resulted from the belief that money buys them the privilege to act as they will.

An instructive parallel for the move to present one's opponent as a tyrant can, however, be found in Aeschines' prosecution of Timarchus. When taken as a whole, the speech *Against Timarchus* aims to prove his unsuitability for public life, but it does so by resting on the claim that the defendant has acted, and continues to act as a male prostitute. This, by law, would make him *atimos*: that is, stripped of the citizen rights that allow a man to speak in the assembly and courts, to hold office, and to take part in religious observances.[54] Whilst reports concerning Timarchus's performance of official duties abroad are thus, strictly speaking, irrelevant to the case, they are nevertheless to be expected in a speech seeking to establish the defendant as a bad citizen. The importance of this passage for the current investigation rests on the kind of behaviour Timarchus exhibited abroad, and his allegedly tyrannical treatment of Athens' allies. Once this has been examined, the question remaining to be answered is, in what ways does Verres' character, as Cicero presents it, derive from a range of *topoi* that are originally Greek?

First, it is important to note that both Aeschines and Cicero allude to the early onset of their opponents' debauched lifestyle, so that their later revelations will come as no surprise. To begin with, both orators are conscious to avert the suspicion that their charges amount to little more than malicious invective. Each states that they will not deal with petty details that occurred before the time their respective opponents entered into public life:[55] of course, this

52 See Corbeill (1996).

53 There is no legal definition to clarify what, for the Athenians, was classed as *hubris*. For a full and comprehensive account of the legal concept see Fisher (1992).

54 For more on *atimia*, see Hansen (1976).

55 Compare Cicero's statement, 'All that time that came before he entered into office and public affairs, he may have free and untouched as far as I am concerned' (*Ver*. 1.33: 'omne illud tempus quod fuit antequam iste ad magistratus remque publicam accessit habeat per me solutum ac liberum'), with Aeschines' remark, 'See, men of Athens, how moderately I intend to deal with this man Timarchus. For all those sins which he committed against his own body as a boy, I remit [...], but those he has committed having reached the age of reason and when he was already a young man and knowing the laws of the state, it is these that I shall make my accusations about' (1.39: σκέψασθε δέ, ὦ ἄνδρες Ἀθηναῖοι, ὡς μετρίως μέλλω προσφέρεσθαι Τιμάρχῳ τουτῳί. ἐγὼ γάρ, ὅσα μὲν παῖς ὢν εἰς τὸ σῶμα τὸ ἑαυτοῦ ἡμάρτηκεν, ἀφίημι [...], ἃ δὲ ἤδη φρονῶν καὶ μειράκιον ὢν καὶ τοὺς νόμους ἐπιστάμενος τοὺς τῆς πόλεως διαπέπρακται, περὶ τούτων ἐγώ τε τὰς κατηγορίας ποιήσομαι). See also Dem. *de Cor.* 129-30 for a similar example of *praeteritio*.

is done in the form of a *praeteritio* so that the defendants are not wholly absolved from their past deeds. At *Ver.* 1.32-33, for instance, Cicero states at some length that he will pass over the sins of Verres' boyhood, be silent about the drunken, night-long orgies, and not make any mention of the pimps, gamblers, and seducers. He will even pass by the losses he inflicted on his father's estate and the dishonour he bore to his own manhood.[56] In contrast, Cicero's own modesty is expressed in his reflection of what it is 'proper' for him to mention, and in his intention to pass over everything that seems too disgraceful to talk about.[57]

When compared to Aeschines' remarks in two passages from the speech *Against Timarchus*, the similarities of form and content alert us to the fact that Cicero must be imitating his predecessor here. First, Aeschines expresses his anxiety that in narrating his opponent's life he might have to transgress the propriety of speech expected in the Athenian court: he claims that Timarchus's behaviour has been so shameful that a man who is describing such behaviour might sometimes have to use equally shameful expressions, even though he may not want to.[58] As noted above, Aeschines has chosen to pass over the sins of Timarchus's boyhood and the sins he committed against his own manhood then. Shortly after the *praeteritio* however, in a second passage, Aeschines immediately reports how, once Timarchus had reached the age of majority, he squandered his patrimony and became a slave to the most shameful pleasures, including extravagant dining, flute-girls, harlots, and dice.[59]

In sum: the correspondences in the passages from the *Verrines* and Aeschines' speech *Against Timarchus* discussed thus far are (1) the rhetorical strategy of *praeteritio* employed to 'pass over' (2) the sins of the accused before he entered public life. (3) The speaker's own anxiety at having to talk about such disgraceful behaviour, which includes (4) squandered patrimony, (5) licentious women, (6) gambling, and (7) the compromising of one's own manhood. The audience is by now in a position to accept the worst the prosecutors can and will come up with regarding their opponents' behaviour.

Following this, the step to presenting Timarchus and Verres as tyrants was not a particularly big one to take. The psychology behind the rhetoric is best illustrated in Plato's *Republic* (9.573b-574). Here, Socrates and his companions are presented as discussing and examining the tyrannical man and what the desires of such men may be. It is agreed that, to begin with, such men go in for feasts, revelries, luxuries, and girlfriends. The costs of such luxuries lead to the borrowing of money and the expenditure of capital. But the desires inside him, especially erotic love, continue to grow, he becomes frenzied and begins to seek out those

56 Cic. *Ver.* 1.32: 'nihil a me de pueritiae suae flagitiis audiet.' *Ver.* 1.33: 'sileatur de nocturnis eius bacchationibus ac uigilis; lenonum, aleatorum, perductorum nulla mentio fiat; damna, dedecora, quae res patris eius, aetas ipsius pertulit, praetereantur.'

57 Cic. *Ver.* 1.32: 'omnia praeteribo quae mihi turpia dictu uidebuntur, neque solum quid istum audire, uerum etiam quid me deceat dicere, considerabo.'

58 Aeschin. 1.38: εἰ αἰσχρῶς οὕτω τυγχάνει βεβιωκώς, ὥστε τὸν τὰ τούτῳ πεπραγμένα διεξιόντα ἀδύνατον εἶναι εἰπεῖν ὡς αὐτὸς βούλεται, ἐὰν μή τι καὶ τῶν τοιούτων φθέγξηται ῥημάτων. εὐλαβήσομαι δ' αὐτὸ ποιεῖν ὡς ἂν δύνωμαι μάλιστα. For more on the rules of propriety in court, see Carey (1994).

59 Aeschin. 1.42: πολλὴν γὰρ πάνυ κατέλιπεν ὁ πατὴρ αὐτῷ οὐσίαν, ἣν οὗτος κατεδήδοκεν, ὡς ἐγὼ προϊόντος ἐπιδείξω τοῦ λόγου· ἀλλ' ἔπραξε ταῦτα δουλεύων ταῖς αἰσχίσταις ἡδοναῖς, ὀψοφαγίᾳ καὶ πολυτελείᾳ δείπνων καὶ αὐλητρίσι καὶ ἑταίραις καὶ κύβοις.

who possess anything that he might take, either by deceit or force. It should be clear that the path to destruction described here – or, more appropriately, the vicious circle – is the same as that by which Aeschines and Cicero present their opponents as already entrapped. The next question is how do these men behave tyrannically when in power?

The first aspect to note is that the would-be tyrant sees his country's allies as a source for plunder and as a means of enriching himself. As much is said of Verres' intentions, whose name, Cicero suggests, was prophetic of his plan to sweep the province clean.[60] Similarly, Timarchus is alleged to have accepted a loan from his friends to bribe his way into the magistracy. The high interest on the loan (approximately 18% *p. a.*) makes it clear that Timarchus expected to extract enough money both to pay back this loan and to enrich himself at the same time.[61]

More instructive, however, is the fact that both Timarchus and Verres use the allies to provide for their debauched lifestyles. As the passage from Plato, cited above, revealed, the tyrannical man is one in whom the capacity to control his desires no longer resides; but the lack of control over sexual urges, which is another mark of the tyrant, is also a manifestation of his *hubris*.[62] References to Verres' sexual misconduct abound in the speeches against him, but when Cicero reports that 'there was not one town out of those towns in which governors were accustomed to stay and to hold court, where some woman had not been selected from some noble family in that town to satisfy his [Verres'] lust', he is explicitly condemning Verres' abuse of his own power as well as the maltreatment of Rome's allies.[63] Aeschines lodges a parallel complaint against Timarchus, who he claims 'displayed a level of licentiousness as great as no other man before in his treatment of the wives of free men'.[64]

To summarize: the above discussion has aimed at alerting the reader of Cicero's *Verrines* as to how the character of Verres, as Cicero presents him, ultimately derives from a range of *topoi* that are originally Greek. From the model of Demosthenes' Meidias, Cicero adapted the make-up of a monster: the wealthy man, who draws an over-inflated sense of his own importance from his wealth. This man believes that the laws do not apply to him and consequently acts without fear or respect for his fellow citizens and the gods: he is hubristic and impious. But, as noted above, Meidias was a bully amongst his own men and, for the presentation of an evil tyrant amongst his nation's allies, Cicero turned to the character of Timarchus presented in Aeschines 1. From the sins of their youth, Timarchus and Verres are deemed to be destined to follow the road to tyranny. The tyrannical use of their respective lands' allies follows naturally from the pleasure they find in material, physical, and carnal

60 Cic. *Ver.* 2.19: 'paratus ex illo omine urbano ad euerrendam prouinciam uenerit.'

61 Aeschin. 1.107; see Fisher (2001) 245.

62 For a discussion on the connection between rape/adultery, *hubris*, and tyranny, as well as how it enters into the discourse of the Attic orators see Omitowoju (1997).

63 Cic. *Ver.* 5.28: 'nam scitote oppidum esse in Sicilia nullum ex iis oppidis in quibus consistere praetores et conuentum agere soleant, quo in oppido non isti ex aliqua familia non ignobili delecta ad libidinem mulier esset.'

64 Aeschin. 1.107: καὶ τοσαύτην ἀσέλγειαν ἐπεδείξατο εἰς ἐλευθέρων ἀνθρώπων γυναῖκας ἡλίκην οὐδεὶς πώποθ' ἕτερος.

pleasures as, again and again, they seek to gratify their lusts. They have, by now, become tyrannical.

Conclusion

Briefly to reiterate the main aim of this paper, I have attempted to show that often in Greek and Roman litigation the situations are sufficiently similar to make it possible for Cicero to re-use the arguments from the Attic orators. In the first section I suggested that Cicero drew upon typically Attic *topoi* and techniques in his self-representation, firstly by presenting himself as a reluctant prosecutor, and secondly by reversing the roles of prosecutor and defendant. In this way the speakers aimed at averting the hostility that usually attached itself to the volunteer prosecutor in both systems.

In the second section I have shown that, in his presentation of Verres, Cicero draws on arguments from character that are originally Greek, even if they have in some cases become Roman commonplaces. While accusations of tyranny were frequently hurled about in the political invective of the Roman Republic, this is no reason to underplay the influence of Attic oratory: the Greek tyrant was grafted onto the Roman attitude to kingship, which goes back into the mists of time.

We could well put the kind of similarities which I have discussed down to a long-standing rhetorical tradition, passed down by word of mouth through the years; or we could put them down to the recognized principles of invective. However, I do not believe that this can account for the number of similarities we find in the works of our orators. When we look at the evidence cumulatively, therefore, I believe that the only explanation is that Greek rhetoric has a greater presence in Cicero's rhetorical practice than has hitherto been appreciated.

Roehampton University

THE RHETORIC OF THE *DE FRUMENTO*

CATHERINE STEEL

> I have had in you in the preceding speeches a most attentive audience – and I found that was most welcome. But it will be much more welcome if you are ready to pay attention to what remains, particularly as there was a certain attractiveness in these earlier matters due to the very variety and novelty of the matter and the charges, whereas I am now beginning to handle the section of my case dealing with corn, which outdoes the other charges in terms of the size and nature of the offence but offers less pleasure and variety in the handling.[1]

In this way Cicero engages, in the opening chapters of the *de Frumento* (his longest surviving speech), in a pre-emptive apology for its tedium. The theme, moreover, recurs (*Ver.* 3.103). The manoeuvre might seem justified: this material on Verres' alleged wrongdoing in relation to the corn supply is complex, technical, and detailed and its location within the *Verrines* as a whole might seem to exemplify the principle of rhetorical organization that weak arguments should come in the middle.[2]

Nonetheless, we should perhaps be wary of taking Cicero's own remarks about the difficulty of the material too literally. The *Verrines* as a whole mark a striking choice on Cicero's part: not simply to disseminate a written version of a forensic speech but to produce versions of speeches that were never delivered and moreover to do so at a length which was almost certainly unprecedented in Latin oratory. These speeches must surely be seen as a marker of Cicero's confidence in his own talent as a speaker and in the potential of Verres' trial and exile to contribute beneficially to Cicero's own developing career.[3] And the *de Frumento*, with its apparently intractable material, is a particularly striking showcase for Cicero's skill: he is an orator who can make even the corn supply appealing and persuasive.

In the first part of this paper I explore how Cicero achieves this feat; the second part suggests, more tentatively, that the striking lucidity of the *de Frumento* enables Cicero to engage in a systematic attempt to confuse and deceive his readers about the nature of Verres' crimes.

1 Cic. *Ver.* 3.10: 'superiore omni oratione perattentes uestros animos hauimus: id fuit nobis gratum admodum. sed multo erit gratius si reliqua uoletis attendere, propterea quod in his omnibus quae antea dicta sunt erat quaedam ex ipsa uarietate ac nouitate rerum et criminum delectatio, nunc tractare causam instituimus frumentariam, quae magnitudine, iniuriae et re criminibus ceteris antecellet, iucunditatis in agendo et uarietatis minus habebit.'

2 *Rhet. Her.* 3.18; Cic. *de Orat.* 2.314.

3 Frazel (2004) has recently restated the case for the *Verrines* as unashamed self-promotion; *cf.* Butler (2002).

I. Structure and Narrative

The structure of the *de Frumento* can be tabulated as follows:

1-11	*Exordium*		1-5	By prosecuting Verres, Cicero is committing himself to good behaviour in the future
			6-9	Despite Verres' crimes, he is still preferred by Hortensius to men like Cicero
			10-11	The jury should not be put off by the tedium of the subject
12	*Partitio*: i) the tithe, ii) grain purchase, iii) valuation			
12-163		The tithe		
		12-20	The arrangments before Verres	
		21-40	Verres' arrangements	
		40-49	Verres' defence: profit for Rome, but …	
			40-48	He has wrecked the province
			48-49	His own profit is as great as that of the Roman people
		50-53	Summary	
		53-63	Examples of injustices against individuals	
			53-57	Sicilians
			58-63	Romans
		64-66	Summary of abuses against individuals	
		67-118	Abuses against cities	
		119-29	Devastation of province; his successor Metellus's efforts to rebuild it	
		130-46	Legal challenges to Verres	
		147-51	Leontini	
		152-63	Attempts by Verres' assistants to control Metellus	
163-87		Grain purchases		
		164	*Partitio*: i) Usury, ii) Non-payment, iii) Underpayment	
		165-69		Usury
		170-79		Non-payment
		180-87		Underpayment
188-225		Abuses in valuations		
226-28		Conclusion		

The initial impression this structure gives is one of great clarity. There is an overarching tripartite structure which provides the basis for the speech; each of these sections is further subdivided into discrete categories. Cicero has done much of the audience's work for it: he has taken the mass of material he had at his disposal from Sicily, analysed it and thus ordered it, and can then present it systematically in clearly identified categories which exemplify a particular malpractice. Not the least of the effects of this clarity is its contribution to Cicero's authority; his ability to present the material so lucidly is a tribute to his mastery of it.

The structure depends upon flexibility in using conventional methods of arrangment. Most notable perhaps is the refutation of Verres' defence, which comes very early: we would normally expect the advocate's own case to be presented before he demolished that of his opponent. In this speech, however, Cicero analyses Verres' defence relatively early on, in chapters 40-49.[4] Verres' defence is that his methods have secured the grain supply. Cicero counters this with two arguments. The cost of this has been to ruin the province's grain-growing capacity, so that a short term benefit has been possible only at the cost of a longer term decline in supplies; and Verres has extracted a personal benefit equal to the benefit he has given the city of Rome.

This organizational device has a number of consequences. One is that there is a controlled release of information. Verres' hypothetical defence comes early, but it is not the initial item in Cicero's exposition. It breaks into Cicero's analysis of what Verres has done wrong; when his defence is presented to us, we have already been prepared, by the earlier recitation of his wrongdoing, to be sceptical. This scepticism is then confirmed, after Verres' defence has been demolished, through the piling-up of example after example of the effects of Verres' practice. This controlled release of information is a way to prevent the mass of evidence from overwhelming the audience, while leading us to be receptive to Cicero's interpretation.

A second element in this early handling of Verres' defence may be the fact that no defence was actually ever offered. Cicero may have wanted to consider the defence early because his reading audience would not already have an idea of what the defence had been – whereas it is fair to assume that, in cases where a written speech related to a trial which had continued until a verdict, the initial reading audience, if they were sufficiently interested in the case to get their hands on a copy, would also have at least a broad idea of the nature of pleading at the trial. Indeed, Cicero here might also be seeking to control what the audience does think Verres' defence might have been, since his summary in 40-49 has no check on it, in terms of what Hortensius did actually say.

Finally, this order enables Cicero to deal with a possible interpretation of the case which, if held by his audience and left unchallenged, would destroy the effectiveness of all his carefully gathered examples. If his audience did happen to believe that the most important aspect of the grain supply was that Rome was efficiently supplied with sufficient quantities of grain, then they might well simply ignore the evidence of the cost of this efficiency to the inhabitants of Sicily. By addressing this problem early on, and by giving his audience solid, self-interested motives for deploring how Verres has handled Sicily, and by stirring up their outrage by pointing to Verres' personal profit, he is attempting to keep them attentive to his case.

In terms of the structure of the third *Verrine*, it is also noticeable that the conclusion of the speech is both brief and relatively restrained: a reminder that this speech, for all its length, is itself only a part of a much larger project. The ordering of topics through the five speeches is carefully designed to produce an ever-increasing level of tension, culminating in Verres'

4 This tactic is even more obvious in the fifth *Verrine*, where Cicero refers in the very first paragraph to Verres' 'magnifica et praeclara [...] defensio' ('an outstandingly impressive defence') and refutes this defence (that Verres' military skill has kept Sicily safe), before turning to his own case.

gross abuses as a military commander. At the mid-point in the project it is important that the conclusion should not bring the forward momentum to a complete halt.

Within this clear overall framework, the evidence in individual sections is presented with considerable variation of pace and use of emotional appeal. The section on the abuses against cities (67-117) can offer a case study. Here, too, tabulation by chapter is the clearest way of showing its structure:

67-74		Agyrium
75-82		Herbita
	81-82	digression: Sulla
83		Acesta
84-85		Lipara
86-87		Tissa
88-89		Amestratus
90		Petra
91		Halicyae
92-93		Segesta: C. Annaeus Brocchus
	94-98	digression: Verres' folly in attacking senators
99		Thermae
100		Imachara
		Henna
101		Calacte
		Mutyce
102		Hybla
		Menae
	103	apology for tedium
104-08		Aetna
109-17		Leontini

The cases handled at the beginning and end of the section are substantial, whereas the ones in the middle are much shorter. There are brief digressions roughly one quarter of the way in, and then again one quarter of the episode's length before the end, and a much more substantial excursus in the middle; these break up the mass of technical information into manageable chunks.

The argument in the case of each city is, in broad terms, the same: the tax-collector who was collecting the tithes took more than was due. This story, if merely repeated over and over again, would become tedious. So there is variation. The first city handled is Agyrium, and the story seems straightforward. The tax-collector in this case is Apronius, whose character has already been discussed at some length earlier in this speech (*Ver.* 3.22-23): he was the chief among the tax-collectors and a great intimate of Verres.[5] He goes to Agyrium and demands a sum of money which will enable him to make a profit on what he has paid for the right to collect taxes. The Agyrians refuse, the matter goes to the governor's court in Syracuse, the

5 On Cicero's invective against Apronius, see Corbeill (1996) 106-12; Steel (2001) 39-43.

Agyrians still refuse to pay up but are threatened with capital punishment and so hand over what Apronius had demanded.

In the case of the second city in this section, Herbita, there is a further outrageous element to what happened. The tithes of wheat were being collected by Aeschrio, the husband of one of Verres' mistresses, and the barley tithes by Docimus, the husband of another one. Furthermore, Verres reduced the sale-price for the tithes after the contract had been awarded. This act provokes Cicero to reflect upon a parallel circumstance relating to the dictator Sulla. Sulla had a habit of offering his friends reductions in the price of confiscated goods after they had been purchased: but the Senate declared that the full purchase price must be handed over to the Treasury. Cicero presents this as the only matter on which Sulla's will was thwarted, thus underlining the importance of preserving the income of the Roman people: consequently, it demonstrates very forcefully how wrong Verres was to make deductions himself in the sale-price of tithes.

The digression on Sulla can thus be seen to play a straightforward part in the argument. But it is perhaps worth asking more generally why Cicero chooses to bring Sulla in at this point, since the case against Verres could have been made perfectly clearly without a supporting *exemplum*: the need to protect the revenues of the Roman people is a convincing argument.

Cicero indicates a general assessment of Sulla's actions: 'we not only maintain all his actions, but even defend them with public authority in fear of greater inconveniences and disasters [...]'.[6] Cicero had engaged with Sulla and his legacy from almost the very beginning of his career, with *pro Roscio Amerino*, and it was presumably useful for him, in terms of the development of his own political ambitions, to reassert a moderate line, which withheld approbration from what Sulla had done but was committed to maintaining his settlement to avoid more upheaval.[7] But it is less obvious that he would have brought in the ambiguous and troubled question of Sulla simply to demonstrate that he held a moderate position.

Verres himself had been a Sullan partisan, who had joined Sulla early in his campaigns in Italy after his return from the Mithridatic War.[8] He was a quaestor or proquaestor at that time, with the proconsul Papirius Carbo, and he took the official cashbox with him when he changed sides: material for fine Ciceronian outrage, indeed, in the first *Verrine*. But many men were finding themselves to be Sullans at this period,[9] and Cicero does not make any explicit reference in this passage of the third *Verrine* to the connection which had existed between Sulla and Verres. Sulla's presence here in the third *Verrine* is perhaps best explained by more general considerations. His dictatorship was marked by profound uncertainty in Italy: property rights were overthrown and individuals executed in ways which seem to have been recalled as frighteningly unpredictable.[10] Cicero sketches this horror out and then proceeds

6 *Ver*. 3.81: 'eius omnis res gestas non solum obtinemus, uerum etiam propter maiorum incommodorum et calamitatum metum publica auctoritate defendimus [...]'. *Publica auctoritate* would suggest that the 'we' Cicero has in mind here is the Senate.

7 Some years later, as consul, Cicero addressed this issue in *On the Sons of the Proscribed* (Crawford (1994) 205-11).

8 Cic. *Ver*. 1.34-40.

9 Badian (1962).

10 Sal. *Hist*. 1.55 (M); Plut. *Sull*. 31.3-6.

to imply that Verres is even worse than Sulla. The comparison contributes to the developing picture of Verres as a man who has devastated Sicily and enables Cicero to move from the very specific details of individual cities to these much broader and more emotionally compelling issues. The comparison hangs on a similar financial manoeuvre, but the emotional hinterland which can thereby be brought into view transforms Verres' scam into an assault on the fundamentals of peaceful life.

After the digression on Sulla, six more cities are then treated comparatively briefly. In each case, however, there is identifying circumstantial detail: the name of the tax-collector and figures for the amount of profit that is extracted are always given. A recurrent feature in these miniature narratives is that the tax-collector is a disreputable or unsuitable figure: at Tissa it is a temple slave, at Petra a man who has been found guilty of assault. Then what happened at Segesta is described. The citizens of this community were exempt from the tithe, but non-citizens who leased land there were liable. Cicero describes the extortion by the tax-collector, another temple slave, of money and corn, first of all from a Sicilian called Diocles Phimus, from Panhormus, and then from a Roman senator called Gaius Annaeus Brocchus.

> C. Annaeus Brocchus, a senator, whose reputation and courage you all recognize, was compelled to give corn and, moreover, money to this Symmachus. When you, Verres, were praetor, was such a man, a senator of the Roman people, an opportunity for profit for a temple slave?[11]

The initial statement of fact gives way to the outraged question; though the apparent straightforwardness of the first sentence is of course carefully designed to prepare our sentiments, with the juxtaposition of 'Symmachus' with 'C. Annaeus Brocchus', the involvement of the audience through the reference to their own opinion of Brocchus, and the introduction of the idea of compulsion.

The outrage a senatorial jury should feel at the thought of a senator being forced to do the bidding of a slave is then nurtured in the digression which follows. In it, Cicero considers what Verres' ill-treatment of a senator might mean, given that the jury is composed entirely of senators. He considers what things were like when the juries were made up of equestrians, and the effect that this had on the behaviour of provincial governors, who became extremely concerned to maintain the goodwill of equestrians in their province. This is implicitly contrasted with Verres' apparent contempt for the senators who will judge him, which Cicero sums up in a sentence which he imagines Verres saying: 'Give me too that senator over there, so that this most dignified title of "senator" may seem created not only for the envy of the ignorant but also for the contempt of wicked men.'[12] Cicero then describes how the wife of another senator also suffered from Verres' impositions, and follows this by suggesting to his audience that the pressures which senators face make it even more important that they are not oppressed by magistrates.

11 *Ver.* 3.93: 'huic eidem Symmacho C. Annaeus Brocchus senator, homo eo splendore, ea uirtute, qua omnes existimatis, nummos praeter frumentum coactus est dare. Venerione seruo te praetore talis uir, senator populi Romani, quaestui fuit?'

12 *Ver.* 3.96: 'cedo mihi etiam istum senatorem, ut hoc amplissimum nomen senatorium non modo ad inuidiam imperitorum, sed etiam ad contumeliam improborum natum esse uideatur?'

This digression provides an important insight into senatorial involvement in land outside Italy, or at least into Cicero's assessment of the issue. The intended audience is, of course, not simply the senatorial jury, given the circumstances of the speeches' dissemination: but this passage only works with any audience if Verres' assault on particular senators seems plausible, and that implies that senators were perceived to have financial interests overseas. Indeed, Cicero implies in this passage that there were senators by this period who lived in Sicily. However, the details may reveal a certain tact. It is unclear whether the law against senators owning land outside Italy was still in force at this point, and neither of Cicero's examples in fact concerns senatorial ownership of land: one of the two cases he mentions (that of Brocchus) concerns land which is rented and the other land owned by the wife of a senator. It may be that these two were all that Cicero had been able to find; but, if there were still some legal difficulty about senatorial land-ownership outside Italy, we would hardly expect Cicero to record for posterity those of his senatorial colleagues who fell into the grey area.

Moreover, the digression on senatorial victims of Verres places senators alongside others who have suffered. Sicilians, *negotiatores*, and equestrians form a list of groups who do not have the resources to defend themselves; but the senators, through their position on juries, do have resources to respond to Verres and Cicero urges them to acknowledge their common identity: 'You, gentlemen of the jury, should consider what we as a group have in common to unite us.'[13] Verres' disregard for their potential to retaliate becomes a further example of his inability to think through the consequences of his actions. The digression thus gives the senatorial jury a personal stake in proceedings, whilst reminding other readers that Verres posed a threat to the whole of civilized society.

There is then a very rapid survey of seven more cities, which are treated even more briefly than those before the digression on senators. As before, Cicero has included headings to mark where evidence would have been produced, although, in this particular case, no opportunity arose to present such material or subject it to scrutiny. The rapidity of the narrative nonetheless includes convincing circumstantial detail: the names of individuals involved, precise figures for amounts of corn and sums of money removed. The impression produced is of someone producing carefully chosen information out of a much wider store of material that he has at his disposal. But the passage is not just an accumulation of detail: it also includes a general reflection on the case.

> My speech is running through all the communities which pay tithes, and I am here occupied not with those individual farmers who have been deprived of all their possessions but with the sums paid by communities to the tithe-collectors, in order that at last, filled up and sated by their fields and towns they might go away with their heap of gain.[14]

13 *Ver.* 3.98: 'uos autem, iudices, putare debetis esse quiddam nobis inter nos commune atque coniunctum.'

14 *Ver.* 3.100: 'nam per omnis ciuitates quae decumas debent percurrit oratio mea, et in hoc genere nunc, iudices, uersor, non in quo singillatim aratores euersi bonis omnibus sint, sed quae publice decumanis lucra data sint, ut aliquando ex eorum agris atque urbibus expleti atque saturati cum hoc cumulo quaestus decederent.'

Thus, even in the most rapid parts of the narrative, Cicero still introduces variety into how the audience is brought to contemplate his case and reminds them that the abuses he is describing at this point are but a part of the overall situation.

After these seven cities in rapid sequence Cicero apologizes again for the potential tedium of his subject: 'I realize that I must put a limit on my speech and avoid wearying you. I shall not spend longer on one subject, but in removing the rest of the material from my speech I shall nonetheless keep it in the case.'[15] Here again, we have a reference to the non-existent presentation of evidence as the essential complement of the speech itself. But, although Cicero here promises the imminent end of the section, there is some more material yet to cover, with the comparatively lengthy narratives concerning Aetna and Leontini.

The greater length of Cicero's treatment of these two cities does not seem to arise from any fundamental difference between events there and elsewhere: the wrongdoing alleged is once again that an excessive tithe and cash sums are extracted from communities. The length comes rather from the handling of material. The land of the two communities is described as 'practically the best and richest'; our attention is secured by the apparently outstanding subject matter. Moreover, Cicero explicitly makes it easier for us by handling only one year out of the three in question: 'I shall choose one year, so that I can explain more easily my subject.'[16] He sets out the position in a very simple sentence: 'The land is fertile, it is the third year, and Apronius is the tithe collector.'[17] In handling Aetna, he repeatedly emphasizes that his treatment is cursory, although Apronius's outrageous behaviour during his visit to the city is described at some length: here Cicero builds on the character sketch he deployed much earlier in the speech (*Ver.* 3.22-23), reinforcing the idea that one of the things which makes Verres' tax-collection particularly oppressive is his close links to individual tax-collectors – who, Cicero suggests, are working for Verres directly. The remainder of the section on Aetna is largely concerned with the juxtaposition of Apronius's name with the enormous sum he is said to have collected, in order to provoke outrage; the details are consigned to the absent section of evidence.

The situation in Leontini is somewhat different. Cicero acknowledges that he has not had the support of the inhabitants of Leontini in constructing his case and that they were not victims of Verres' government. However, he then explains that the reason they were not affected is that hardly any of the inhabitants of Leontini actually farm the city's territory. As a result, they have not presented any evidence in support of Cicero's case; he, therefore, will explain what happened at Leontini himself. This allows him to engage in a detailed exposition of the figures and their relation to a putative level of grain production in the area; he also continues in his attack on Apronius's methods, including his lack of accounts and his use of force to extract the tithe. The handling of Leontini, and indeed the entire section on abuses against cities, comes to a splendidly rousing climax with a series of rhetorical questions about Apronius's actions, concluding with his indefensible practice of charging extra fees: 'He had

15 *Ver.* 3.103: 'sentio, iudices, moderandum mihi esse iam orationi meae fugiendamque uestram satietatem. non uersabor in uno genere diutius, et ita cetera de oratione mea tollam ut in causa tamen relinquam.'

16 *Ver.* 3.104: 'unum annum eligam, quo facilius id quod institui explicare possim.'

17 *Ver.* 3.104: 'agri sunt feraces, annus tertius, decumanus Apronius.'

no precedent for this practice and no right to do it, nor did he provide accounts for this money; nor will anybody ever be able to work out how the man is going to defend himself against this little charge.'[18]

This section of the speech dealing with abuses against cities is worth attention in some detail, in order to show how Cicero structures the material to make it seem clear and to keep his audience's interest. He varies the length of episodes; he includes personal material to rouse emotions and to provide a contrast with the detailed figures; there are digressions which bring in wider issues of interest to the audience; and he regularly relates the material he is presenting to the general case against Verres – particularly important in an area where Verres was not directly involved in what was going on. This episode offers a splendid example of how to make difficult material palatable; and one could analyse other parts of the third *Verrine* in similar ways.

Nonetheless, the apparent lucidity of the third *Verrine* is, arguably, only superficial: part and parcel of a systematic obfuscation of the issues in the case.[19] That is, this attractive and accessible style of narration also enables Cicero to conceal and confuse, in order to put Verres and his actions in the worst possible light.

II. Lucid confusion

That there is some degree of concealment and obfuscation at work in the speech is surely in itself not in question. At the very least, the third *Verrine* does not provide particularly clear evidence for the management of the corn supply in Sicily, despite being the major source on the subject; and a number of the papers in this volume are concerned with some of the interpretative problems that the speech raises, precisely because there are issues which are not fully explained in it. It is debatable, for example, how far Verres' actions were illegal, as opposed to unprecedented; to what extent he was personally involved in the corn supply; and how far we are dealing with fraud as opposed to heavy, but nonetheless transparent, exactions.

Three aspects of Cicero's narrative methods in this speech are particularly worth noting in this respect. They are his use of names and places; his description of the mechanisms of fraudulent behaviour; and the relationship claimed in the written speech between it and the evidence.

It is not possible to come to a full assessment of the order in which Cicero names the different communities which he handles in the section discussed above, because the exact location of some is unknown. But even with this *caueat* it is difficult to discern any obvious ordering principle. Other speeches, outside the *Verrine* corpus, show that Cicero was very alert to the possibilities of manipulating his audiences' responses through the careful placing of geographical names.[20] The apparently random order here is thus unlikely simply to be the result of carelessness or indifference; possibly the order is deliberately random, in order to make it more difficult for a reader of the speech to take control of the information in it and thus begin to interrogate it himself – and so even a reader who knew Sicily well and did know

18 *Ver.* 3.118: 'hoc neque exemplo cuiusquam neque ullo iure fecit, neque eam pecuniam rettulit; neque hoc paruum crimen quem ad modum defensurus sit homo quisquam umquam excogitabit.'

19 *Cf.* Steel (2004).

20 Vasaly (1993) 218-43.

where all these places were would find themselves somewhat unsure of the situation, given Cicero's presentation, precisely because of its lack of a coherent geographical underpinning.

The description of the mechanisms of profiteering is also a source of potential confusion. Cicero's use of two different measures, the *modius* and the *medimnum*, may not on its own have been a serious problem for his audience, however daunting it may seem for a modern reader, even though it is not clear that Cicero has any reason for his choice of one term rather than the other at any specific point. But, where matters get more complex, the narrative does not always aid comprehension. An example comes in the section on grain purchasing dealing with the city of Halaesa.[21] Verres ordered the Halaesini to sell him 60,000 *modii* of wheat, at the price fixed by Rome. He rejected the corn that they offered him as sub-standard, and so took from them a sum of money equal to the current market price of wheat. He then sent the 60,000 *modii* of grain from his own supplies to Rome, and kept the money he had been given by the state to purchase the grain.

Verres is engaging in two different processes in this transaction. One is what a governor did when a community which was facing the demand of compulsory purchase did not have enough grain, or enough of sufficiently high quality, to meet the demand: it seems that the governor demanded a cash equivalent to buy grain elsewhere. The purpose of the mechanism was presumably to protect the Roman state from local fluctuations of price, since if one community was having difficulty in supplying enough grain it might point to wider shortages, which would push up the price; and clearly a governor needed a veto over quality to stop the Romans from being the recipients of sub-standard grain. The second process is the governor supplying wheat out of his own supplies and thereby keeping the state funds, which had been allocated for grain purchase, for himself. Verres used both in this case, rejecting the grain of Halaesa and demanding a cash supplement, and then fulfilling the actual requirement for grain from supplies which he had already purchased, thus retaining the state cash allocated for this purchase. Cicero takes this interconnectedness and turns it into a wonderfully entwined confusion: 'A praetor, who ought to be buying grain, doesn't buy it but sells it, and takes away and carries off all the money which he ought to be handing out to states.'[22] Crucially, his initial telling of the story omits Verres' provision of the required grain from his own supplies: hence it appears that he is taking cash both from Halaesa and from Rome without giving anything in return to either side. It is probably worth noting, too, that Cicero does not tell us how much money the people of Halaesa handed over to Verres to compensate for the absence of suitable corn, which would suggest that it was not very great and possibly therefore amounted only to the excess of the market price over the state-fixed price, if the former were higher. The language of the passage appears simple and straightforward, and as readers we are borne along by the indignation which Cicero stirs up; but, as soon as one begins to reflect upon the actual transactions involved, it becomes far from clear that Verres did engage in any

21 *Ver.* 3.170-71.

22 *Ver.* 3.171: 'ut praetor, qui frumentum emere debeat, non emat sed uendat, pecunias, quas ciuitatibus distribuere debeat, eas omnis avertat atque auferat.'

behaviour which would have been regarded as inappropriate; which does not, of course, preclude his use of mechanisms which could lead to substantial private profits.[23]

The final trait in this speech which is potentially misleading is the impression that the speech gives of offering, quite legitimately, only a part of the relevant information. The speech is full of headings, which mark points at which evidence would be given. I noted above a reference, in the section on abuses against communities, to information which was given during the evidence and so did not need handling in the speech, and another place where the lack of evidence becomes a justification for Cicero to treat a topic at length himself. In a normal case, the evidence would have been presented at the trial and then excised from the written version, in what seems to have been a generic convention. The same convention is at work in the *Verrines*: but the evidence has not been subjected to the same tests. The consequence for the reader is a sense that there is an enormous amount of further material which supports Cicero's case: that the material presented is only the tip of the iceberg.

There are thus a number of devices that Cicero uses, which make it more difficult to establish exactly what might be going on. It is in relation to this that the apparent lucidity and attractiveness of his narration become so important. The speech gives the impression of being clear; it is also agreeable, because there is variety and interest; and, as readers, we know that the author is taking care for our well-being, because he remarks on the steps he is taking to avoid boring us. If these traits operate successfully on us, we will be well-disposed towards Cicero, more inclined to trust him, and more inclined to believe that what he is saying makes perfect sense – even if we ourselves cannot quite follow the details.

Concluding remarks

It remains to ask why this speech is constructed with such misleading art. The answer, I would suggest, lies in the particularly fluid potential of charges arising out of the handling of the grain supply. In this area of provincial government, above all, the interests of provincials and of Romans were directly opposed. The more taxation that was levied, the better for the Romans and the worse for the provincials; and *uice uersa*. This conflict of interests provided a strong defence for any magistrate accused of exploitation in this area, since they could claim to be securing the interests of Rome – as Verres did. By ensuring the sale of tithes at a high rate, he benefited the people of Rome. Hence, indeed, the importance for Cicero of demonstrating Verres' wrong-doing over grain. But the competing interests also provided the means to construct a multi-faceted attack. Given the many different interests involved, there were many individuals and groups who could claim to have been badly treated by Verres: Sicilian communities, individual farmers, but also the Roman people. That is, Cicero manages to argue both that too much grain was taken from the Sicilian people and that the Roman people were defrauded. A striking example of this is in the digression on Sulla, in which Cicero uses the fact that not even Sulla was allowed to undersell property, the proceeds of which were going to the Roman treasury, as a demonstration of the extraordinary wickedness shown by Verres in doing just that. The charge is that Verres reduced the taxes due to Rome. But this comes in the midst of a long section where the basic issue is that Verres allowed too

23 Famously, Cicero himself accumulated 2,200,000 *sesterces* by the end of his governorship of Cilicia 'saluis legibus' (*Fam.* 5.20.9 = SB 128).

much taxation to be levied, with bad consequences for the Sicilians. One might suspect a degree of inconsistency.

The device which Cicero uses to skate over the inconsistency is his inclusion of the tax-farmers. By accusing them of appropriating money, he is able to argue both that too high a sum was taken from farmers in Sicily and that too low an amount reached the Roman people. And of course this also brings in Verres: he too is accused of profiteering alongside the tax-farmers. So it is very important for Cicero's strategy to spend time early in the third *Verrine* establishing the character of Apronius, and to refer to dubious appointments of tax-farmers, such as the spouses of Verres' mistresses, because Cicero needs a corrupt group of tax-farmers in order to explain what is going on; but, even though the nominal jury for this speech was entirely senatorial, he does not wish to accuse the equestrians of wholesale misbehaviour. This central explanatory weight on the tax-farmers is supported by the overall impression Cicero creates of having handled the grain charges in a thorough and lucid fashion, which nonetheless makes it a matter of considerable effort to create hypotheses which explain what is going on in ways other than Cicero's. The case in the third *Verrine* is weak, complex, and confusing; Cicero's rhetorical transmutation makes it powerful, straightforward, and clear.

University of Glasgow

LES DONNÉES CHIFFRÉES DANS LE *DE FRUMENTO* DE CICÉRON[1]

SYLVIE PITTIA

Appréhender les données chiffrées dans le *corpus* cicéronien n'appelle pas les mêmes méthodes selon le type de texte qu'on affronte. Ainsi la correspondance offre-t-elle une multitude d'informations chiffrées; ce sont surtout des sommes d'argent, intéressant aussi bien les affaires publiques que les finances privées. Ces renseignements sont épars, le plus souvent il n'est guère possible d'établir entre eux des corrélations. Dès lors, la cohérence des chiffres est souvent considérée *in abstracto*, en tout cas en sortant du texte cicéronien lui-même, et par comparaison avec d'éventuels autres témoignages contemporains.[2]

Dans les discours au contraire, on peut trouver plus facilement des séries de chiffres. Par exemple, le plaidoyer *pro Q. Roscio comoedo*, quoique lacunaire, permet de reconstituer, dans le déroulement propre de l'affaire, les données chiffrées, qui sont souvent répétées et mises en corrélation.[3] Dans ce cas, la fiabilité de ces chiffres est assez plausible. En l'occurrence, ce sont des paiements, pour l'essentiel. Face à ce type de mentions

[1] Cette enquête fut présentée lors du séminaire organisé par J. Prag à l'*Institute of Classical Studies* de Londres (6-7 février 2004). Les observations ou objections qu'avaient avancées J. Andreau, M. H. Crawford, J. Patterson, D. Rathbone et C. Steel m'ont été profitables. Depuis lors, J. Dubouloz et R. Robert m'ont, par leurs critiques, permis d'amender le propos dont je leur ai infligé l'austère relecture. Qu'ils en soient ici chaleureusement remerciés, ainsi que J. Prag.

[2] Pour citer seulement un cas, évoquons les prix des maisons achetées par les riches sénateurs au temps de Cicéron. Pour la maison de Cicéron sur le Palatin, il suffit de rétablir les coefficients multiplicateurs pour avoir un prix plausible (*Fam.* 5.6.2 = SB 4): depuis Mendelssohn, tous les éditeurs corrigent XXXV en $\overline{\text{xxxv}}$, soit 3,500,000 sesterces. D'autres affaires immobilières en revanche ont suscité plus de polémiques, ainsi celle qui concerne de prestigieux membres de la noblesse romaine, comme la maison d'Autronius acquise en 61 av. J.-C. par le consul M. Valerius Messala Niger. La lettre Cic. *Att.* 1.13.6 = SB 13 indique le prix de la maison. Aucun manuscrit n'a conservé les barres de multiplication. Constans (1934) proposait de substituer simplement les barres multiplicatives à la première et à la dernière lettre de la somme donnée par la principale tradition manuscrite, passant de CXXXIIII à $|\overline{\text{xxxiii}}|$ soit 3,300,000 sesterces. Shackleton Bailey (1987) rétablit de façon plus audacieuse les multiplicateurs $|\overline{\text{cxxxiiii}}|$ soit 13,400,000 sesterces. Cette somme est ainsi comparable à celle payée par Clodius, d'après un texte de Pline (*Nat.* 36.103). Je me limite ici à évoquer les débats entre éditeurs du texte. Peu d'historiens prennent finalement la peine de discuter les deux lectures, *cf.* entre autres Shatzman (1975) 23 et 308 n. 137.

[3] Dans le *pro Q. Roscio comoedo*, on peut citer comme exemples de sommes récurrentes: la deuxième traite de 50,000 HS due par Roscius à Fannius au titre de l'arbitrage de Pison (*Q. Rosc.* 11, 12, 22, 23, 24); le dédommagement de 100,000 HS dû par Flavius à Fannius pour compenser la mort de l'esclave Panurge (*Q. Rosc.* 39, 40, 41, 42, 43, 48, 49, 51, 55).

récurrentes, la cohérence est surtout examinée d'un point de vue interne au texte cicéronien.

L'équipe française qui prépare une nouvelle édition du troisième livre des *Verrines*, s'est trouvée confrontée à ces questions de la compréhension et de la fiabilité des chiffres.[4] Le *de Frumento* présente, en comparaison des précédents exemples, des points communs et des traits originaux. Là encore, les données chiffrées sont très nombreuses, elles le sont même plus que dans aucun autre discours des *Verrines*.[5] Leur variété surtout est frappante: prix, taux, rendements, délais, surfaces, volumes, chiffres bruts ou données relatives, *etc.* Il est rare qu'une plaidoirie contienne autant de quantités ou de nombres. Devant ce matériau, plusieurs approches sont possibles.

L'éditeur du discours doit assurément examiner un par un ces passages, mettre au service de l'établissement du texte toutes les ressources de la science philologique: dès lors la hiérarchie des supports de transmission, la valeur intrinsèque des manuscrits tend à prévaloir sur les autres considérations, de caractère plus historique. Cette démarche n'est pas évitable pour qui édite le discours, elle est même un point de passage obligé.

Une autre approche consisterait à insérer ces données dans un patient travail d'inventaire. Cette enquête, très analytique, inscrite dans les méthodes inductives, peut, malgré l'hétérogénéité des informations recueillies, déboucher sur des comparaisons extérieures au texte. Et l'on comparerait alors les données fournies par le *de Frumento* aux revenus procurés par d'autres provinces romaines, dans le but d'évaluer les recettes fiscales par exemple. Telle est, entre autres, la démarche qu'avait suivie Tenney Frank,[6] qui retenait de la plaidoirie que la dîme du blé en Sicile rapportait environ trois millions de *modii*, et qu'à raison de trois sesterces le *modius*, cela représentait neuf millions de sesterces.[7] Dans la mesure où les céréales constituaient la principale des denrées prélevées dans l'île, le tribut sicilien n'aurait donc pas dépassé les quatre millions de deniers. Cette présentation, pour le moins synthétique, des revenus procurés par la Sicile éludait totalement nombre de questions, comme la régularité du prélèvement en fonction des récoltes annuelles. Et les données fournies par le seul Cicéron étaient juxtaposées avec celles d'autres textes littéraires, jamais contextualisés. De la sorte, le tableau des revenus était inscrit dans une dimension synchronique. Les chiffres étaient réputés vrais, sûrs et pour tout dire, parlants.[8]

D'autre part, étudier des chiffres et *a fortiori* des chiffres qui intéressent l'histoire de l'agriculture sicilienne ou de la fiscalité romaine, pourrait aussi conduire l'enquête vers une perspective cliométrique: les grands noms de l'histoire économique antique ont

[4] Dans le cadre d'un programme de l'UMR 8585-CNRS (Centre G. Glotz), auquel collaborent J. Andreau, J. Dubouloz, J.-L. Ferrary, J. France, J. Prag et l'auteur.

[5] Nous recensons une bonne centaine de cas.

[6] Frank (1933-40) I 322-24.

[7] Le calcul se fonde sur *Ver.* 3.163.

[8] La même démarche est suivie dans le chapitre consacré à la Sicile par V. M. Scramuzza (1937).

marqué de leur empreinte ce type de débat,[9] tantôt en appréhendant l'existence de statistiques antiques, tantôt en s'interrogeant sur les mérites et les dangers d'une approche quantitative,[10] toujours perçue comme nécessaire et toujours sentie comme dangereuse.[11] Je ne me risquerai pas sur ce terrain, d'abord et surtout parce que les renseignements fournis par le seul *de Frumento* ne peuvent valablement concourir à un traitement statistique de dénombrements. Comment les débats sur les productions agricoles, la part des surfaces cultivées, le nombre d'exploitants pourraient-ils encore progresser sur la base des seules données textuelles, déjà tirées dans tous les sens et surexploitées? La méthode qui consisterait à extraire du discours de multiples renseignements ponctuels, réputés objectifs et indépendants du contexte de leur citation, puis à les insérer dans des séries, paraît exposée à bien des périls. Et il est une autre raison, à savoir que cette documentation tirée des *Verrines* est très spécifique: le *de Frumento* est à sa façon unique en son genre. La situation fiscale de la Sicile et des prélèvements que l'État romain peut y opérer, comparés à ceux des autres territoires provinciaux, présentent une originalité que Cicéron lui-même avait pris soin de bien souligner.[12]

Aucune des démarches précitées n'est finalement retenue ici. Il ne s'agit pas de discuter telle ou telle leçon (ce que fera l'édition commentée que nous préparons), ni de produire le catalogue des données chiffrées dans le *de Frumento*, ni de tenter un tableau comparatif plus large. Qui plus est, nous voudrions nous garder de deux visions irréductiblement antagonistes: celle qui sacraliserait le texte et validerait n'importe quel chiffre pourvu que la tradition manuscrite unanime en fît mention. À l'opposé, mais reflétant un même manque de nuances, la position qui récuserait en bloc toutes les données chiffrées ne semble pas plus acceptable: on ne saurait systématiquement accuser les copistes d'erreurs, ni invalider du coup l'ensemble des données chiffrées, quand bien même les risques d'altérations sont importants.

Pour échapper à ce débat biaisé, qu'il nous soit permis de rappeler quelques vérités d'évidence. *Primo*, philologues et historiens partagent souvent la même erreur, celle qui fait postuler systématiquement une vérité antique des chiffres à un moment donné, vérité altérée éventuellement au cours des siècles antiques ou lors des copies médiévales. C'est oublier au moins trois réalités: il y avait des chiffres erronés dans les documents antiques dès le départ, par simple erreur de documentation, de lecture, de calcul, *etc.* En outre, certains chiffres antiques furent en leur temps contestés, soit par les contemporains soit par les historiens eux-mêmes: qu'il suffise de mentionner le nombre de morts dans les batailles, pour lesquels les contradictions et débats remontaient sans doute au moment même des faits.[13] Ensuite, il y avait dans les chiffres antiques des manipulations et des

[9] En particulier A. H. M. Jones en 1948 dans sa leçon inaugurale pour la chaire d'histoire économique antique. Parmi les divers travaux qui ont alimenté la réflexion, citons Finley (1974) et (1982); *cf.* aussi les travaux pionniers de Duncan-Jones (1982) et (1990).

[10] Par exemple Garnsey et Saller (1987) 95-102.

[11] Un exposé synthétique est donné par Andreau (2001) 229-34.

[12] *Ver.* 3.12.

[13] Pour ne citer qu'un exemple, celui de la retentissante bataille de Sentinum (295 av. J.-C.), dont Douris de Samos propagea l'écho jusque dans le monde grec, évoquant 100,000 morts au combat (*FGrHist* II A 76, *cf.* Diod. Sic. 21.6.1). Liv. 10.29-30 ramène le chiffre de morts chez les Gaulois à

trucages qui peuvent avoir été perpétués sans le savoir. Dans ce cas, la transmission du texte peut être irréprochablement fidèle, il n'en demeure pas moins que le chiffre est inexact. Enfin, il y a, dans les chiffres du *de Frumento*, un certain nombre de situations qui n'entretiennent aucun lien avec la réalité des faits. Ainsi disposons-nous de raisonnements virtuels, modélisés, de constructions hypothétiques pour lesquels les chiffres sont par définition faux, ou du moins fictifs. Ils ne visent pas, dès l'origine du discours, à transposer une quelconque réalité.

Secundo, beaucoup d'historiens, même s'ils s'en défendent dans l'absolu, continuent d'utiliser ces textes comme des banques de données, et, en tant que de besoin, ils extraient des chiffres pour illustrer leur étude. Et quand bien même ces historiens contestent la probabilité de telle ou telle donnée, il est bien rare qu'ils s'interrogent sur les raisons de la présence d'un chiffre dans une plaidoirie.[14] Pourquoi l'auteur a-t-il sur tel point quantifié? Comment le fait-il et que veut-il montrer à travers ces chiffres? Aucun orateur antique n'avait le souci de laisser à la postérité des statistiques ou des informations chiffrées. C'est l'évidence. Loin de travailler ici sur une documentation épigraphique, nous devons prendre en compte la spécificité littéraire de cette source écrite. Nous ne sommes pas directement en face d'inventaires ou de comptabilités, ou bien devant la matérialisation d'une déclaration fiscale, ou encore devant une disposition réglementaire ou légale. Les documents officiels s'inscrivaient (du moins peut-on le supposer) dans une perspective d'exhaustivité, d'exactitude, ils étaient soumis à des contrôles et des vérifications. A l'inverse, nous ne pouvons perdre de vue, dans le *de Frumento*, que les chiffres sont tous inscrits dans une anthologie: l'accusateur et, très probablement le défenseur, sélectionnaient dans un matériel documentaire les chiffres qu'ils mettaient au service d'une démonstration, qu'ils inscrivaient dans la construction de la preuve pour l'accusateur Cicéron, ou dans la défense de Verrès pour Hortensius.[15]

Aussi le traitement des données chiffrées dans le *de Frumento* appelle-t-il naturellement les précautions habituelles devant les données chiffrées et les investigations philologiques sur chacun des passages en particulier. Mais, parce que ce texte est d'abord une plaidoirie, je voudrais appréhender ici la question sous un autre angle: après avoir précisé les conditions du dépouillement, je m'interrogerai sur la typologie des données chiffrées que l'accusateur choisit de retenir et de citer; cela m'amène à préciser les sources

25,000 et surtout il raille les historiens qui exagèrent les chiffres de combattants et de morts, et dépassent ainsi les limites de la vraisemblance: 'Magna eius diei, quo in Sentinati agro bellatum, fama est etiam uero stanti; sed superiecere quidam augendo fidem, qui in hostium exercitu peditum sexiens centena milia, equitum sex et quadraginta milia, mille carpentorum scripsere fuisse, scilicet cum Vmbris Tuscisque, quos et ipsos pugnae adfuisse; et ut Romanorum quoque augerent copias, L. Volumnium pro consule ducem consulibus exercitumque eius legionibus consulum adiciunt.'

[14] Ainsi dans l'article de Pritchard (1972). D'un côté Pritchard met certes en doute certains chiffres, en insistant sur le souci d'émouvoir l'auditoire, par exemple pour la situation des cultivateurs sur l'*ager Leontinus*. Mais émouvoir n'implique pas de chiffrer. D'un autre côté, Pritchard passe en revue des prix maximum, des prix moyens, fait des calculs sophistiqués sur les cours ou les superficies cultivées ou le nombre de cultivateurs par district, à partir des chiffres antiques. L'étude présente un intérêt certain et ses conclusions restent prudentes, mais la dimension rhétorique du plaidoyer, sa construction même, sont ignorées.

[15] Sur la partialité des données dans les *Verrines*, voir Coarelli (1981) 14-15, 17-18.

auxquelles Cicéron a emprunté les chiffres. Puis je voudrais réinscrire ces informations dans la construction de la preuve et l'utilisation des témoignages ou des pièces versées au dossier. Enfin je m'efforcerai d'interpréter le sens de l'utilisation des données chiffrées par l'accusateur et de mesurer leur fiabilité.

Dans cette enquête, le principal souci de méthode est de ne pas séparer l'interprétation singulière des données d'une réflexion plus englobante sur la construction du discours, sa logique, les règles qui président à sa composition. C'est au prix de ce détour que l'historien pourra à notre sens utiliser avec plus de pertinence certaines des données chiffrées qu'il rencontre dans le *de Frumento*.

I. Les caractéristiques du dépouillement

Dans les dépouillements, nous avons relevé les données chiffrées quelle que soit leur nature (valeur relative ou valeur absolue), quelle que soit l'unité dans laquelle elles sont exprimées (jugères, *modii*, médimnes, sesterces, deniers, délais ou durée, *etc.*). En outre, nous avons jugé utile pour l'enquête de ne pas seulement relever les données chiffrées mais, de façon générale, toutes les formes de quantification ou toute expression des rapports de proportionnalité.

Avant d'examiner les résultats de relevé, on voudra bien autoriser quelques brefs commentaires philologiques. En premier lieu, la variété avec laquelle les nombres sont notés dans les manuscrits latins est bien connue. Un même nombre peut être transcrit de plusieurs façons concurrentes dans un même manuscrit à quelques lignes d'intervalle et le *de Frumento* n'échappe pas à cette pratique.[16] Par exemple, au §55, la notation des 50,000 sesterces est HS IↃↃↃ, tandis qu'au §106 la notation des 50,000 sesterces est HS $\bar{\text{L}}$. En deuxième lieu, rappelons qu'on trouve des nombres exprimés de façon développée[17] et des nombres transcrits sous forme numérisée, avec les habituels symboles (par exemple ∞) ou les barres de quantification (horizontales ici), pour les multiplicateurs. Quelquefois, et pour un même *codex*, dans la même phrase, les deux modes de transcription des chiffres coexistent sans qu'on puisse déceler la moindre logique dans ces choix.[18]

Quelques constatations se dégagent du relevé global. Pour les mesures, nous trouvons des quantités volumétriques, exprimées en médimnes[19] ou en *modii*, selon le système de référence métrologique dans lequel Cicéron se place;[20] remarquons d'ailleurs, comme

[16] Sur la variété de la notation chiffrée, il reste utile de recourir aux articles de Mommsen (1909a), (1909b), et Zangsmeisters (1887). Plus récemment, voir aussi Macve (1985).

[17] *Ver.* 3.69: 'In singulos HS quinquagenis milibus damnari mauultis' ('Vous préférez chacun être condamné à payer 50,000 sesterces').

[18] *Ver.* 3.56: '[Polemarcho] cum pro iugeribus quinquaginta medimna DCC decumae imperarentur [...] qui DCC medimnis decidere noluisset, mille promisit.' ('Comme on lui ordonnait, pour 50 jugères, de verser, au titre de la dîme, 700 médimnes, [...] lui qui avait refusé un compromis à 700 médimnes, en promit 1000.')

[19] *Ver.* 3.54, 3.56, 3.72, 3.73, 3.77, 3.84, 3.89, *etc.*

[20] Le médimne (unité de superficie) représente pour les anciens Grecs de Sicile et de Cyrénaïque l'étendue de terres qu'on peut ensemencer avec un médimne (unité volumétrique) de céréales ce qui revient à peu près à l'équivalent du jugère; *cf.* Hultsch (1882) 654. C'est surtout le deuxième sens,

c'était prévisible, qu'il n'y a pas de denrées pesées.[21] Sont également exprimées maintes fois des quantités correspondant à des surfaces.[22] Pour les sommes, on repère aussi bien des taxes légales,[23] des surtaxes illégales ou des bénéfices illicites,[24] des montants d'adjudication,[25] des loyers,[26] des revenus,[27] des prix,[28] des cours moyens,[29] des pénalités,[30] des montants d'amende,[31] des sommes d'argent versées pour corruption,[32] ou encore des promesses de versement.[33] En tout cas, il y a une extrême hétérogénéité des données. Ensuite, on relève l'inégale répartition de l'utilisation des données chiffrées (et soulignons bien que nous avons affaire à un discours non lacunaire). Sur la bonne centaine de passages où des données chiffrées sont présentes, plus des deux tiers des informations quantifiées figurent dans la partie consacrée aux dîmes, le blé acheté et le blé estimé

unité de capacité, qui est utilisé dans le *de Frumento.* Il correspond à 52.53 litres (Hultsch (1882) 703). Le médimne est utilisé pour mesurer des denrées sèches et son invention est rapportée aux réformes soloniennes (Arist. [*Ath. Pol.*] 7, où Aristote utilise μέτρον mais vraisemblablement, le médimne était utilisé pour les denrées sèches, tandis que le métrète l'était pour les denrées liquides). L'équivalence entre le médimne et six *modii* est connue par *Ver.* 3.54 précisément. Hultsch (1882) 107 n. 3 et 655, à la suite de Böckh et de Mommsen, pose que les systèmes attique, sicilien et romain sont globalement identiques, sauf dans leurs divisions. Pourtant les auteurs antiques prennent bien soin de préciser à quel système ils font référence: par exemple, Polybe en 2.15.1 mentionne spécifiquement le Σικελικός μέδιμνος, tandis qu'il utilise en 6.39.13 le médimne attique pour évoquer les rations des soldats.

21 Sur ce point, je reste perplexe devant la mention de denrées pesées faite par Nicolet (2000a) 279. Pour les matières sèches comme les céréales, les Anciens mesurent en volume, non en poids. On trouve certes dans un texte de Pline (*Nat.* 18.62) des considérations sur le 'poids' des différentes céréales (dans une perspective scientifique, on raisonnerait aujourd'hui plutôt en termes de densité). Pline écrit que l'orge est la plus 'légère' des céréales, avec un poids de quinze livres par unité de mesure. Mais précisément, le texte ne dit pas de quelle unité volumétrique il est question! H. Le Bonniec, dans son édition de Pline l'Ancien, *Histoire naturelle, livre 18*, C. U. F. (Paris 1972) 78 propose 'boisseau', ce qui est très plausible, mais demeure une restitution (restitution avancée dans le texte français car aucun éditeur n'a corrigé le latin). Dans le passage de Pline, on trouve en fait une sorte de hiérarchie des densités: l'*hordeum* est le plus léger, puis le *far*, puis le *triticum.*

22 Exprimées surtout en jugères: *Ver.* 3.56, 3.112-14, 3.116-17.

23 *Ver.* 3.56, 3.202.

24 *Ver.* 3.56, 3.72, 3.73, 3.76, 3.78, 3.79, 3.83, 3.86, 3.88, 3.89, 3.90, 3.91, 3.93, 3.100, 3.106, 3.107, 3.116, 3.117, 3.118, 3.140, 3.173, 3.181-83, 3.184, 3.197, 3.201, *etc.*

25 *Ver.* 3.75, 3.76, 3.77, 3.83, 3.84, 3.89, 3.90, 3.91, 3.99, 3.100, 3.110, 3.117, 3.148, 3.151, *etc.*

26 *Ver.* 3.93.

27 *Ver.* 3.119.

28 *Ver.* 3.163, 3.174, 3.179, 3.188, 3.189, 3.191, 3.193, 3.194, 3.196, 3.214, *etc.*

29 *Ver.* 3.90, 3.174, 3.189, 3.194, 3.196, 3.214-15, *etc.*

30 *Ver.* 3.26, 3.28, 3.34, 3.70, *etc.*

31 *Ver.* 3.54, 3.55, 3.69, 3.184, *etc.*

32 *Ver.* 3.145.

33 *Ver.* 3.135.

totalisant, à eux deux, plus du quart des occurrences. On ne sait s'il y a là une inégalité inhérente à la documentation récoltée par Cicéron dans son enquête sicilienne aussi bien qu'à Rome,[34] ou s'il faut voir dans cette inégalité de répartition une intention touchant à la composition même du discours.

Peut-on arriver à une typologie? En premier lieu, l'enquête montre la forte présence de données quantifiées mais non chiffrées. Nous avons pris en compte les expressions touchant à des formes d'évaluation quantitative et force est de constater que, très souvent, Cicéron se contente de donner des indications de tendance, sans chercher la précision du chiffre. C'est vrai pour l'expression de quantités indéfinies relatives comme pour l'expression de quantités indéfinies absolues. Par exemple, à propos de quantités ou de données relatives:

> [§43] Metellus a adjugé les dîmes *à un prix bien inférieur* non seulement au tien, mais aussi à celui de tes prédécesseurs.[35]
> [§70] Je [= Apronius] dis que ta déclaration *sous-évalue* la surface de tes terres [= le cultivateur].[36]
> [§225] Vous trouverez, Juges, que [Verrès] a réquisitionné auprès des cités pour son grenier privé *cinq fois plus* qu'il ne lui était permis de percevoir.[37]

On attendrait ici des indications chiffrées précises, or le chiffre est volontairement absent. Les deux premiers exemples présentent un point commun, l'ellipse du chiffre, et une différence nette. Dans le premier cas, c'est Cicéron qui élude les détails tout en cherchant à confondre Verrès. L'accusateur n'a pas besoin de la donnée précise pour prouver que l'accusé a agi contrairement aux intérêts de Rome. Le raisonnement ne requiert pas la présence du chiffre. Dans le deuxième exemple, le contexte est celui d'un discours fictif attribué à Apronius. Ce dernier s'adresserait à un cultivateur sicilien et contesterait sa déclaration de surface.[38] C'est une situation de mauvaise foi caractérisée, où Apronius lèse les agriculteurs en truquant les chiffres. Ni les vrais ni les faux ne sont cités: d'une part, parce que la situation était récurrente et les cas d'extorsion nombreux; d'autre part, parce que Cicéron entend démonter un mécanisme, et non reconstituer méticuleusement un épisode particulier. Et même quand il donne des détails sur l'identité des victimes et sur les procédés, la quantification n'est pas nécessaire à l'établissement de la culpabilité de Verrès et ses comparses. Ainsi en est-il des malversations de Symmaque, un esclave de Vénus, dépêché à Segesta. Il extorque une somme comptant, en plus du blé, à un

[34] Pour une reconstitution de l'enquête, de sa chronologie, des interlocuteurs rencontrés, de l'itinéraire parcouru *etc*., il est utile de consulter Marinone (1950).

[35] *Ver.* 3.43: 'Multo minoris uendidit non modo quam tu, sed etiam quam qui ante te uendiderunt.'

[36] *Ver.* 3.70: 'Minus te iugerum professum esse dico'.

[37] *Ver.* 3.225: 'Reperietis quinquiens tanto, iudices, amplius istum quam quantum in cellam ei sumere licitum sit ciuitatibus imperasse.'

[38] Il ne faut évidemment pas exclure que des contestations de ce type aient été, du point de vue romain, fondées: des agriculteurs tentaient sûrement de tricher. Les malversations d'Apronius, telles que Cicéron les présente, ne doivent pas pousser le commentateur moderne à présenter tous les cultivateurs siciliens comme exempts de toute tentative de fraude.

personnage de rang sénatorial, C. Annaeus Brocchus.[39] Aucun détail chiffré n'est donné, seule la mention du procédé compte. La preuve ne paraît pas requérir la précision chiffrée.

D'autres passages mentionnent des quantités ou des estimations absolues:

> [§39] [...] enlever [à beaucoup d'agriculteurs] *une importante quantité* de blé et exiger d'eux *de fortes sommes*.[40]
> [§49] Oui, tu [= Verrès] as adjugé *à haut prix* les dîmes.[41]
> [§70] Laissons dire à Hortensius, s'il y tient, que Verrès a adjugé les dîmes *à prix élevé*.[42]

Là encore, on est loin du détail de la reconstitution judiciaire. Implicitement, ces propos se réfèrent à une norme. Mais cette norme n'est pas explicite. C'est celle du juste milieu, de la proportion raisonnable, de l'équité. Ceci amène à souligner que, pour les besoins de l'argumentation, l'orateur a au moins autant besoin de dégager des tendances, de globaliser, que de donner des renseignements précis et vérifiables. Cela ne signifie pas du tout que ces données exactes n'existaient pas, mais Cicéron choisit ou non de produire dans la plaidoirie ces chiffres réels.[43] La force de conviction du discours ne repose pas entièrement sur la présentation de faits tangibles et de données concrètes. Le but est surtout de suggérer les mécanismes frauduleux et les immenses profits qu'ils dégagent, tout en étant très précis sur les individus qui tirent le bénéfice de ces malversations, d'autant que Verrès n'est pas intervenu personnellement dans toutes les extorsions. Identifier les coupables et leurs complices reste une priorité. Verrès n'a pas agi seul, même s'il est le seul à comparaître au procès. Ce réseau d'individus louches et malhonnêtes ne vient pas exonérer la responsabilité de Verrès, au contraire, elle est aggravée par l'existence même de cette organisation illégale qu'il aurait mise en place en Sicile. La dénonciation est celle des personnes, des manoeuvres criminelles, et il paraît moins important d'établir exactement les montants détournés que de prouver le crime lui-même et ses procédés.

Cicéron n'avait pas besoin de donner tous les chiffres. Conséquemment, nous ne pouvons pas raisonner sur les données chiffrées du *de Frumento* sans garder en tête que l'accusateur précise uniquement les chiffres qui servent à sa démonstration et qu'il n'a pas besoin de donner systématiquement la preuve chiffrée ou quantifiée de ce qu'il avance. Sans doute l'avait-il en sa possession. Ou du moins le laissait-il entendre. Et bien plus, les quantités incommensurables, les profits inestimables, les détournements innombrables, tout cela était finalement plus convaincant que les réalités mesurées.[44] La précision du

[39] *Ver.* 3.92-94. Sur le personnage, mal connu par ailleurs, voir Fraschetti (1981) 66.

[40] *Ver.* 3.39: 'Magnus [...] frumenti numerus ablatus magnaeue pecuniae coactae'.

[41] *Ver.* 3.49: 'Magno tu decumas uendidisti.'

[42] *Ver.* 3.70: 'Dicat licet Hortensius, si uolet, magno Verrem decumas uendidisse.'

[43] Voir *infra* pour la discussion sur les actes officiels existant.

[44] *Ver.* 3.49: 'Cognoscite nunc innumerabilem pecuniam frumentario nomine ereptam' ('Connaissez maintenant les sommes incalculables arrachées au titre de l'approvisionnement'); 3.163: 'Ex quo intellexistis innumerabilem frumenti numerum per triennium auersum ab re publica esse ereptumque

chiffre brut pouvait aussi affadir le propos, elle ancrait dans la banalité du quotidien un raisonnement où Cicéron tentait de confondre en justice l'*auaritia* et la *cupiditas* incarnées, Verrès, l'homme de la démesure.[45]

II. Esquisse de typologie des données

La typologie des données chiffrées est plus complexe à établir qu'il ne paraît au premier abord. Il ne suffit pas de regrouper des prix avec des prix, des surfaces avec des surfaces, des volumes avec des volumes, *etc.* Et on ne peut pas non plus se limiter à une approche simpliste et binaire, les chiffres fiables qu'on opposerait aux chiffres manipulés ou faux. Si nous cherchons à nuancer le classement, nous trouvons d'abord des données peu contestables, au premier rang desquelles les chiffres intéressant des formules d'action judiciaire, comme la poursuite au quadruple ou à l'octuple.[46] Une altération du texte est ici peu probable et d'un point de vue typologique, ces chiffres sont aux marges de notre thème.

Ensuite, nous pouvons également admettre les chiffres de conversion, dans lesquels le deuxième chiffre est forcément dépendant du premier, et il apparaît cohérent avec lui. Ainsi la conversion de médimnes en *modii* est-elle particulièrement fréquente ou bien encore la simple transposition par un changement d'unité de compte, de sesterces en deniers ou inversement. Par exemple, au §116, les 90,000 médimnes sont banalement convertis en 540,000 *modii*, pour transposer la réalité dans les unités de mesure familières aux Romains. De même, les §191-94 montrent une cohérence totale des chiffres: le raisonnement consiste à montrer que Verrès a fait payer trois deniers aux cultivateurs par *modius*, alors que le cours du marché est de trois sesterces par *modius*. En permanence, nous retrouvons les équivalences entre trois deniers et douze sesterces, il s'agit bien de simples conversions. On ne peut évidemment exclure la possibilité d'une mise en cohérence par un copiste vraiment fort consciencieux et bien informé, mais globalement, la duplication de données sous formes de totaux convertis en unités de comptes romaines écarte les suspicions. D'un point de vue strictement rhétorique, cette tautologie favorise la compréhension par l'auditoire et contribue surtout à marteler dans les esprits les accusations contre Verrès. La répétition tautologique crée un effet d'objectivité, donc fait croire à la vérité globale de ce qui est dit par l'accusateur.

D'un autre côté, nous sommes face à des données situées d'emblée dans des raisonnements déconnectés du réel, des modélisations ou des constructions hypothétiques. Ces chiffres-là s'inscrivent dans un discours dont la modalité est clairement conditionnelle. La question de la fiabilité ne se pose pas car elle n'a pas de sens. Il s'agit de donner des chiffres qui ont des qualités de divisibilité, des rapports de proportion faciles à dégager. En voici quelques exemples:

aratoribus' ('[Mon argumentation] vous a permis de comprendre que, pendant trois ans, une quantité incommensurable de blé a été détournée de l'État, arrachée aux cultivateurs').

[45] *Ver.* 3.21, 3.52, 3.103, 3.120, 3.126-27, 3.131, 3.152, *etc.*

[46] *Ver.* 3.26, 3.28, 3.34, 3.70, *etc.*

> [§49] *Si je montre que ce que tu* [= Verrès] *as détourné vers ta maison n'est pas inférieur* à ce que tu as envoyé à Rome au titre de la dîme, quelle faveur populaire t'assurera ta défense, puisque tu auras prélevé sur une province romaine, pour ton propre intérêt, une part égale à celle que tu auras envoyée au Peuple romain? Eh bien? *Et si je montre que tu as soustrait une part deux fois plus grande de blé* que celle que tu as envoyée au Peuple romain, pensons-nous que, devant cette accusation, ton défenseur hochera encore avec grâce la tête et se présentera devant le public et l'auditoire?[47]
> [§111] *Et que dire si je démontre* que dans cette seule adjudication, le profit est de 100,000 *modii* de froment? *Que dire s'il est de* 200,000? *Et que dire pour* 300,000? *Et que dire pour* 400,000?[48]
> [§119] *Faisons une comparaison*: si d'une propriété qui a rapporté 10,000 sesterces, après avoir arraché et vendu les arbres, ôté les tuiles, cédé le matériel et le troupeau, un intendant tire 20,000 sesterces qu'il envoie au maître, au lieu des 10,000, tandis qu'il s'est gardé pour lui 100,000, la première réaction du maître, qui ignore le préjudice, est de se réjouir, d'être ravi par cet intendant, puisqu'il a retiré de la propriété un revenu bien supérieur; mais ensuite, quand il apprend qu'on s'est débarrassé et qu'on a vendu les éléments sur lesquels reposaient les fruits et la mise en culture de la propriété, alors il inflige à l'intendant les derniers supplices et considère qu'il s'est mal conduit envers lui.[49]
> [§225] *Vous trouverez, Juges, qu'il a réquisitionné* pour son grenier privé *cinq fois plus* qu'il ne lui était permis de percevoir.[50]

Aucun des chiffres cités dans ces passages ne peut passer pour objectif ou reflétant une réalité. Ce sont des chiffres ronds, des multiples, qui donnent au discours une dimension plus véridique. D'ailleurs, le rapport au temps lui-même est occulté: ainsi dans le §119, on peut supposer que les bénéfices évoqués sont annuels, mais rien ne situe ces chiffres dans un contexte ou une situation réels. Quant au §49, là encore, on ne peut dire si les exactions de Verrès sont rapportées à la durée de son gouvernement ou à une année en particulier. On est bien là confronté à la fascination du chiffre, à l'apparence d'objectivité ou de

[47] *Ver.* 3.49: 'Si doceo te non minus domum tuam auertisse quam Romam misisse decumarum nomine, quid habet populare oratio tua, cum ex prouincia populi Romani aequam partem tu tibi sumpseris ac populo Romano miseris? Quid? si duabus partibus doceo te amplius frumenti abstulisse quam populo Romano misisse, tamenne putamus patronum tuum in hoc crimine ceruiculam iactaturum et populo se ac coronae daturum?'

[48] *Ver.* 3.111: 'Quid, si ostendo in hac una emptione lucri fieri tritici mod. C? quid, si CC? quid, si CCC? quid, si CCCC milia?'

[49] *Ver.* 3.119: 'Vt si qui uilicus ex eo fundo qui sestertia dena meritasset, excisis arboribus ac uenditis, demptis tegulis, instrumento, pecore abalienato, domino XX milia nummum pro X miserit, sibi alia praeterea centum confecerit, primo dominus ignarus incommodi sui gaudeat uilicoque delectetur, quod tanto plus [sibi] mercedis ex fundo refectum sit, deinde, cum audierit eas res quibus fundi fructus et cultura continetur amotas et uenditas, summo supplicio uilicum adficiat et secum male actum putet.'

[50] *Ver.* 3.225: 'Reperietis quinquiens tanto, iudices, amplius istum quam quantum in cellam ei sumere licitum sit ciuitatibus imperasse.'

science qu'il porte, et que dénonçait Moses Finley pour les analyses des Modernes.[51] Cette magie du chiffre valait aussi, consciemment ou inconsciemment, pour les Anciens.

Un troisième type de données est constitué par celles qui sont inscrites dans de véritables calculs arithmétiques: les nombres se comprennent alors dans un raisonnement global, avec des opérations mathématiques. Mettre en cause un élément de la chaîne revient à mettre en cause tout le calcul et son résultat. Les éléments de comparaison, de cohérence sont fournis simultanément. Supposer des erreurs dans ces chiffres revient à postuler une correction intermédiaire, une réharmonisation par un copiste, ou un scholiaste dont on aurait inséré les rectifications directement dans le texte. Le §116 en est l'illustration la plus probante.[52] Ces données inscrites dans des opérations de calcul me paraissent plus sûres que les données isolées. Elles sont immédiatement vérifiables par le copiste, le lecteur, *etc.* Du moins sont-elles plus fiables quant à la transmission du texte. Cela n'écarte pas l'hypothèse d'une manipulation volontaire des chiffres: comme toujours, nous travaillons sur deux niveaux de fiabilité, celui de l'historicité en elle-même et celui du document transmis.

Un quatrième groupe est formé par les données totalement isolées. Il est alors impossible, ou en tout cas difficile, d'apprécier leur fiabilité. Tout au plus peut-on donner des éléments sur leur caractère plausible. Ces informations sont celles qui embarrassent le plus l'historien car elles sont incontestablement le matériau de toute analyse sur la production agricole, la fiscalité, les prix, *etc.* Parmi les illustrations les plus significatives, on peut mentionner d'abord des versements, comme au §79, où il s'agit du supplément exigé par Verrès pour Tertia et versé par les habitants d'Herbita: '[§79] Versez 12,000 sesterces en liquide.'[53] Dans des cas de ce genre, on ne peut guère aller plus loin que juger du caractère vraisemblable de la somme. Et les variantes de la tradition manuscrite ne sont guère signifiantes: l'hésitation entre 12,000 et 15,000 maintient le versement dans des proportions comparables. Ce type de donnée isolée est invérifiable, ce qui ne veut pas dire fausse, non plus que vraie.

De même, le nombre des cultivateurs subsistant à Leontini après les exactions de Verrès constitue un type de renseignement isolé dans les sources littéraires:

> [§120] En vertu de la loi de Hiéron, le nombre des cultivateurs est chaque année enregistré devant les magistrats. Pour finir, donne lecture du nombre de cultivateurs que Verrès a trouvé sur le territoire de Leontini: 84. Combien font leur déclaration au bout de trois ans? 32. Ainsi 52 cultivateurs ont été chassés par la force sans trouver le moindre successeur, même parmi leurs aides. Combien d'agriculteurs y avait-il sur le territoire de Mutycè à ton arrivée? Constatons-le d'après les documents officiels: 187. Et bien, et la troisième année? 86. Les injustices commises par l'accusé, rien que sur un seul territoire, l'ont privé de 101 cultivateurs [...]. Le territoire d'Herbita, la première année, a compté 252 cultivateurs, la troisième année 120. 132 chefs de famille ont dû s'enfuir, privés de leurs terres. Le territoire d'Agyrium – faut-il souligner sa population nombreuse,

[51] Finley (1982) 70.

[52] Cité et analysé *infra* n. 102.

[53] *Ver.* 3.79: 'Numerate HS $\overline{\text{XII}}$ ' (avec une difficulté d'établissement du texte).

son honorabilité, sa richesse – comptait 250 cultivateurs après la première année de ta préture. Et alors? La troisième année? 80. Les envoyés d'Agyrium ont exposé dans quelles conditions d'après leurs registres publics, vous les avez entendus. [§121] Par les dieux immortels, si tu avais expulsé de la province dans son ensemble 170 cultivateurs, pourrais-tu échapper à la sévérité des juges? Or le seul territoire d'Agyrium est vidé de 170 cultivateurs: dès lors, ne pourrez-vous deviner le résultat pour l'ensemble de la province?[54]

Les commentaires sur ces nombres n'ont pas manqué. Pris singulièrement, pour tel ou tel territoire, ou ensemble, pour un tableau de la Sicile au temps de Verrès, ces chiffres constituent des données qu'on a tirées dans tous les sens: d'abord, pour qu'un aussi grand nombre de cultivateurs disparût en si peu de temps, il fallait, disait-on, très probablement qu'ils fussent de petits ou à la rigueur de moyens propriétaires.[55] Et on touche là au débat, initié par Theodor Mommsen,[56] continué dans le livre de Jérôme Carcopino,[57] poursuivi entre autres dans les articles du colloque de Pise en 1979:[58] il s'agit de la discussion sur la nature des victimes de Verrès (petits, moyens ou grands propriétaires?[59]) et aussi des calculs sur la taille moyenne des propriétés avant et après le gouvernement de Verrès.

[54] *Ver.* 3.120-21: 'Lege Hieronica numerus aratorum quotannis apud magistratus publice subscribitur. Recita tandem, quot acceperit aratores agri Leontini Verres: LXXXIIII. Quot anno tertio profiteantur: XXXII. Duo et quinquaginta aratores ita uideo deiectos ut iis ne uicarii quidem successerint. Quot aratores aduentiente te fuerunt agri Mutycensis? Videamus ex litteris publicis. CLXXXVII. Quid? anno tertio? LXXXVI. Centum et unum aratores unus ager istius iniuria desiderat, atque adeo nostra res publica, quoniam illa populi Romani uectigalia sunt, hunc tot patrum familias numerum desiderat et reposcit. Ager Herbitensis primo anno habuit aratores CCLII, tertio CXX: hinc CXXXII patres familias extorres profugerunt. Agyrinensis ager – quorum hominum, quam honestorum, quam locupletium! – CCL aratores habuit primo anno praeturae tuae. Quid? tertio anno? LXXX, quem ad modum legatos Agyrinensis recitare ex publicis litteris audistis. [§121] Pro di immortales! si ex prouincia tota CLXX aratores eiecisses, possesne seueris iudicibus saluus esse? Vnus ager Agyrinensis CLXX aratoribus inanior cum sit, uos coniecturam totius prouinciae nonne facietis?'

[55] Coarelli (1981) 16-17.

[56] Mommsen (1985) 421. Le savant allemand admet sans discussion les chiffres du texte cicéronien. Il en tire un pourcentage: 59% des propriétaires ont préféré laisser leurs terres en jachère sous la préture de Verrès. Mommsen tirait argument du nombre peu élevé de cultivateurs mentionnés pour conclure que 'ces propriétaires n'étaient point de petits et pauvres paysans' et qu''ils appartenaient tous à la classe des gros planteurs, presque tous ils étaient citoyens romains'. Mommsen a beau écrire que 'des documents précis l'attestent', son traducteur Ch. Alexandre ajoute en référence ce seul passage des *Ver.* 3.120. On reste perplexe devant cette argumentation.

[57] Carcopino (1919) 233-34, 242-43.

[58] Voir en particulier l'article de Coarelli (1981) et celui de M. Mazza (1981). L'article de Mazza (42-43) fait le point sur les parallèles fournis par la documentation épigraphique. *Cf.* aussi Mazza (1980).

[59] Carcopino (1919) 243 pensait que les victimes de Verrès à Leontini étaient surtout 'les détenteurs des domaines les moins considérables', mais il avait posé (233) que l'*ager Leontinus* était 'une exception aux formes de la propriété en Sicile', partagé 'en quelques lots considérables affermés à un petit nombre de tenanciers'. Par ailleurs, il soulignait le cas limite de Leontini en Sicile, où la majorité des possesseurs étaient de petits propriétaires.

Pour le second de ces débats, si on pose la superficie de l'*ager Leontinus* comme constante,[60] on passerait, selon les calculs des modernes, d'une superficie moyenne[61] de 2342 jugères (588 ha) à 892 jugères (223 ha).[62] La probabilité d'une moyenne tournant autour de 500 ha serait selon Filippo Coarelli raisonnablement acceptable, qui en juge aussi d'après les données reconstituées pour Dioclès de Panhormus[63] et Nymphon de Centuripae.[64] Mais les textes ne disent rien de précis sur des superficies moyennes en distinguant les territoires (ou plutôt les passages envisagent seulement quelques cas particuliers dont la représentativité mérite au moins d'être mise en question[65]) et les commentateurs finissent, sur cette question de la taille moyenne des propriétés, par comparer entre elles surtout des hypothèses formulées à l'époque contemporaine, en tirant dans tous les sens l'interprétation de données antiques isolées.[66] Ainsi, là où Carcopino concluait à la diminution des propriétés latifundiaires après la première révolte servile, Coarelli penchait pour la conclusion opposée:[67] je n'entends pas réouvrir ici le débat mais souligner *primo* que personne ne conteste la réalité historique de ces chiffres, tout au contraire, ils sont la plupart du temps admis comme le serait un postulat;[68] *secundo* je

[60] Coarelli (1981). La modélisation de Coarelli se fonde sur les superficies cultivées, 30,000 jugères, et suppose, pour intégrer l'assolement et la jachère, un total de 75,000 jugères pour les propriétés. Ce chiffre de 30,000 jugères (7500 ha) est tiré du §116 et de la *professio sationum*; quant au calcul supposé de 75,000 jugères (18,750 ha) au total, il vient de Carcopino (1919) 242-43, qui toutefois intégrait uniquement la jachère dans son hypothèse. Comme le remarquait le même Carcopino, ces emblavures correspondent à une année précise, à savoir 71 av. J.-C., année où le nombre de cultivateurs n'était plus que de 32, après avoir été de 84 dans les époques antérieures aux ravages exercés par le gouvernement de Verrès. Or il y a évidemment corrélation entre la diminution du nombre de cultivateurs 'disposés à ensemencer' et la superficie des terres emblavées.

[61] Je laisse volontairement de côté le débat sur la pertinence même d'un calcul sur des superficies moyennes ('moyennes' par rapport à quoi?), dans un contexte où les disparités peuvent être fortes, donc l'écart type par rapport à ces moyennes est assez significatif.

[62] Cette surface moyenne est mise en rapport avec les assignations faites par Antoine en 43 av. J.-C., au bénéfice d'un rhéteur et d'un médecin (Cic. *Phil.* 2.101), respectivement de 2000 et 3000 jugères soient 500 et 750 ha.

[63] *Ver.* 3.93. Il s'agit de terres cultivées sur le territoire de Ségeste.

[64] *Ver.* 3.54. Les terres ne sont pas localisées sur un territoire précis et rien ne dit qu'elles soient toutes situées sur le même territoire.

[65] Leontini est-il ou non un cas limite comme le soulignait Carcopino (1919) 233 n. 2, à savoir celui des territoires siciliens où se concentrent les plus grosses propriétés individuelles?

[66] Pour une comparaison, voir la synthèse récente concernant Leontini à la période antérieure, avec la bibliographie récapitulative dans de Angelis (2000) 128-29. L'article ne prend pas pour point de référence la période d'occupation romaine, mais se limite à la fin de l'âge grec classique, *i.e.* la fin de l'indépendance des cités grecques par rapport à Carthage. Le territoire de Leontini est évalué à 83,000 ha, dont 80%, soit 66,400 ha auraient été exploitables pour l'agriculture, mais les études archéologiques aboutissent à des proportions oscillant entre 75 et 95%.

[67] Coarelli (1981) 17. Sur ce débat, *cf.* aussi Pritchard (1969) 554-56; Manganaro (1972) 449-51; Mazza (1980) 230-35.

[68] Il faut signaler l'exception que constituent les concises nuances de Scramuzza (1937) 260, et surtout les propos de Pritchard (1972) 648. Pritchard, sur la base de comparaisons avec Pline

crois qu'on gagnerait à poser plus clairement la nature des données sur lesquelles ces reconstructions sont appuyées, en soulignant l'interdépendance des calculs fondés sur les §116 et 120. Et surtout il me paraît essentiel de rappeler que la finalité des chiffres mentionnés par Cicéron pour Leontini est de mesurer un écart significatif entre deux dates très rapprochées, pour un territoire classé *ager publicus* et dont la mise en culture est affermée. Le flou, dans les commentaires modernes, est de surcroît souvent entretenu entre deux notions distinctes: la taille des propriétés (au sens juridique du droit de propriété sur le sol) et la superficie des exploitations (ce qui prend en compte la location de terres). D'où le pas que beaucoup de commentateurs ont franchi: passer des chiffres connus pour Leontini à un tableau de la propriété en Sicile.

Parmi les autres données potentiellement les plus intéressantes pour l'histoire économique et sociale, intéressantes mais totalement invérifiables, on peut relever le montant supposé de la corruption des juges:

> [§145] Alba Aemilius, qui se tient assis à l'entrée du marché, dit publiquement que Verrès a gagné, qu'il tient les juges pour achetés, l'un 400,000 sesterces, l'autre 500,000 sesterces, le moins bien payé 300,000![69]

Si on connaît des parallèles quant à la corruption des tribunaux eux-mêmes, les éléments de comparaison manquent pour connaître les sommes grâce auxquelles les tribunaux, tout spécialement ici pour les procès de concussion, étaient soudoyés.[70] Ce type de situation n'était pas rare,[71] et le cas de l'acquittement de Clodius en 61 av. J.-C., dans le procès sur la profanation des Mystères de la *Bona Dea* est un des plus notoires.[72] Toutefois le 'prix d'un juge' reste inconnu, non seulement pour des personnages de rang sénatorial, mais aussi, en fonction des lois successivement en vigueur, pour les juges des jurys 'mixtes'. Ceci étant, les accusés jouaient la suite de leur carrière, dans une compétition politique

l'Ancien *Nat.* 18.95 (rendement de 100/1 dans les plaines de Leontini), considère que Cicéron a minimisé les gains des cultivateurs exploitant des terres à Leontini et manipulé d'autre part les chiffres concernant le rendement des terres elles-mêmes (*Ver.* 3.112). L'intention de l'accusateur était de gagner la sympathie du jury pour ses clients siciliens.

[69] *Ver.* 3.145: 'Albam Aemilium sedentem in faucibus macelli loqui palam uicisse Verrem, emptos habere iudices, alium HS $\overline{\text{CCCC}}$, alium HS $\overline{\text{D}}$, quem minimo, $\overline{\text{CCC}}$!'

[70] On peine à déduire du texte cicéronien la somme réelle évoquée pour le procès du sénateur P. Septimius Scaevola dans *Ver.* 38. Cicéron dit que l'amende et les dépens auxquels il a été condamné sont calculés, au moment de la *litis aestimatio*, d'après le montant d'un versement qui avait servi à l'acheter comme juge. Mais il n'est point fait mention d'une somme exacte.

[71] Voir les rappels effectués par Gruen (1995) 31-32 et 524-33.

[72] Cic. *Att.* 1.16.2 (= SB 16): Cicéron prétend que la pauvreté des juges (*egestas iudicum*) peut seule expliquer l'acquittement, ce qui est une façon spirituelle de dire qu'ils ont été achetés. Mais rien n'est dit sur les sommes dépensées par Clodius pour obtenir malhonnêtement cette sentence. Et plus loin, évoquant ceux des juges qui étaient tribuns du Trésor, Cicéron plaisante en disant que ces juges avaient perdu leur propre trésor (*non tam aerati quam aerari*), pourfandant le caractère notoirement misérable de leur conduite (§3). Pour finir, il rapporte comment Catulus les provoque en ironisant sur la demande d'une garde armée (§5): c'était pour éviter qu'on ne volât aux juges l'argent corrompu qu'ils avaient touché!

très serrée. Les tarifs de corruption que mentionne Cicéron dans ce passage des *Verrines* ont un caractère plausible. Peut-être faut-il voir dans la hiérarchie des sommes mentionnées au §145 une forme dévoyée de *gradus dignitatis* ou en négatif, l'échelle des responsabilités exercées? Le prix moyen de corruption du juge changeait-il selon le stade de la carrière auquel il était parvenu? C'est très plausible.

Enfin, il est des séries de chiffres parmi les plus 'historiques' mais qui sont aussi parmi les plus embarrassants, parce que non contextualisés. Par exemple, le texte comporte des prix ou des cours mais, souvent, les passages ne mentionnent pas forcément la nature ou la variété des grains (*hordeum, frumentum, triticum*).[73]

> [§173] Je vois, d'après les registres publics, que, pour chaque médimne, les gens d'Halèse t'ont donné quinze sesterces.[74]
> [§174] Légalement, le prix du *modius* était en effet de trois sesterces et demi, mais, sous ta préture, comme tu t'en vantes toi-même dans beaucoup de lettres écrites à des amis, il était de deux sesterces.[75]

En revanche, l'attention est prêtée à la variation des cours selon les périodes de l'année:

> [§214] Sacerdos, à son arrivée dans la province, réquisitionna du grain pour sa réserve. Alors que le *modius* de *triticum* était, avant la nouvelle récolte, à cinq deniers, les cités lui demandèrent de donner une estimation. Son estimation fut notablement inférieure au cours du marché, car il la donna à trois deniers.[76]

Et une attention comparable est accordée aux variations selon les années. Les trois deniers mentionnés au §214 pour la préture de 75 av. J.-C. (Caius Licinius Sacerdos) constituent un prix inférieur au cours du marché, qui plus est au moment de la 'soudure' entre les récoltes de deux années; en revanche, les trois deniers exigés sous la préture de Verrès représentent quatre fois le cours moyen de trois sesterces.[77] Ici le chiffre est sans doute fiable car tout le raisonnement, qui court sur de longs paragraphes, n'est compréhensible que si ce montant de trois deniers est juste dans le texte.

[73] Pour les variétés de céréales antiques, voir Pline *Nat.* 18.63-104.

[74] *Ver.* 3.173: 'In medimna singula uideo ex litteris publicis tibi Halaesinos HS quinos denos dedisse.'

[75] *Ver.* 3.174: 'Est enim modius lege HS IIIS aestimatus, fuit autem te praetore, ut tu in multis epistulis ad amicos tuos gloriaris, HS II.'

[76] *Ver.* 3.214: 'Sacerdos ut in prouinciam uenit, frumentum in cellam imperauit. Cum esset ante nouum tritici modius denariis V, petiuerunt ab eo ciuitates ut aestimaret. Remissior aliquanto eius fuit aestimatio quam annona; nam aestimauit denariis III.'

[77] De même, l'attention est portée au prix en fonction du moment de l'année, voir *Ver.* 3.215: 'Eodem tempore praetor Antonius III denariis aestimauit post messem, summa in uilitate, cum aratores frumentum dare gratis mallent, et aiebat se tantidem aestimasse quanti Sacerdotem, neque mentiebatur; sed eadem ista aestimatione alter subleuarat aratores, alter euerterat.' À la même époque, le préteur Antonius donna une estimation après la récolte à trois deniers, à un moment où le prix était au plus bas, alors que les cultivateurs préféraient donner du grain pour rien; il disait avoir donné une estimation équivalente à celle de Sacerdos et disait vrai, mais avec cette même estimation, le premier avait soulagé les agriculteurs, le second les avait mis à genoux.

Pour certains chiffres concernant les récoltes, en revanche, la qualité des terres n'est pas toujours précisée, ni ce que le cultivateur a précisément ensemencé.

> [§56] Comme on lui [= Polemarchus] ordonnait, *pour 50 jugères*, de verser, au titre de la dîme, *700 médimnes* [...].[78]

Si on admet que les cinquante jugères sont emblavées et que les 700 médimnes forment une dîme, on a une proportion de 14 médimnes de blé dîmé par jugère. Donc en principe 14 x 50 multiplié par 10 soit 7000 médimnes de récolte. Mais dans la suite du texte, Polémarque promet 1000 médimnes au lieu des 700 demandés. Soit une imposition de 20 médimnes par jugère. Il faut bien prendre en compte qu'il s'agit d'une situation d'extorsion. Cela ne veut pas dire que les chiffres en eux-mêmes sont faux, simplement on ne peut pas tirer de la dîme perçue le total de la récolte, puisqu'ici, en fait, on a une dîme qui n'est pas *stricto sensu* un dixième, c'est un prélèvement de plus de 14% (1000/7000)!

D'autres chiffres constituent des indications de rendement, mais sans considération des productions réelles sur les territoires en question.

> [§112] Dans le territoire de Leontini, on sème à peu près un médimne de *triticum* par jugère, cette quantité de semence est constante d'année en année. Quand la récolte a un rapport de un pour huit, c'est une bonne année. Si tous les dieux s'y mettent, le rapport est de un pour dix. Quand cela arrive, alors on doit donner comme dîme exactement ce qu'on a semé, c'est-à-dire on doit à la dîme autant de médimnes que de jugères ensemencés.[79]

Le passage a évidemment été abondamment glosé et commenté, non sans comparer ces chiffres avec les données de l'époque moderne.[80] Avec un taux d'ensemencement d'un peu plus de 160 kg/ha (6 *modii* par jugère), le rendement serait ainsi, pour une bonne année, de 8 pour 1, soit environ 1300 kg/ha. Dans le cas d'une année exceptionnelle, avec un rendement de 10 pour 1, on dépasserait les 1600 kg/ha. Faut-il prendre ces chiffres comme des moyennes, indépendamment de la qualité des terres? La question posée ici est finalement assez semblable à ce qu'on trouve pour la signification de certains chiffres dans les traités des agronomes (pour ne citer qu'un exemple, les chiffres de rendement avancés par Columelle pour la vigne[81]).

[78] *Ver.* 3.56: '[Polemarcho] cum pro iugeribus quinquaginta medimna DCC decumae imperarentur [...].'

[79] *Ver.* 3.112: 'In iugero Leontini agri medimnum fere tritici seritur perpetua atque aequabili satione; ager efficit cum octauo, bene ut agatur; uerum ut omnes di adiuuent, cum decumo. Quod si quando accidit, tum fit ut tantum decumae sit quantum seueris, hoc est ut, quot iugera sint sata, totidem medimna decumae debeantur.'

[80] Scramuzza (1937) 260-61.

[81] Col. 3.3.4. Voir spécialement Carandini (1983) 186-94; pour une synthèse des débats, voir Garnsey et Saller (1987) 140-46 et Marcone (1997) 142-43. Rappelons que Varron insistait lui sur la variété des rendements selon les terrains (Var. *R.* 1.44.2).

Un autre exemple d'imprécision touche aux surfaces cultivées, pour lesquelles on peine à distinguer entre les propriétés et les terres à bail. On ne peut donc évidemment déduire des surfaces cultivées la taille réelle des propriétés. De plus, quelle est la prise en compte de la jachère? Ainsi au §54, à propos de la condamnation de Nymphon de Centuripae, on ne sait pas si la quantité contestée correspond seulement aux terres prises à bail par Nymphon ou à toutes ses propriétés arables. La saisie-amende est de 7000 médimnes de *triticum*. La peine n'est pas proportionnelle à la quantité de froment qui aurait été dissimulée pour telle ou telle parcelle, elle paraît globale.[82] De même au §56, dans le cas de Polémarque de Murgentia (?= Morgantina), étudié ci-dessus, on ne sait pas si ces cinquante jugères correspondent ou non à l'ensemble des terres qu'il met en culture. Et au §55, Xénon de Mènes (Menae) a bel et bien fondé sa défense sur le fait qu'il n'était ni le *dominus*, ni même le *locator*.

Plusieurs mises en garde s'imposent pour qui veut exploiter historiquement ces indications: d'abord et surtout, on a affaire à des cas limites, puisque précisément, ce que Cicéron veut montrer, ce sont les exactions et les méfaits de Verrès. Il ne faut pas prendre pour des moyennes, ou des situations ordinaires ce qui constitue par nature une exception. Cela ne veut pas dire que les données sont en elles-mêmes fausses: les chiffres peuvent être justes, mais ils ne sont pas représentatifs de situations ordinaires et transposables. La question de la fiabilité des chiffres ne tient pas forcément aux chiffres eux-mêmes. En tout cas, fiabilité des chiffres et représentativité des situations sont deux questions distinctes, on l'a vu en particulier pour le nombre d'exploitants à Leontini. Du coup, l'utilisation du *de Frumento* pour des considérations générales sur les structures de la propriété en Sicile ou sur la productivité des agriculteurs de l'île suscite la perplexité, si elle n'est assortie de nuances prudentes et de contextualisations détaillées.

III. Les sources des chiffres cités

Une autre difficulté de l'interprétation tient à l'origine des informations recueillies par Cicéron. Une bonne partie d'entre elles a été réunie sur place, en Sicile, durant les quelques dizaines de jours d'enquête de terrain. En effet, l'accusateur assumait largement l'instruction du dossier et il se voyait confier une mission de caractère public: quand Cicéron avait obtenu le droit d'accuser Verrès au terme de la *diuinatio*, il dut présenter, par écrit vraisemblablement, au magistrat un énoncé rassemblant le nom de l'accusé, les motifs de la poursuite judiciaire. Le magistrat procéda alors à la *receptio nominis* et rendit publics les chefs d'accusation. Ce même magistrat fixa le délai et donna à l'accusateur les moyens de rassembler les preuves. Cicéron était investi officiellement d'une autorité qui permettait de faire citer les témoins, mais aussi de se faire remettre des documents, des registres, des lettres, *etc*. En cela, l'accusateur se trouvait temporairement investi d'une délégation de puissance publique.[83]

[82] En tout cas, Cicéron affirme qu'on saisit toute la récolte sur l'aire. Est-ce parce que Nymphon se serait abstenu de toute déclaration comme le laisse entendre le §53 ('[decumanus negabat] numerum iugerum professum esse')? Pour des déclarations minorées ou réputées telles, ce qui est le cas de Xénon de Mènes (Menae) au §55, la condamnation prononcée est une amende de 50,000 sesterces.

[83] David (1992) 502-08.

On peut de fait, dans tous ces chiffres, identifier en propre des renseignements de caractère public. Certains éléments semblent venir de sources officielles romaines, des archives de l'État, par nature très contrôlées.[84] Ainsi, lorsqu'il est question de montants décidés au Sénat, et dont les totaux sont forcément archivés dans l'*Aerarium*:

> [§163] Ainsi, pour le grain réquisitionné, une somme de deux millions huit cent mille sesterces était allouée annuellement à Verrès, à verser aux cultivateurs et, pour les secondes dîmes, une somme d'environ neuf millions de sesterces. Donc, sur trois ans, a été prélevée sur le Trésor, pour ces achats de grain en Sicile, une somme de presque douze millions de sesterces.[85]

D'autres informations, de caractère tout aussi public, étaient recueillies auprès des cités de Sicile et leurs témoignages étaient selon toute vraisemblance appuyés sur leurs propres documents publics. Cicéron choisit parfois de citer des données très précises, ainsi à propos du blé dîmé dans le territoire de Tissa:

> [§86] La deuxième année, les citoyens de Tissa sont contraints de verser, malgré eux, 21,000 sesterces à titre de bénéfice. La troisième année, ils ont été contraints de verser 12,000 boisseaux de blé à Diognetus, l'esclave de Vénus, à titre de bénéfice. [... §87] Ces faits, prenez-en donc connaissance par le témoignage officiel des citoyens de Tissa. TEMOIGNAGE OFFICIEL DES CITOYENS DE TISSA.[86]

De fait, une multiplicité de renseignements à caractère public devait bien figurer dans les archives des cités de Sicile, et les données fournies par Cicéron ne représentent en réalité qu'un modeste échantillon de la documentation disponible. Ainsi les cultivateurs étaient recensés tous les ans dans le cadre de la *subscriptio*[87] et Cicéron n'a cité que les chiffres de Leontini.[88] Lors de cette déclaration, les cultivateurs précisaient la superficie

[84] Pour autant, les cas de falsifications sont attestés, même pour l'*aerarium*. Voir Coudry (1994) 71. Même des sénatus-consultes étaient parfois falsifiés, Cic. *Phil.* 12.12.

[85] *Ver.* 3.163: 'Ita in frumentum imperatum HS duodetriciens in annos singulos Verri decernebatur quod aratoribus solueret, in alteras decumas fere ad nonagiens. Sic per triennium ad hanc frumenti emptionem Siciliensem prope centiens et uiciens erogatum est.'

[86] *Ver.* 3.86-87: 'Anno secundo Tissenses HS $\overline{\text{XXI}}$ lucri dare coguntur inuiti; tertio anno $\overline{\text{XII}}$ mod. tritici lucri Diogneto Venerio dare coacti sunt. [... §87] Atque haec ex publico Tissensium testimonio cognoscite. TESTIMONIVM PVBLICVM TISSENSIVM'.

[87] *Ver.* 3.113 et surtout 120: 'Id adeo sciri facillime potest ex litteris publicis ciuitatum, propterea quod lege Hieronica numerus aratorum quotannis apud magistratus publice subscribitur.' Il est facile de l'apprendre d'après les documents officiels des cités, puisqu'en vertu de la loi de Hiéron, le nombre des cultivateurs est chaque année enregistré devant les magistrats. Voir Carcopino (1919) 5-6, 165 et 280-81. Carcopino justifiait la nécessité annuelle de ce recensement par le fait que dans un territoire de culture extensive comme l'était la Sicile, l'alternance entre jachère et mise en culture était forte et le nombre de cultivateurs variait selon lui sensiblement d'une année sur l'autre. L'exactitude des données n'était possible que par la régularité des enregistrements. Cette variation attendue du nombre de cultivateurs a été aggravée sous la préture de Verrès.

[88] Voir *supra* n. 54.

ensemencée[89] et ces données individuelles, après avoir été rassemblées dans chaque cité, étaient très probablement transmises à Syracuse, afin que le gouverneur pût en disposer.[90] Là encore, nous ne trouvons citées que les déclarations de Leontini au §116. Nous avons bien affaire à une sélection de chiffres, sans doute les plus probants et point les seuls disponibles, loin s'en faut. Ajoutons à ces informations les conditions d'adjudication des dîmes que le préteur portait dans ses registres et rendait publiques: un témoignage en fut donné par lecture du greffier, afin de comparer les données de la cité d'Acesta et les registres du gouverneur.[91] Là encore, un exemple, sans doute bien choisi, venait illustrer le procédé frauduleux en faisant éclater au grand jour les différences entre les témoignages des cités et les archives falsifiées du préteur. Le raisonnement valait pour les autres cités sans que la production de toutes les données fût nécessaire. D'autres éléments complétaient la *lex decumis uendundis*, le cahier des charges des dîmes, à savoir l'enregistrement des adjudications effectives, le prix concrètement offert par le décimateur et approuvé par le préteur. Une fois de plus, seul l'exemple de Leontini est retenu, dans la mention faite à propos de C. Norbanus.[92] De nouveau, le lecteur butte sur la mention d'une lecture du document réputée être faite au procès, mais dont le détail n'a pas été conservé. Plus avant dans la procédure, les décimateurs passaient des conventions privées avec les cultivateurs:[93] les exemples d'Hybla et de Menae attestent que ces *pactiones* étaient consignées par écrit et ces documents sont lus lors des procès. Claude Nicolet a supposé que ces conventions particulières étaient rassemblées et centralisées dans la capitale provinciale, en sorte que le gouverneur pût chaque année connaître le total des dîmes de blé et d'orge qu'il avait vendues.[94]

Et dans le cas des secondes dîmes, le Sénat devait allouer au gouverneur une somme, et avant cela, la déterminer par rapport au montant des premières dîmes; il fallait bien qu'il existât aussi des documents comptables publics très précis, d'où les calculs mentionnés par Cicéron, qu'il tire sans doute des archives même du Sénat romain et du Trésor, donc d'une source contrôlable par les juges:

> [§163] Verrès devait acheter du grain en Sicile, en vertu d'un sénatus-consulte et de la loi frumentaire Terentia et Cassia. Il existait deux façons d'acheter: la première, une dîme, la seconde, le grain qui, en plus de cela, avait été réparti équitablement entre les cités. Pour ce qui est de la dîme, la quantité était équivalente à celle qui avait été tirée des premières dîmes, pour ce qui est du grain réquisitionné, la quantité annuelle était de 800,000 *modii* de *triticum*, mais, si, pour la dîme, le prix avait été fixé à trois sesterces par *modius*, pour le grain réquisitionné, il était de trois sesterces et demi. Ainsi, pour le grain réquisitionné, une somme de deux millions huit cent mille sesterces était allouée annuellement à

[89] *Ver.* 3.102 (*professio sationum*).

[90] Nicolet (2000b) 256-58. L'essentiel est repris dans Nicolet (2000a) 278-82.

[91] *Ver.* 3.83.

[92] *Ver.* 3.117.

[93] *Ver.* 3.102.

[94] Nicolet (2000b) 256.

> Verrès, à verser aux cultivateurs et, pour les secondes dîmes, une somme d'environ neuf millions de sesterces. Donc, sur trois ans, a été prélevée sur le Trésor, pour ces achats de grain en Sicile, une somme de presque douze millions de sesterces.[95]

Ces chiffres-ci n'appellent donc guère contestation, sauf à considérer que la tradition manuscrite serait peu fiable ou que les chiffres auraient été falsifiés avant même que Cicéron s'en fût emparé pour les besoins de la cause à plaider. Ces données étaient de celles que Cicéron pouvait le moins manipuler: non seulement parce qu'il s'agissait de documents publics, mais aussi parce qu'ils émanaient des archives même de Rome. Et avant même d'être archivés, ces montants avaient donné lieu à des débats publics; des témoins de ces discussions au Sénat étaient à Rome, sur place, et ils étaient de la plus haute honorabilité. Donc la fiabilité des chiffres peut être considérée comme presque certaine dans ce dernier cas. Dès lors, l'historien aujourd'hui ne peut mettre tous ces renseignements tirés des documents publics sur le même plan, ou s'en tenir au critère public/privé. La manipulation, le mensonge par omission, la sélection tendancieuse de données étaient évidemment plus faciles pour les renseignements venus de Sicile à proprement parler que pour des éléments tirés de la comptabilité publique de l'État romain.

Finalement, il est patent que beaucoup de documents publics contenant de multiples données chiffrées existaient et pouvaient avoir été utilisés pour l'enquête. Mais de cette masse d'informations, Cicéron pouvait évidemment ne retenir que des éléments sélectionnés, soit qu'ils fussent les plus convaincants, soit que la collation même des informations dans son enquête de terrain eût été d'inégale qualité ou ampleur. Le cas de Leontini doit-il dans ces conditions être pris comme emblématique? Ou, au contraire, comme révélateur des injustices les plus criantes, donc les plus propres à emporter la conviction des juges pour faire condamner Verrès? Je pencherais pour la seconde hypothèse.

À côté de ces documents publics, Cicéron a retenu des renseignements de caractère privé, des témoignages de particuliers sans doute. On peut citer le cas de Dioclès de Panhormus, qui cultivait une terre prise à bail sur le territoire de Segesta:

> [§93] [Dioclès de Panhormus] avait loué pour 6000 sesterces. Lorsqu'il eut été malmené par un esclave de Vénus, il consentit en guise de dîme à verser 16,000 sesterces et 654 médimnes.[96]

[95] *Ver.* 3.163: 'Frumentum emere in Sicilia debuit Verres ex senatus consulto et ex lege Terentia et Cassia frumentaria. Emundi duo genera fuerunt, unum decumanum, alterum quod praeterea ciuitatibus aequaliter esset distributum; illius decumani tantum quantum ex primis decumis fuisset, huius imperati in annos singulos tritici mod. $\overline{\text{DCCC}}$; pretium autem constitutum decumano in modios singulos HS III, imperato HS IIIS. Ita in frumentum imperatum HS duodetriciens in annos singulos Verri decernebatur quod aratoribus solveret, in alteras decumas fere ad nonagiens. Sic per triennium ad hanc frumenti emptionem Siciliensem prope centiens et uiciens erogatum est.' Pour un commentaire du passage, voir Nicolet (2000a) 280-81.

[96] *Ver.* 3.93: '[Diocles est Panhormitanus] conductum habebat HS sex milibus. Pro decuma, cum pulsatus a Venerio esset, decidit HS $\overline{\text{XVI}}$ et <medimnis> DCLIIII.'

De tels témoignages ne devaient pas être difficiles à obtenir sur le terrain. La précision même des chiffres leur donne aujourd'hui une certaine vraisemblance. Mais surtout, par delà ces témoignages plus ou moins spontanés, l'accusateur disposait d'un droit d'investigation dans son enquête de terrain. Cicéron en usa y compris chez les particuliers.[97] Ainsi, il a littéralement perquisitionné au domicile de Carpinatius en Sicile, à Syracuse, où il a récupéré une lettre compromettante pour Verrès; L. Carpinatius est un publicain lui-même et il n'est rien moins que le *magister scripturae et sex publicorum*. De même, Cicéron a eu le droit de prendre à Rome, chez L. Tullius (un *magister* lui aussi et un familier de l'accusé) copie d'une correspondance. Le commentateur moderne ne peut considérer comme systématiquement subjective voire falsifiée la documentation privée car elle pouvait être prise auprès des victimes témoignant de plein gré, tout comme elle pouvait être saisie en fonction des pouvoirs d'injonction de l'enquêteur, qui disposait du droit de sceller tous actes et objets indispensables au procès. Divers passages tirés des *Verrines* illustrent ces pouvoirs d'enquête:[98] par exemple, dans le *de Signis*, Cicéron évoque son audience auprès du Sénat de Syracuse, qui vote le décret supprimant l'éloge en faveur de Verrès, au cours d'une session mouvementée durant laquelle Cicéron a pris la parole en grec.[99] Devant la résistance du préteur en charge et celle des partisans de Verrès, au nombre desquels un certain Théomnaste, Cicéron fait mettre sous scellés et emporter le registre des délibérations. Pour venir à bout des opposants, il invoque une *lex* lui conférant le droit de saisir tous registres et documents.[100] Adolf Holm, sans citer de sources précises, voyait là une allusion à une disposition de la *lex Cornelia de repetundis* permettant des sanctions pénales contre ceux qui auraient retenu par devers eux des documents nécessaires aux procès d'extorsion.[101] La conclusion de l'incident syracusain laisse bien voir en tout cas que la loi, quelle qu'elle fût, était redoutée car Théomnaste céda. L'enquêteur avait donc les moyens de collecter des renseignements, auprès des cités ou des particuliers.

[97] *Ver.* 3.167.

[98] *Ver.* 1.50 (Cicéron examine les statues volées dans la propre maison de Verrès, lorsqu'il vient lui signifier l'acte d'accusation); 1.60 (saisie des livres de comptes ayant appartenu à Verrès et même à son père jusqu'en 73); 1.149 (Cicéron a posé des scellés sur un registre de Verrès); 2.182-90 (registres saisis au domicile d'un *magister* d'une société de publicains); 3.154 (lettre saisie dans la demeure d'Apronius); 4.36 (saisie incomplète des comptes de Verrès); 4.146-49 (registre des délibérations du Sénat de Syracuse). Voir aussi *Flac.* 36 (évocation des droits de l'accusateur, D. Laelius Balbus) et Pseudo-Asconius 236 Stangl (scholie sur la mise sous scellés des preuves au domicile même de Verrès).

[99] *Ver.* 4.138-49.

[100] *Ver.* 4.149: 'Ego legem recitare omnium mihi litterarum et litterarum fieri potestatem. [...] nisi legis sanctionem poenamque recitassem tabularum mihi potestas facta non esset.'

[101] Holm (1898) 186; Rotondi (1912) 360 reconstitue peu d'éléments pour la *lex Cornelia de repetundis*. C'est peut-être encore en vertu de cette loi qu'aurait été jugé L. Valerius Flaccus en 59 av. J.-C. (*cf.* notice complémentaire de Ph. Moreau dans Cicéron, *Pro Flacco*, éd. F. Gaffiot, C. U. F. (Paris 1989^2) 72f-g).

IV. Le rôle des données chiffrées dans l'argumentation et la preuve

Il y avait des avantages et des dangers à multiplier les chiffres. Les chiffres étaient destinés à servir l'accusation, ils devaient donc en principe rendre claire la culpabilité de Verrès. Ils concouraient à réifier le débat, à ancrer la présentation dans un contexte: des personnages identifiés produisaient telle quantité de céréales par an, devaient donner telle quantité au titre de la dîme, pouvaient recevoir telle indemnisation pour le blé acheté, *etc.* Il fallait recréer une réalité convaincante qui suscitât indignation envers Verrès et sympathie pour les victimes de son administration.

Pourtant l'utilisation de chiffres était loin de servir uniquement à clarifier le débat et elle pouvait même desservir la cause. À cela plusieurs raisons: d'abord citer une multiplicité de chiffres embrouillait l'auditoire, leur accumulation pouvait faire décrocher l'attention du public. Ainsi en est-il ici:

> [§116] Les déclarations du territoire de Leontium se montent environ à 30,000 jugères, c'est-à-dire à 90,000 médimnes, soit 540,000 *modii*; une fois déduits 216,000 *modii* de *triticum*, qui sont la somme à laquelle furent adjugées les dîmes, il reste 324,000 *modii* de *triticum*. Ajoutez à la somme globale de 540,000 *modii* trois cinquantièmes, soit 32,400 *modii* de *triticum* (en effet, chacun devait verser trois cinquantièmes), cela donne à la fin environ 360,000 *modii* de *triticum*. Mais j'avais dit que le bénéfice se montait à 400,000: c'est que je ne prends pas en compte ici ceux à qui il n'a pas été permis de transiger à trois médimnes par jugère. Mais, dans le présent calcul, pour parvenir au total auquel je me suis engagé, pour chaque médimne, nombreux étaient contraints d'ajouter deux sesterces, nombreux un sesterce et demi de supplément, au moins un sesterce. En restant au minimum, puisque nous comptons 90,000 médimnes, s'ajoutent à cet exemple jamais vu et infâme 90,000 sesterces.[102]

L'effet d'un tel passage était à double tranchant. L'auditoire qui suivait parfaitement l'orateur dans tout son développement adhérait au raisonnement. Il était d'ailleurs moins convaincu par les chiffres eux-mêmes que par la logique de la construction argumentative. Mais, dans un discours très long comme l'aurait été la *Deuxième action*, il n'est pas non plus interdit de penser que le plus souvent, le public pouvait être littéralement perdu sous cette avalanche de chiffres. L'attention de l'auditoire était-elle vraiment soutenue ou au contraire égarée par une telle énumération de données? La réponse n'est pas univoque bien sûr.

[102] *Ver.* 3.116: 'Professio est agri Leontini ad iugerum $\overline{\text{XXX}}$; haec sunt ad tritici medimnum $\overline{\text{XC}}$, id est mod. $\overline{\text{DXXXX}}$; deductis tritici mod. $\overline{\text{CCXVI}}$, quanti decumae uenierunt, reliqua sunt tritici $\overline{\text{CCCXXIIII}}$. Adde totius summae DXXXX milium mod. tris quinquagesimas; fit tritici mod. $\overline{\text{XXXII}}$ CCCC (ab omnibus enim ternae praeterea quinquagesimae exigebantur); sunt haec iam ad $\overline{\text{CCCLX}}$ mod. tritici. At ego $\overline{\text{CCCC}}$ lucri facta esse dixeram; non enim duco in hac ratione eos quibus ternis medimnis non est licitum decidere. Verum ut hac ipsa ratione summam mei promissi compleam, ad singula medimna multi HS binos, multi HS singulos semis accessionis cogebantur dare, qui minimum, singulos nummos. Minimum ut sequamur, quoniam $\overline{\text{XC}}$ med. duximus, accedant eo nouo pessimoque exemplo HS $\overline{\text{XC}}$.'

Un deuxième danger était inhérent à la multiplication des données chiffrées, le fait que le public était confronté à des difficultés métrologiques. Il fallait en permanence convertir des unités, volumétriques en particulier, selon des unités en usage dans le monde romain, c'est-à-dire des unités 'parlantes' pour l'auditoire. Le médimne n'était pas une unité vraiment utilisée en Italie péninsulaire, en tout cas pas en Italie centrale, elle l'était en revanche en Sicile. D'où les nombreuses transpositions effectuées par l'orateur, pour que les quantités évoquées demeurassent, en ordre de grandeur, intelligibles pour le public. Ces conversions faisaient parfois doublons et constituaient de pures répétitions, pour mieux marteler l'information. Ainsi en est-il aux §77 et 78, où les médimnes sont rapidement convertis en *modii* avec le rapport de 1/6 entre les deux, donc une corrélation entre les données chiffrées, que l'éditeur aujourd'hui doit accepter ou rejeter en bloc par conséquent.

> [§77] [Verrès] réduit le total de 600 médimnes [...]. [§78] [... les gens d'Herbita] sont contraints de donner à Aeschrion [...] autant que ce qui avait été enlevé au total, 3600 boisseaux de blé.[103]
> [§110] La troisième année, les dîmes du territoire de Leontini ont été vendues 36,000 médimnes, c'est-à-dire 216,000 *modii* de *triticum*.[104]

On peut encore citer une troisième source de confusion pour le public. Le mélange des données formait une constante dans le discours, qui citait volontiers les données relevant de catégories disparates: Cicéron mélangeait des surfaces, des volumes, des sommes d'argent. La mise en relation de deux informations hétérogènes était difficile et aggravait l'incapacité de l'auditeur à vérifier sur le champ les données et leur cohérence. Ainsi, dans le paragraphe où il était question des habitants de Tissa, Cicéron additionnait-il les sesterces et les volumes:

> [§86] La deuxième année, les citoyens de Tissa sont contraints de verser, malgré eux, 21,000 sesterces à titre de bénéfice. La troisième année, ils ont été contraints de verser 12,000 *modii* de blé à Diognetus, l'esclave de Vénus, à titre de bénéfice.[105]

Nous ne devons pas perdre de vue, dans une réflexion sur la compréhension des chiffres par ceux auxquels ils étaient destinés, les deux dimensions de la plaidoirie: la dimension originelle, celle de l'*actio* et celle que nous lisons aujourd'hui, l'*oratio*. Une chose est de comprendre au fil du prononcé du discours, dans le rythme continu de la version orale, sans retour possible sur un chiffre mal compris, au milieu d'une foule bruyante. Une autre est de publier des données – et peu importe que le livre antique soit destiné à la récitation plus qu'à la lecture proprement dite, au sens où nous l'entendons. Il

[103] *Ver.* 3.77: 'Demit de capite medimna DC [...]. [§78] [... Herbitenses] coguntur Aeschrioni [...], tantum dare quantum erat de capite demptum, tritici modium $\overline{\text{III}}$ DC.'

[104] *Ver.* 3.110: 'Agri Leontini decumae tertio anno uenierunt tritici medimnum $\overline{\text{XXXVI}}$, hoc est tritici mod. CC et XVI milibus.'

[105] *Ver.* 3.86: 'Anno secundo Tissenses HS $\overline{\text{XXI}}$ lucri dare coguntur inuiti; tertio anno $\overline{\text{XII}}$ mod. tritici lucri Diogneto Venerio dare coacti sunt'.

nous faut nous interroger sur ce qui était vraiment dit et sur ce qui pouvait être ajouté après coup. Non seulement parce que la multiplication de données chiffrées imposait à l'orateur des efforts supplémentaires en termes de *memoria*, mais aussi pour deux autres raisons: la tentation de sélectionner à l'oral était toujours plus forte, pour tenir compte de l'attention et de la réceptivité du public. Enfin, les possibilités de vérification étaient différentes, entre le procès proprement dit, avec ses pièces susceptibles d'être contrôlées par le tribunal, et la lecture déconnectée du contexte judiciaire.

Il est hautement probable que les données chiffrées furent réagencées dans la version composée du discours, comme n'importe quelle autre information qui figurait dans les témoignages. À côté des mentions simplifiées du type *testimonium publicum*, *litterae publicae*, nous trouvons dans le discours des paraphrases.[106] Nous ne possédons plus rien des éventuelles discussions ou contestations auxquelles prêtaient ces chiffres au cours de l'*altercatio*. On ignore s'ils étaient simplement lus, ou commentés oralement par l'accusateur ou les témoins, ou les deux.

Il n'en demeure pas moins que certains chiffres importaient au déroulement même du procès, en particulier à l'acte d'accusation. Ainsi dans la *Première action*, Cicéron évalue à quarante millions de sesterces les prévarications commises par Verrès.[107] Ce montant était-il le résultat d'une totalisation rigoureuse ou une estimation? Correspondait-il à ce qu'on supposait être la somme des détournements ou à ce qu'on pouvait prouver strictement, et en ce cas le détournement aurait été bien supérieur. Les quarante millions de sesterces sont de nouveau mentionnés dans la *Deuxième action*.[108] Les commentateurs ont mis en rapport cette somme avec celle que Cicéron réclamait, en vertu de la loi, en dédommagement à Verrès: cent millions de sesterces.[109] On en a déduit alors que la loi prévoyait une pénalité égale à deux fois et demi les montants détournés. L'estimation initiale des vols et exactions, dans ces conditions, n'aurait donc pas dû être calculée avec des méthodes si peu rigoureuses, voire avec une approximation récurrente. La preuve de la culpabilité importait en priorité à Cicéron, mais, dans son rôle d'accusateur, pouvait-il se passer de l'établissement précis des faits? On reste en peine d'élucider la question car, pour ne prendre que les montants détournés par Verrès au titre du *frumentum in cellam*, le lecteur qui mettrait bout à bout les chiffres cités par Cicéron totaliserait bien plus de cent millions de sesterces.[110] La contradiction interne du texte est indépassable. Il n'est pas

[106] Ainsi au §83, la déposition elle-même n'est pas reproduite mais le contenu en est paraphrasé et les données chiffrées sont reprises par l'orateur (sans qu'on puisse avoir le moindre élément sur le caractère sélectif ou non de cette paraphrase).

[107] *Ver.* 56: 'quadringentiens sestertium'.

[108] *Ver.* 1.27: 'HS quadringentiens'. Dans ce passage, comme dans celui cité n. 107, les manuscrits ne présentent pas de variantes.

[109] *Diu. Caec.* 19: 'sestertium miliens ex lege repeto.'

[110] Voir la démonstration de Holm (1898), 418-19. Le détournement se monte à trois deniers par *modius* (*Ver.* 3.188-225). Holm admet d'ailleurs qu'on ne peut étendre le calcul aux trois ans du gouvernement de Verrès, sous peine d'atteindre une somme improbable. Il faut plutôt admettre que ce bénéfice de 1200% correspond à une escroquerie ponctuelle. Verrès en effet, dans ce cas, additionnait le détournement de la somme que lui versait directement le Sénat romain pour le *frumentum aestimatum* et les montants qu'il extorquait, sur les mêmes grains, aux cultivateurs

interdit de croire que Cicéron a additionné pour la totalité du gouvernement de Verrès des gains qu'il aurait réalisés ponctuellement sur une des années. Les chiffres sont faux parce que des opérations frauduleuses singulières sont présentées comme récurrentes. Et l'accusateur a aussi probablement cumulé des sommes que les complices de Verrès, dont des fermiers de l'impôt, ont détournées pour leur compte.

On peut s'étonner qu'Hortensius n'ait pas répondu dans une défense argumentée, serrant de près les chiffres.[111] Sans doute y avait-il assez de vérité d'ensemble dans les accusations portées par Cicéron pour que les réfutations de détail devinssent inutiles. Le fait que Cicéron ait pu présenter ainsi, de façon assez technique, presque comptable, de nombreux détails chiffrés pouvait aussi prendre l'allure d'une innovation de style. Par delà l'affrontement entre l'ancien gouverneur et les Siciliens, les *Verrines* constituaient aussi une lutte entre Hortensius et Cicéron pour la suprématie dans l'éloquence judiciaire. Leur opposition était aussi une opposition de style.[112] L'utilisation massive de démonstrations appuyées sur les chiffres serait-elle passée pour un nouveau mode de plaider, une façon moderne de conduire l'accusation, qu'un orateur de l'ancienne école, aurait plutôt boudée? Ce n'est pas exclu mais ne suffit point à expliquer le silence d'Hortensius.

Qui plus est, l'accusateur avait plus de moyens à sa disposition pour instruire le dossier que l'accusé et son défenseur n'en avaient. En effet, là où le *delator* s'était vu délégué une forme de puissance publique pour collecter des preuves, saisir des documents, emporter des registres, *etc.*, l'accusé n'avait à sa disposition que ses propres moyens pour réunir des preuves ou des contre-témoignages. Hortensius n'avait pas mené de contre-enquête, il ne le pouvait pas, alors que l'accusateur assumait un rôle public et s'en voyait officiellement confier les moyens.[113] Évidemment, un ancien préteur comme Verrès, soutenu par le brillant Hortensius et une bonne partie des sénateurs, pouvait opposer au modeste édile désigné qu'était Cicéron la force de ses soutiens, le poids de ses réseaux, *etc.* Et concrètement, l'un, Cicéron, devait obligatoirement chercher des preuves, amasser des documents, et avait juridiquement les pouvoirs d'investigation pour y parvenir. L'autre, Verrès, n'avait pas les moyens juridiques d'instruire un dossier à décharge et

siciliens. Verrès faisait un double bénéfice sur le *frumentum in cellam* (tout comme il en avait fait un double bénéfice sur le *frumentum emptum*, voir *Ver.* 3.179). Les variations annuelles du prix des grains, que Cicéron ne manque pas de souligner, poussent aussi à ne pas étendre de façon systématique aux trois ans de gouvernement les sommes connues pour un procédé frauduleux bien particulier. Le fait que le gouverneur soit poursuivi devant le tribunal par les seules cités de Sicile n'enlève rien au fait qu'il a cumulé les malversations. Verrès n'est pas comptable dans ce procès-ci de tous ses actes criminels (*Ver.* 1.11-14 énumère toutes les autres actions dont il serait passible s'il était acquitté devant le tribunal *de repetundis*, parmi lesquelles le péculat et la lèse-majesté): même si une partie des faits rappelés est à proprement parler juridiquement délictueuse au regard d'un procès en récupération des biens extorqués, la démonstration ne manque pas de cumuler ce qui est moralement et légalement répréhensible.

111 Du *pro Verre* qu'il prononça, nous ne possédons que la citation de Quintilien *Inst.* 10.1.23. Indépendamment des chiffres eux-mêmes, rappelons qu'Hortensius esquiva l'affrontement, même lors de la *Première action.* Sur sa défense de Verrès, voir Alexander (1976).

112 Cic. *Brut.* 25.

113 David (1992) 507 n. 36.

pouvait s'en passer de toutes façons. Les modes d'action de l'accusateur et les procédés de défense ne se concevaient pas en miroir. Il fallait à Cicéron beaucoup d'énergie et de ténacité, un certain courage même, pour exercer ses droits d'enquête. Il avait potentiellement tous les moyens d'investigation dans un délai certes limité. Il n'en demeure pas moins, comme le souligne avec raison Jean-Michel David,[114] que cette enquête était une forme de défi envers l'aristocratie sénatoriale et ses réseaux. Aller chercher ces informations qui étayaient l'accusation nécessitait assurément de l'audace. Face à un accusateur de rang encore médiocre, l'accusé, lui, devait surtout réunir ses plus prestigieux partisans ou protecteurs.

La réalité de la faute apparaissait en tout cas patente, la preuve de la culpabilité du défendeur pouvait même s'accommoder de la manipulation des chiffres, y compris par l'accusateur. Sur ce point, rappelons le passage de Plutarque où le biographe mentionne l'accusation portée contre Cicéron, celle d'avoir rabaissé l'évaluation des détournements commis par Verrès. De la sorte, l'amende encourue eût été moindre pour l'ancien gouverneur. Les détracteurs de Cicéron le soupçonnaient d'avoir négocié un bénéfice personnel, en contrepartie d'une sous-évaluation.[115] Il n'est pas complètement exclu qu'il faille voir dans ce chiffre (trois millions de sesterces) l'amende réelle à laquelle Verrès, déjà exilé, aurait été condamné, mais aucune source ne le dit expressément.[116] Et il n'est pas impossible que dans la version publiée, Cicéron ait changé des chiffres en fonction du résultat du procès. La somme utile pour prouver la culpabilité de Verrès n'était pas forcément le montant réel des détournements. Enfin, il reste difficile de rapprocher Cicéron lui-même de son biographe Plutarque, qui ne lui vouait pas une grande estime: il y a autant contradiction des chiffres que divergences de l'historiographie elle-même.

En tout cas, Verrès ne fut probablement pas ruiné par le procès et la condamnation qu'il entraîna. Quand il mourut, toujours exilé,[117] en décembre 43 av. J.-C., peu de jours après Cicéron, il était encore très riche. C'est d'ailleurs son refus de céder à Antoine des vases corinthiens qui aurait suscité la colère du triumvir et l'inscription de Verrès sur la liste des proscriptions, alors même qu'il était retiré de la vie publique depuis plus de vingt-cinq ans.[118]

[114] David (1992) 507-08.

[115] Plut. *Cic.* 8.1.

[116] Le chiffre cité par Plutarque (*supra* n. 115), 750,000 drachmes, soit 3,000,000 sesterces, peut paraître peu crédible pour le montant de l'amende, si celle-ci correspond bien à deux fois et demi les montants détournés. Disons que si Verrès avait été présent et si le procès avait été mené à terme, cette pénalité semblerait dérisoire. Ou alors, il faudrait supposer que Plutarque aurait confondu le montant de l'amende réclamée à Verrès et l'argent qui aurait servi à acheter la complicité de Cicéron. Il n'y a pas eu de *litis aestimatio* de toute façon.

[117] Ps.-Asconius 205 et 225 Stangl.

[118] Plin. *Nat.* 34.6; Hinard (1985) 543.

V. La fiabilité en question

Dans l'interrogation qui est la nôtre sur la véracité initiale des chiffres, la question des sources même de Cicéron compte beaucoup. Les possibilités de falsification étaient en théorie moindres pour des comptes soumis à reddition publique et à archivage officiel, en tout cas à Rome. En même temps, dans une univers civique où le contrôle des fortunes privées était très étroit, du fait même de l'organisation ploutocratique des cités, il ne faut pas considérer avec suspicion les déclarations individuelles. La tenue de registres de comptes privés, l'enregistrement des entrées et dépenses sur un *codex* étaient obligatoires pour les Romains. Ces documents devaient être soignés, mis à jour au fur et à mesure, et pouvaient être produits en justice.[119] Bien sûr, on est vite renvoyé à la question de la disparité des pratiques entre les citoyens grecs de Sicile et le monde romain *stricto sensu*. Le fait que Cicéron fasse vigoureusement reproche à Verrès de n'avoir point tenu à jour certains registres laisse croire cependant que pour les citoyens romains au moins, il était vraiment attendu que la tenue des comptes fût rigoureuse et pût servir de preuve, donc que les données chiffrées fussent exactes.[120]

En tout état de cause, les sources de l'orateur étaient disparates et cette hétérogénéité se traduisit aussi par la sélection des cités et des témoins: en arrière-plan, se pose la question de savoir si toute la Sicile était vraiment mobilisée contre Verrès, par delà les deux exceptions notables de Syracuse et de Messana.[121] Les chiffres mentionnés par Cicéron étaient évidemment ceux qui tendaient à confondre l'accusé, à le faire condamner. Les exploiter en tant que révélateurs de l'économie de la Sicile, significatifs sur le nombre des cultivateurs, *etc.*, est incontestablement risqué. Il manque à tout le moins les chiffres qu'aurait cités Hortensius. Et l'ensemble ne constituerait de toute façon qu'un tableau très subjectif. Hortensius aurait lui aussi sélectionné ce qui disculpait Verrès ou atténuait sa responsabilité. La logique du plaidoyer reste déterminante. Nous ne lisons pas un dossier d'instruction à charge et décharge établi par un enquêteur indépendant, mais un pan de procès.

Certains passages relèvent à l'évidence de la manipulation des chiffres par Cicéron: en soi, ils ne sont pas faux, mais leur agencement entretient la confusion et incite le public à additionner les sommes détournées. Ainsi, à propos du *frumentum in cellam*, il y avait deux sources de recettes pour Verrès: le prix versé par le Sénat (quatre sesterces le *modius*), que Verrès conservait au lieu de le reverser aux cultivateurs; les sommes que le gouverneur faisait payer aux Siciliens au lieu de les dédommager (huit sesterces le *modius*). Cicéron joua sur les deux tableaux, en mêlant ce qui était à proprement parler la somme extorquée aux Siciliens, à savoir deux deniers,[122] et le bénéfice total, à savoir trois

[119] C'est tout l'objet du *pro Q. Roscio comoedo* par exemple que de contester une dette qui n'a pas été correctement reportée sur le *codex accepti et expensi*, et qui ne peut être valablement prouvée. Une bonne partie des réfutations produites par la défense tient au fait que le plaignant produit en justice non point un *codex* ou des *tabellae* mais des *aduersaria*, des brouillons de comptes, une sorte de bloc-notes. *Cf. Q. Rosc.* 5-9.

[120] *Ver.* 3.112.

[121] Cette unité est contestée par Dilke (1980).

[122] *Ver.* 3.197 et à moindre titre 201.

deniers, qui résultait de l'addition des sommes publiques détournées et des montants volés aux cultivateurs.[123] Il n'y a pas de contradiction dans le texte, mais une confusion subtilement entretenue pour discréditer l'accusé.

Il faut maintenant revenir sur la question posée initialement: les chiffres sont-ils vrais ou sont-ils faux? J'aurais tendance à penser que beaucoup d'entre eux sont probables, plausibles de façon absolue. Mais ils sont faussés par la construction même de la plaidoirie judiciaire, par les critères qui ont présidé à leur sélection, leur inscription dans une démonstration partisane qui voulait faire condamner le gouverneur Verrès. Ils sont faux ou manipulés en ce que Cicéron était peut-être incapable de dire exactement, ou plutôt ne cherchait pas à dire avec exactitude, l'ampleur de la perte pour l'État, ou à calculer de façon arithmétique la somme des profits de Verrès. Le crime n'était pas d'avoir détourné des sommes ou des grains, tous les gouverneurs le faisaient sans doute, l'important était les proportions prises par les exactions. Le crime de Verrès était la démesure, plus que le détournement à des fins d'enrichissement privé. Et les données chiffrées que Cicéron choisissait de citer, soulignons-le, constituaient souvent des extorsions, des écarts considérables par rapport à la norme, des situations d'exception. Aucune de ces données ne doit être utilisée sans une recontextualisation scrupuleuse, elles prennent sens dans un raisonnement qui se fonde sur des rappels internes: rien ne serait plus dangereux que d'extraire les chiffres pour une interprétation isolée de leur signification.

J'ai volontairement laissé de côté dans cette enquête les indications de nature chronologique. Elles se situent aux marges du thème et surtout, dans l'ensemble des *Verrines*, le *de Frumento* est celui des discours qui n'en comporte pratiquement pas. Pourtant, je voudrais faire un bref détour sur le sujet, car la comparaison entre les données chiffrées et les indications chronologiques est assez éclairante. Il n'est pas lieu de rouvrir ici le débat complexe sur la reconstitution chronologique des différentes phases du procès, sur les dates précises des épisodes successifs.[124] Mais il est remarquable que les indications temporelles soient elles aussi très floues, y compris pour des faits que le jury ou l'auditoire étaient à même d'apprécier et de vérifier. Le temps de présence de tel ou tel personnage officiel à Rome ou dans la province, la durée de telle ou telle mission d'enquête effectuée dans les semaines précédant la séance au tribunal, les délais d'acheminement entre Rome et les provinces, ce type de renseignements fait lui aussi l'objet d'une évocation contradictoire ou imprécise. Prenons l'exemple d'une question pourtant au coeur de la procédure juridique, le *tempus inquirendi*. Le délai d'enquête officiellement accordé à Cicéron était de 110 jours,[125] ce qui est une donnée précise, d'autant que le procès prétexte entrepris contre un pro-préteur d'Achaïe obtient le droit de

[123] *Diu. Caec.* 30 et *Ver.* 3.188, 3.189, 3.191-94.

[124] Il faut surtout se reporter à l'article de Zielinski (1894) 248-58 avec des vues assez personnelles (et très contestables) sur une double *sortitio* des jurés; et pour un point de vue contraire sur les phases du procès ainsi que leur calendrier, *cf.* Marinone (1950). Un état comparatif de la question était présenté de façon assez commode (dans un livre par ailleurs discutable) par Cowles (1917) 192-204.

[125] *Ver.* 1.30: 'C et X dies solos'.

passer avant le procès contre Verrès grâce à une enquête resserrée sur 108 jours.[126] La bataille de procédure repose tout entière sur l'écart de deux jours. Or, dans le même passage et juste à la suite, Cicéron reprend la mention des 108/110 jours par *menses tres*, trois mois. Le texte a été compris de deux façons par les commentateurs: soit ces trois mois sont ceux de l'enquête, qu'on admettra parallèle, en Sicile et en Achaïe pour chacune des deux causes; soit il s'agit du temps qu'aurait occupé le procès contre le propréteur d'Achaïe et qui aurait donc d'autant retardé l'accusation contre Verrès.[127] Dans un cas comme dans l'autre, les *tres menses* sont une indication générique. En effet, 108 ou 110 jours ne font pas trois mois! Et quant au procès sur l'Achaïe, s'il est passé en premier et en admettant qu'il a bien eu lieu, il n'a pas duré trois mois, mais se serait déroulé en mai-juin et se serait achevé au pire début juillet (la *reiectio iudicum* du procès de Verrès aurait en effet eu lieu entre le 14 et le 26 juillet). Donc les trois mois sont une indication vague.

De la même façon, on trouve un calcul étonnant à propos du délai nécessaire au défenseur de Verrès pour répondre à l'accusation (*comperendinatio*), délai allongé par les nombreux jours de vacance du tribunal: environ quarante jours,[128] dit Cicéron dans la *Première action*, puis quarante jours exactement dans la *Seconde action*.[129] En réalité, il s'agit de désigner la période de fêtes religieuses entre le 16 août et le 19 septembre inclus,[130] soit une trentaine de jours.[131] On pourrait citer un dernier exemple, qui constitue un calcul sur les années: pour la période où la *lex Sempronia iudiciaria* fut en vigueur, Cicéron indique *annos prope quinquaginta continuos*;[132] dans les faits, la loi s'appliqua de

[126] *Ver.* 6. Il s'agit de l'accusation menée par un personnage inconnu contre un pro-préteur d'Achaïe. Cette manoeuvre de diversion servait à retarder le procès contre Verrès mené par Cicéron. On reste étonné de la contradiction formulée par Cicéron lui-même qui, d'un côté, présente le délai d'enquête comme une durée très courte (*dies inquirendi perexigua*) et d'un autre côté, quelques lignes plus bas, se vante d'avoir parcouru la Sicile tout entière et mené l'enquête en 50 jours (*quinquaginta diebus*). La contradiction est levée si on considère que ces 50 jours correspondent au séjour sur le terrain sicilien, à l'exclusion des voyages d'aller et de retour. Voir Marinone (1950) 28-29.

[127] Je me contente ici de rappeler que la réalité historique du procès d'Achaïe est l'objet de controverses. Contre la *communis opinio*, Zielinski (1894) 251 et 256-59 a défendu l'historicité de cet épisode judicaire. Il le fait commencer le 4 mai et se terminer fin juin. Pour une réfutation des analyses de Zielinski, voir Holm (1898) 422-23.

[128] *Ver.* 31: 'propre XL diebus'.

[129] *Ver.* 1.30: 'quadragesimo post die'.

[130] C'est le 16 août que commençaient les *Ludi uotiui* et le 19 septembre que se terminaient les *Ludi Romani*. Dans *Ver.* 31, Cicéron donne le nombre de jours pour chaque série de jeux, jusqu'en octobre.

[131] Dans ce calcul, je suis évidemment dans la nécessité de prendre parti sur la reconstitution du calendrier. Je choisis de suivre les propositions de Marinone (1950), de façon constante pour la série d'exemples chronologiques. Ce qui m'intéresse ici, est de montrer le caractère très approximatif des calculs de durée dans le texte lui-même. Bien évidemment, le principe même de la reconstitution chronologique des phases du procès s'en trouve affecté. Le commentateur est face à un cercle vicieux.

[132] *Ver.* 38.

122 à 81 av. J.-C., soit 42 ans. Il ne faut pas en conclure que toutes les indications chronologiques évoquées dans le procès sont fausses, mais elles s'inscrivent parfois dans une appréciation volontairement floue, dans une temporalité générique où il ne faut pas chercher la précision.[133] Toutes les données mesurées, quantifiées, datées, *etc.*, n'avaient pas vocation à former la preuve ou à concourir à l'établissement des faits. Nombre d'entre elles pourraient bien entrer dans la mise en place d'une contextualisation générale des événements, avec ce qu'il y avait, volontairement ou non, d'à-peu-près ou d'exagéré.

Conclusion

Il y a eu une fiabilité antique ou du moins une crédibilité de ces données mesurées. Les chiffres avancés par Cicéron étaient sans doute assez vraisemblables pour obtenir soit la fuite, soit la condamnation de Verrès. Ils ont concouru à la démonstration de sa culpabilité. Il ne faut pas oublier que le jeune questeur, édile désigné, affrontait Hortensius, au faîte de sa gloire comme patron judiciaire, consul désigné, orateur expert. Cicéron ne pouvait avancer sans déployer une véritable 'artillerie lourde' de l'éloquence judiciaire.

On ne saurait trop rappeler, pour évaluer l'intérêt des données quantifiées et chiffrées, la nécessité d'une enquête qui conjugue les approches philologique et historique. Les deux démarches se répondent et prémunissent le chercheur contre certaines dérives inhérentes à une enquête monodisciplinaire. En effet, la difficulté du sujet est qu'il faut à la fois tenter de voir d'où Cicéron tenait lui-même les chiffres rapportés dans la plaidoirie; ensuite, mesurer comment il manipulait ces données dans le contexte oratoire; enfin, prendre en compte la transmission du chiffre et ses éventuelles déformations au fil de la tradition manuscrite. En plus de cela, l'exploitation des renseignements fournis par le discours est inséparable d'une réflexion sur la nature même du texte, sur les règles qui président à l'éloquence judiciaire, sur les caractéristiques de la procédure aussi.

Au terme de cette étude, il faut souligner que la démarche de l'accusateur consistait à reconstituer des mécanismes, quitte à les déformer, pour dénoncer des pratiques. Les chiffres sont toujours là pour illustrer les procédés, pour donner une image de l'ampleur des profits réalisés ou des malheurs endurés par les Siciliens, au plan individuel comme au niveau des cités. L'argumentation cherche à révéler le crime du gouverneur, ses torts envers l'État romain lui-même et envers ses sujets. Le texte n'est pas en soi un inventaire ou un tableau. Bien au contraire, toutes les données s'inscrivent dans une anthologie d'illustrations et d'exemples, qui cherche à rendre vivant un raisonnement général austère, portant sur des questions techniques, fiscales pour l'essentiel.

Les données rassemblées ne servent que modestement à dessiner un authentique bilan de l'économie sicilienne, elles ne révèlent pas vraiment non plus la perte de fortune des cultivateurs: les éléments de comparaison manquent, l'état de leur fortune avant l'arrivée de Verrès n'est pas connu. Ce qui ressort, c'est qu'il n'y a plus intérêt à mettre des terres en culture en Sicile dans de telles conditions de prélèvements, donc que les intérêts vitaux de la République romaine et son ravitaillement sont en cause. La ruine individuelle de tel ou tel propriétaire sicilien importait sans doute assez peu au jury. La dîme, les réquisitions ne sont pas contestées dans leur principe bien sûr et Verrès n'a d'ailleurs pas forcément

[133] Marinone (1950) 20-21.

adjugé au plus haut. Ses profits personnels sont illicites, ils ont porté tort aux Siciliens autant qu'à Rome, puisqu'il devait adjuger les dîmes à des complices (pour garantir son bénéfice propre) et pas systématiquement au mieux-disant.

Finalement, on ne peut aborder cette question de la fiabilité des chiffres avec pour seule perspective celle de leur utilisation pour écrire aujourd'hui une histoire de la Sicile ou de la fiscalité romaine. Pour essayer de comprendre ces données, pour évaluer leur fiabilité, on ne peut se passer d'établir ce à quoi elles servaient dans l'économie même du discours. Pourquoi tel ou tel type d'information quantifiée était retenu ou passé sous silence? La sélection même des données chiffrées par l'orateur est en soi significative. L'orateur cherchait l'effet de persuasion. L'enquête menée ici voulait, elle, éviter la confusion entre la fiabilité des renseignements chiffrés et la représentativité des cas qu'ils illustrent.

Le sujet étudié dans le *de Frumento* vaut d'être étendu à l'ensemble des *Verrines*. Bien des questions en suspens touchent aux conditions de l'enquête menée par Cicéron en Sicile et à la nature des sources qu'il a collectées. Qui plus est, le lecteur moderne est vite confronté à une difficulté générale, celle de la constitution de la preuve dans les procès de concussion. Enfin, bien sûr, l'historien peine à retracer comment ces éléments concrets, recueillis pour confondre Verrès, étaient produits devant le tribunal, soumis à sa vérification et conservés. Nous sollicitons le texte au delà de ce qu'il peut donner: nos interrogations ne correspondent pas à ce que le défenseur voulait exposer à ses contemporains et nous demandons au document bien davantage de renseignements que ceux que Cicéron entendait laisser à la postérité. Mais c'est bien le discours, en tant qu'oeuvre complète, qui peut donner des clés de compréhension, non les extraits voire les bribes que nous isolons dans des reconstructions fragiles. C'est dans une approche de la globalité du texte que nous pouvons espérer rendre compte de ses difficultés et même de ses contradictions. Le *de Frumento* n'est assurément ni un manuel de droit fiscal, ni un recueil de données touchant à l'économie. Trop souvent sans doute, dans le souci de mieux comprendre ce qui résiste à l'interprétation des modernes, nous oublions cette évidence. La subjectivité de la plaidoirie et ses imperfections, ses ellipses et ses contradictions n'offrent pas moins d'intérêt que les *Realien* qu'elle peut aussi, parfois, retracer.

Université de Reims / CNRS - UMR 8585 Centre Gustave Glotz

REGISTERS, ACCOUNT-BOOKS, AND WRITTEN DOCUMENTS IN THE *DE FRUMENTO*

JEAN ANDREAU

In the *Verrines*, and particularly in the *de Frumento*, we often see references to written documents. Cicero himself writes in the first action: 'Now let us accuse the man with account-books, with witnesses, with public and private documents.'[1] And, in the *de Praetura Urbana*, he speaks of the abundance of documents and witnesses.[2] Some of these documents were prepared specifically for the trial; recently, they have been studied by Philippe Moreau.[3] Others existed before the accusation and the trial. Cicero bases arguments on them, but they were not generated with the trial in mind. My paper is about this second category of documents. In the first part, I am going to deal with the quantity of the documents and of the copies that were normally made of them. After that, I will consider the way in which Cicero refers to them and presents them. The third part will be devoted to falsification of documents.

I

During the 1990s, Claude Nicolet greatly emphasized the profusion of public and private written documents and archives at the end of the Republican period and under the Empire. Of course, apart from a very few fragments, these documents have been lost. Nicolet organized a project on that topic, 'La Mémoire perdue'; the intention was to collect all the traces of such documents that have survived in ancient evidence. Two books and a set of papers were published as a result of this project.[4] In one paper, Nicolet sharply criticized a famous sentence written by A. H. M. Jones and quoted by Moses Finley: according to Jones, there were no statistics in Antiquity.[5] To tell the truth, the two opinions are not actually contradictory, and I think Jones and Nicolet are both right on this matter. The existence of numerous written documents, kept in archives, does not necessarily imply that they were made public. Neither does it necessarily imply that the information they provided gave rise to any

1 Cic. *Ver.* 33.

2 Cic. *Ver.* 1.16.

3 Moreau (2000); this paper is connected with the research 'La Mémoire perdue', directed by Cl. Nicolet, and then by Cl. Moatti.

4 Demougin (1994); Nicolet and Moatti (1998); *MEFR(A)* (2000) 112: 647-779.

5 Nicolet (2000b) 248 n. 6.

statistical analysis. As for the publication of information, I have recently argued that it was very limited, even nearly nonexistent.[6]

But, none the less, I think we are justified in using the word 'archive', and Rudolph Haensch, for instance, expresses the same conclusion in his long paper about the 'Statthalterarchiv'.[7] What is at issue is the intentional preservation of administrative and fiscal documents, in order potentially to employ them in the administration of the province. The members of the city councils and the magistrates were responsible for this preservation, but several texts show that, in practice, decisions could be taken by *apparitores* and even by public slaves. What Plutarch writes on Cato the Younger's quaestorship shows that, in Rome, at the end of the Republic, the scribes of the quaestors used to play a more major role than the magistrates themselves (who were very young).[8] And, in the first century AD, in the province of Lycia and Pamphylia, a public slave, Tryphon, was punished by the governor, Q. Veranius, because he had agreed to insert documents with erasures and additions into the archives of Myra.[9] In the last part of the paper I shall again allude to this episode.

In Sicily, we do not have any original document which had been kept in public archives. But several copies of official documents, on stone or metal, have been found. For instance, there are cadastral inscriptions from Halaesa and Acrae, and the accounts from Tauromenium, which date back to the first century BC.[10] One must refer also to the Entella and Nakone tablets, bronze plates on which several decrees of Entella and one of Nakone are copied.[11]

As regards the quantity of documents, the Sicilian situation, as the *Verrines* and especially the *de Frumento* depict it, surpasses our expectations. The collection of the tithe involved making out and keeping a surprising quantity of public documents, as Cicero himself wrote;[12] and several copies were made of many of them. For instance, in the archives of the Sicilian cities there were the lists (*subscriptiones*) of the landowners and farmers (*aratores*) who produced grain, and the farmers' statements (*professiones*) regarding the surface areas and sowing. For each city, the praetor every year used to auction the right to collect the tithe to a tax-collector, the *decumanus*.[13] The schedule of conditions concerning this *uenditio,* the *lex uendundis decumis*, existed necessarily in three copies: one was kept in the city archives, one in the archives of the praetor's offices, and one by the purchaser of the tithe. This purchaser (*decumanus*) used to conclude an agreement with every landowner or farmer, the *pactio*. The

6 Andreau and Virlouvet (2002) 1-18.

7 Haensch (1992).

8 Plut. *Cat. Min.* 16-17.

9 See Wörrle (1975) (=*SEG* 33 (1983) 1177) and Meyer (2004) 186-87.

10 Halaesa: *IG* XIV 352 (*IGSI* no. 2) with Di Giovanni, *Archivio Storico Siciliano* 10 (1885) 123-29 and *SEG* 31 (1981) 825; Acrae: *IG* XIV 217 (*IGSI* no. 3); Tauromenium: Manganaro (1988) (=*SEG* 38 (1988) 973).

11 *SEG* 30 (1980) 1117-23; 32 (1982) 914; 35 (1985) 999; and Ampolo *et al.* (2001).

12 Cic. *Ver.* 3.112: 'ratio decumanorum [...] sine plurimis litteris confici non potest' ('the business of tithe-collection [...] cannot be managed without very full accounts').

13 Nicolet (2000a).

pactio was made in triplicate and signed by both parties. One copy remained with the *decumanus*, another with the farmer, and the third was lodged with the city officials.[14]

The praetor's office had to keep every *lex uendundis decumis*, and it kept them for many years. Either in the archives of the province, or in those of the city of Leontini, Cicero found the *lex uendundis decumis* of the praetor Gaius Norbanus for Leontini. We know that Gaius Norbanus had been the governor of Sicily during the Social War. He had stayed there for at least two years, very probably in 90 and 89 BC, and perhaps even longer. But, at the latest, he had gone back to Rome in 85 BC, for in 84 he was a candidate to the consular elections for 83, and was elected.[15] Moreover, the bid for collecting the tithe took place every year, and every year all the documents I have just mentioned had to be renewed. Besides the *lex uendundis decumis* of the city and the *pactiones*, I suspect the tax-collectors had to keep copies of the *subscriptiones* and *professiones*.

One may imagine the impressive quantity of documents that were kept by the various actors involved in tithe-collection. As regards Leontini, Mutyce, Herbita, and Agyrium, Cicero provides the number of farmers who were growing grain during the first year of Verres' praetorship, in 73 BC, and the number of those who were still producing grain in 71 BC. In 73 BC, he says there were 84 farmers in Leontini, 187 in Mutyce, 252 in Herbita, and 250 in Agyrium.[16] Of course, such figures have to be considered with a critical eye, because Cicero tries to show that Verres has completely ruined Sicilian agriculture. On the other hand, it is nearly impossible, from information concerning four cities, to obtain a general view of all the cities which had to pay the grain-tithe. But, all the same, such figures give us a rough idea of the numbers. So, every year, probably somewhere between ten and twenty thousand documents (some of them rather short, others longer) were needed, and that simply to run the grain-tithe, without taking copies into account.

What Cicero writes about the correspondence of the *societates publicorum* is very interesting for a number of reasons.[17] As Haensch has remarked, Cicero's text implies that this correspondence was considered to belong to the whole *societas*. The decision to throw away or to hide a part of the letters could only be taken by the company collectively, and not by one of its *magistri*. Each of the *magistri* and *promagistri* could only keep the letters and pass them on to his successor.[18] Even the letters each of them had written as a *magister* were not his personal property. However, several copies of such letters were made.

The letter that the *magister* Publius Vettius Chilo had written to Carpinatius was among Carpinatius's papers, but a copy of it had theoretically to be kept in the head office of the *societas publicorum*, in Rome. And, if we believe Cicero, when the *magistri* were no longer in office and had to pass the archives on to their successors, they used to keep a copy of their correspondence. It seems that they could often keep it in a lighter, less bulky form (papyrus

14 Rickman (1980) 38.

15 Cic. *Ver.* 3.117; on Norbanus, see also *Ver.* 5.8; Badian (1964) 84-86; Manganaro (1989) 178-81; *MRR* III 149.

16 Cic. *Ver.* 3.120.

17 On the role of correspondence in the *Verrines*, see Butler (2002) 45-48.

18 Haensch (1992) 245-46.

instead of wax-tablets), but that does not affect the quantity of written texts in the slightest. In the correspondence of a man who had been *magister* of that company, Cicero found a copy of Vettius Chilo's letter. Let us remember that, in relation to this company, which dealt with customs (*portorium*) and with the cattle tax (*scriptura*), Cicero provides the names of at least five previous *magistri* (Gaius Antistius, Publius Servilius, Lucius Tullius, Publius Vettius Chilo, and Lucius Vibius) who had been in office betwen 73 and 71 BC.[19] On top of that, Cicero makes an allusion to a *magister* who had helped Verres, but he does not mention his name.[20] That particular *magister* had managed to ensure that letters which could harm Verres had been removed. Either the anonymous *magister* is one of the five already detailed, or he is a sixth, who was in office during the same years.

The taxes on wine, on oil, on vegetables, on cattle, customs dues, and so on, also required many documents to be written out, and Cicero does not mention these documents at all. Neither does he go into details about the many documents established for the collection of *frumentum imperatum*, the requisitioned grain, nor for the *in cellam* grain. In addition to all these, we have to add the copies Cicero himself managed to make in the course of his investigation, for instance the copies of the registers of the *societas publicorum*. He speaks of these copies in the famous passage of which the point at issue is the identity of Gaius Verrucius.[21] It is, of course, impossible to guess the total number of pages of registers that were kept and copied, and frequently copied several times.

II

In this paper, my purpose is not to study all the written documents that Cicero mentions in the *Verrines* – I limit myself to the *de Frumento*. Moreover, Shane Butler, believing that scholars have usually tended to underestimate the importance of the written texts referred to in the *Verrines*, has recently provided a very useful catalogue.[22]

When one thinks of the way in which Cicero presents these different documents and makes comments on their contents, at least two observations may surprise us. The first is that, regarding the archives of the Sicilian cities, Cicero remains as general and as imprecise as possible. Each time, he mentions the *litterae publicae* of the Sicilian cities without saying anything about their structure, or the way they were kept in archives, or the places where they were kept. He explains only which documents were required to collect the tithe and has some of them read out from the *litterae publicae* of the cities, but without saying anything more about these *litterae*. It is the same for the *rationes*, the public account-books which were kept both by Roman magistrates and by the cities.[23]

According to Butler, *litterae publicae* should be a Latin translation of the Greek expression τὰ δημόσια γράμματα, which was already used in Athens in Demosthenes' time, whereas the

19 Cic. *Ver.* 3.166-69.

20 Cic. *Ver.* 2.173.

21 Cic. *Ver.* 2.186-91.

22 Butler (2002) 35-60.

23 Cic. *Ver.* 3.171, 175, 177, and 181.

Romans used to prefer *tabulae publicae*.[24] I am not convinced by such an observation, but, that notwithstanding, it is certain that Cicero does not provide a lot of information on these documents.

It is probably not very difficult to explain his silence. On the one hand, in this speech, Cicero has to speak of a number of institutional details that concern fiscality, and he has to quote many figures. So, he has to make a very strict selection of topics and to eliminate whatever is not useful. On the other hand, there were sixty-five cities in Sicily, and fifty-seven among them had to pay the tithe. Probably, the names of the public documents and the way they were managed differed somewhat from city to city and he could not easily describe such a variety. Cicero never gives the titles of the Sicilian magistrates, as Carcopino noticed;[25] in the same way, he does not provide any detail on the manner in which the cities prepared and maintained their public documents.

No less surprising are the very few details which Cicero provides on the function and content of several official Roman documents, which by no means all his readers could have known very well (far from it!). For instance, the register that the praetor used to prepare, in the context of his judicial activity, and which Cicero calls *tabulae* or *codex*. In such a register, Verres, according to Cicero, had falsely stated that Sthenius of Thermae was condemned in his own presence.[26] Cicero also calls the document in which the praetor had to register his edicts *codex* or *tabulae*.[27] The context shows us that he is making a point about registers of this kind, but he does not allow us to understand the relationship between such categories of books.

In the *de Frumento*, and in the *Verrines* in general, the vocabulary of registers and documents is so fuzzy that, sometimes, it is not easy to understand which document is concerned, and whether it is private or public. In the trial of Sthenius of Thermae, we find such an example with Gaius Claudius's tablets. This Gaius Claudius, whom we do not know further, is described as very close to Verres, a docile auxiliary of Verres' operations. Cicero shows him holding tablets, writing, in the service of Verres: 'illum qui tabulas tenet, qui scribit [...]'.[28] But the nature of the tablets is not stated. In the case of Heraclius's inheritance it is not stated either. In that context, Cicero writes that the *tabulae* will allow him to prove that the 300,000 *sesterces* which had to be paid to the Syracusans had finally fallen into Verres' hands.[29]

According to Elizabeth Meyer, when Servius Tullius created the *census*, but much later as well, and even in Cicero's time, state and household, public and private, were not considered as distinct. As an argument, she uses two texts written by Florus and Dionysius,[30] and the fact

24 Butler (2002) 36-37.

25 Carcopino (1919) 27-33; on the titles of Sicilian magistrates, see Cordano (1999).

26 Cic. *Ver.* 2.101-07; 3.41.

27 For example, Cic. *Ver.* 3.25-26.

28 Cic. *Ver.* 2.108.

29 Cic. *Ver.* 2.50.

30 Flor. *Epit.* 1.6.3 and Dion. Hal. *Ant. Rom.* 20.13.2-3.

that *publicae tabulae* were sometimes stored in the censors' homes.[31] As regards the account-books which are mentioned in the *Verrines*, Meyer says that this confusion between public and private is frequently visible: the words by which private and public documents are referred to are the same (for instance, *tabulae*), and they provide the same kinds of information. '[Cicero] does not draw meaningful or substantive distinctions between *publicae* and *privatae tabulae*. [...] The spheres of private and public are intermingled.'[32] I think many different things are mixed and intermingled, but in such a conclusion and not in Cicero's text. The fact that both categories of documents were called *tabulae* does not mean that they were confused; if some public documents were kept in private houses, it does not necessarily mean that either. And it is not at all certain that the same information could be found both in private and public *tabulae*. Contrary to Meyer, I am convinced that the Romans (and especially Cicero) established a very clear-cut distinction between the public field and the private one. For instance, what I have written above (part I) on the publicans' letters, shows that they very clearly divided the personal documents of the *magistri* from the letters written on behalf of the society; these latter letters, for that reason, belonged to the society.[33]

Through other evidence, for instance through Cato the Elder, we know that private persons used to keep various inventories and account-books, for example in the management of their rural estates, and that such inventories and account-books did not constitute a unity. But, at that period among the Romans, the main document, as regards the management of private patrimonies, was the *codex accepti et expensi*, which was also called *tabulae accepti et expensi*. This was certainly a cash-book, in which every item of income and expenditure was registered, but it was not only a cash-book, for some of the items that were written in it constituted the *litteris* contract.[34] There are many discussions on its nature and on the way it worked. This is not the occasion to discuss it, because the *de Frumento* does not provide any precise information on it. One may find more evidence about it in the *pro Roscio comoedo*.

When Cicero refers to such a register, he uses the two expressions, both *codex accepti et expensi* and *tabulae accepti et expensi*, and he writes *codex* or *tabulae* too. Neither the *Verrines* nor Cicero's works in general are the only texts where one may observe such an imprecision in the vocabulary of registers. But, sometimes, he uses this imprecision in the frame of his case. For instance, he pretends to be surprised that Apronius declares that he does not keep any *codex accepti et expensi*. And he refers to the quantity of documents that must be made out for the tithe-collection, and especially to *subscriptiones* and *professiones*. By mixing up two kinds of documents, he tries to suggest that it was outrageous for Apronius not to keep a *codex*, whereas actually it was probably not.

All the documents that are referred to as *tabulae* were written on wooden tablets, and all the documents called *codices* had the structure of a book or of a register. But the expressions *codex accepti et expensi* and *tabulae accepti et expensi* were only used to qualify the cash-

31 See Rawson (1985) 238-39.

32 Meyer (2004) 29-30.

33 See Haensch (1992) 245-46.

34 On the *litteris* contract, see Watson (1965) 18-39; Thilo (1980) 276-318.

book of Roman *patres familias*, the cash-book through which, moreover, the *litteris* contract was constituted.

If the *codex accepti et expensi* and the *tabulae accepti et expensi* are part of all *codices* and *tabulae*, the contrary is not true. There are *codices* and *tabulae* that do not belong to that traditional category of Roman cash-books. On such issues, Ralf Thilo, who has studied the *codex accepti et expensi* very accurately and makes many judicious remarks in his book, is not always sufficiently clear-cut and rigorous.[35]

The *Verrines* help to bring to the fore three conclusions that concern the *codex accepti et expensi*. The first one regards the private documents of Sicilian notables. When he speaks of them, Cicero refers to their *tabulae*. For instance, it is in the registers of rich grain-growers that the price of wheat in Sicily during the years of Verres' administration was mentioned.[36] What were those *tabulae*? They are private account-books, which, just like the Roman *codex accepti et expensi*, played a central role in the management of their ownings. But they were not the Roman *codex accepti et expensi*, for that register, however we may imagine it, was very specific. On the Sicilians' account-books, Cicero does not provide any detail. He implicitly refers to them as to non-Roman equivalents of the *codex accepti et expensi*, but he does not say that they were exactly similar to the Roman *codex*. For that reason, he only uses the word *codex*. If he does not say anything more, one may explain that in the same way as his silence on Sicilian magistrates or on Sicilian *litterae publicae*: he refuses to go into useless detail and to indulge in a kind of ethnographic description of the Sicilian way of life.

The second issue, which Thilo explains and treats very well, regards public documents.[37] The words *codex* and *tabulae* are used, without any specification, to refer to public documents, because they are composed of big, rigid wooden tablets and they are linked up in a register; but this does not mean at all that they are *tabulae accepti et expensi*. When we find expressions like *acceptum ferre* or *referre*, *expensum ferre* or *referre*, these are not sufficient to identify a *codex accepti et expensi*. Such expressions may be employed for any account-book. If I am not mistaken, a public document is never referred to as a *codex accepti et expensi*, neither in Rome, nor in any city of the Roman Empire. The public documents must not be assimilated to this traditional and patrimonial private cash-book.

On the contrary, a passage of the *de Praetura Siciliensi* proves, in my view, that the *societates publicorum*, the publicans' companies, used to keep *tabulae accepti et expensi*. It is the famous passage in which Cicero speaks of Carpinatius's business with the so-called Verrucius.[38] Admittedly, in that passage, there are no specific details that would help us to identify a *codex accepti et expensi*, but the way in which the register is referred to is meaningful, in my view. The *sociorum tabulae accepti et expensi* are the same account-book as the *societatis tabulae* that are referred to a little further on. So, at that date, the publicans' companies were keeping this patrimonial cash-book, just like many rich, private *patres familias*.

35 Thilo (1980).

36 Cic. *Ver.* 3.173 and 189.

37 Thilo (1980) 170-81.

38 Cic. *Ver.* 2.186-91; see Thilo (1980) 217-21.

Why did the Romans not have a richer and more precise vocabulary at their disposal, to denote the various private and public documents? I must confess that I have no answer to such a question.

III

In Cicero's speeches, and especially in the *Verrines*, the issue often concerns the falsification of documents. As Cicero considers Verres to be the champion of falsification and has bothered accurately to assemble and analyse the evidence necessary to reveal his frauds, the *Verrines* provide us with a very good sample of every kind of adulteration of documents.[39] But Cicero's works are not the only texts that testify how much importance the Romans attached to conserving public and private documents. In Egypt, for instance, when M. Mettius Rufus was prefect of the province, from AD 89 onwards, an action was brought against those who were in charge of the Public Record Office in the Arsinoite, because many documents had been partly or completely destroyed.[40] These included official correspondence, tax rolls, land registers, and census lists. I have already alluded to the punishment that the governor of the province of Lycia and Pamphylia, Q. Veranius, meted out to a public slave, Tryphon, who had inserted documents with erasures and additions into the archives of Myra (first century AD).[41] Such examples show both how much value was attached to written documents, particularly in trials, and how fragile they were.[42]

One of the means to cheat consisted in not keeping registers, in having no *codex accepti et expensi*, or at least in pretending not to keep one; if there are no registers, there is no possible control. This tactic was of course easy to carry out, all the more so since it was not legally compulsory to keep a *codex accepti et expensi*. Cicero writes that not to keep one was *minime probandum*, which proves that, even for a high-ranking man, the absence of a *codex* was entirely possible.[43] So, Verres declares he keeps no *codex accepti et expensi*. But at the same time, if we believe Cicero, Verres strangely says that he had kept one until 73 BC and that he had stopped at that date, that is at the beginning of his *praetura* in Sicily. Of course, Cicero argues from that that he is lying.[44] Apronius too claimed not to keep a *codex*.[45] As I have said above, it is not clear whether Apronius was lying and if he used to keep a *codex*. But, Apronius had to keep the specific documents of tithe-collection. If he had claimed not to keep such documents either, he would surely have been lying.

Another manner in which to cheat was not to enter every operation in the *codex accepti et expensi*.[46] Verres does that in the case of the statues and paintings he had brought back from

39 Butler (2002) 90.

40 On this example and on the organization of archives in Roman Egypt, Burkhalter (1990).

41 See above, n. 9.

42 Fezzi (2003) and Moreau (1994).

43 Cic. *Ver.* 1.60; see de Ste Croix (1956) 44.

44 Cic. *Ver.* 4.36 and 43.

45 Cic. *Ver.* 3.112.

46 Cic. *Ver.* 1.60-61.

Asia and Greece. Neither his *codex accepti et expensi*, nor his father's mentions them, according to Cicero. If subsequently, one had, at all costs, to write down the forgotten operations, then the item, the *nomen*, was not written at its normal chronological place. It was an example of *extraordinaria pecunia* and that transaction, that transfer of money, was suspected to be illegal. But, whatever the etymological sense of *extraordinarius* was, I am convinced, like Pierre Jouanique,[47] that in Cicero's time the *pecuniae extraordinariae* were not only those that were not registered in their normal chronological order. The *Verrines* provide us with a strong argument in favour of such a conclusion. The expression is used by Cicero in reference to transactions that, precisely, were not written down in Verres' *codex*, although they dated back to before 73 BC: transactions between Quintus and Gnaeus Curtius Postumus and himself.[48] In my view, the *pecuniae extraordinariae* were payments that did not conform to the regulations, that did not contain all the necessary information, for instance the name of the person and the reason for the operation.

If one cheated by modifying the content of the document, five different ways are mentioned in ancient texts. The first was to add something inside the document or at the end of it (*adiectio*, *interpolatio*, *adicere*, *interpolare*).[49] The second was to strike a few words through (in Latin, in some texts, *inductio, inducere*). The third way consisted in writing new words on top of the previous ones, without erasing them (*superductio*, for example in Ulpian's texts).[50] The fourth consisted in erasing a few words or sentences, which produced an empty space. Finally, the empty space could be filled up with new words, which replaced the original ones. Most of the time, all these processes left a trace, a visible alteration (*litura*). The most discreet was the first one, especially if the new writing had been added at the end of the document; however, in such a case one could detect the fraud from the logical order of the text. As regards wax-tablets, *litura* meant that the wax had been smeared and rubbed, in order to erase something previously written.

The *Verrines*, and particularly the *de Frumento*, provide us with examples of nearly all these kinds of frauds, and particularly of items that were added afterwards,[51] and of items that were deleted and then replaced by others, both in public documents[52] and in *codices accepti et expensi*. Verres is shown by Cicero to be a man who cannot help falsifying every document, 'semper aliquid demendo, mutando, interpolando'.[53] The best example, and the most famous one, is the correction of the name of Verres, which, in the publicans' account-books, has been transformed to Verrucius.[54] This same passage gives us very concrete information about the way to get a certified copy of a document that is going to be used in a trial. Another very fine

47 Jouanique (1968) 8, 18, 29-30.

48 Cic. *Ver.* 1.100.

49 Bülow-Jacobsen, Cuvigny, and Worp (2000).

50 *Dig.* 28.4.1 (Ulpian).

51 Cic. *Ver.* 1.92.

52 For example, Cic. *Ver.* 1.149 and 2.101-07.

53 Cic. *Ver.* 1.158 ('always scratching out, or altering, or interpolating something').

54 Cic. *Ver.* 2.186-91.

example may be found in the *pro Cluentio*: according to Cicero, Oppianicus was induced to write a whole *testamentum* again, in order to hide the traces that his erasures had left.[55]

As Dario Mantovani has noticed,[56] the integrity of a register is an important indicator of its credibility. Every erasure casts doubts on the value of the register and on the honesty of its owner. For that reason, Cicero emphasizes the erasures, the *liturae* that one may see, according to him, in Verres' documents. He insists upon it even when the existence of *liturae* does not seem to be of great importance. For instance, in the case of Malleolus's will, Cicero makes it explicit that Verres had added an item with an erasure at the extreme end of the *codex*.[57] The erasure, in that case, is of very little importance, for this item is not the result of the deletion of a previous one that Verres would have liked to correct or to suppress. Cicero only aims at showing that Verres' registers were very badly kept, and so betrayed dishonest behaviour. Just like the order of items, the erasures are a symptom. If an item is not in the regular chronological order, it does not prove that the owner of the register has done something dishonest. But, just like the presence of erasures, it is a symptom which has to be stressed in a speech.

In a passage of the *de Frumento*, Cicero contrasts Verres' behaviour with the way in which the Sicilian cities used to keep their documents, that is very precisely and accurately.[58] Even the public documents of the Syracusans are very fairly kept, Cicero says (although their city had not taken part in the delegation that asked him to sue Verres); and in their *litterae publicae*, he has found clues against Verres.[59] In his praise of the *rationes* of all the Sicilian cities (*Ver.* 3.175), that is their financial registers, their account-books, Cicero says that everything he mentions has been recorded 'in order' (*ordine relata atque confecta sunt*) in the account-books of the cities, for they are neither *interpositae*, nor *perturbatae*, nor *repentinae*. On the contrary, they are *certae* and *institutae*. The precise meaning of some of these words is not completely certain and, generally, the translators and commentators do not explain them adequately. *Ordo* may apply either to the listing of items in the *rationes* or, more generally, to an established means of organizing the accounts. Butler chooses this second interpretation. It cannot be excluded. Nevertheless, I would rather think that to keep documents according to an established and institutional means is expressed by *institutae* ('organized'), and that *ordo* is here applied to the listing of the items. As regards *certae*, I think one must translate it by 'precise', as Butler does.[60] The three adjectives at the beginning, *interpositae, perturbatae,* and *repentinae*, denote what the cities took care not to do. All three of them refer to the listing of the items in the account-book: *interpositae* means items that are added subsequently between previous items (Butler's translation is 'interpolated'); *repentinae* means unexpected items, which have been written down in a place where one would not

55 Cic. *Clu.* 41.

56 Mantovani (2000) 686-90.

57 Cic. *Ver.* 1.92.

58 Cic. *Ver.* 3.175.

59 Cic. *Ver.* 4.140-44; see Butler (2002) 29-32.

60 Butler (2002) 68.

expect them; and *perturbatae* expresses a disorder, a confusion in the way in which the items are presented.

IV

As Mantovani has noted,[61] it is not easy to produce a unified conclusion to such a topic, which lends itself more to fragmentary observations concerning details. I would like, however, to end my paper with two more general remarks. These two remarks seem to be in conflict, but I think both of them are characteristic of what one sees in the *Verrines*.

On the one hand, the importance of written documents is fundamental. Their very quantity signifies the role they played in the institutional and juridical life of the Romans, even if only one contract, the *litteris* contract, was constituted, as such, by a written text. But on the other hand, in Roman eyes, oral testimonies and written documents have both much value and some limitations. We cannot say that written documents were systematically highlighted, or that oral testimonies were systematically depreciated. And we cannot say the opposite either. In Meyer's recent book there is an excellent passage in which she shows that, for second- and third-century jurisconsults, oral and written were complementary and each of them could stand in for the other.[62] According to Paul's fragment in the *Digest*, it seems that a stipulation written by the respondent allows the legal presumption that the questioner had spoken, even if he had not.[63] And, according to a text that dates back to Antoninus's reign, 'if a *promissio* of interest given *interrogatione praecedente* is proved to have been given, although not written in *instrumenta*, by the best law monies are owed'.[64] Meyer's comment is very good:

> Ulpian and Paulus were not implying that stipulation was written *rather than* oral or oral *rather than* written. [... They] are instead tackling a difficult problem by implicitly reminding their audience that *verba* could be both written and spoken, and clearly stating that one could compensate for defects in, or absence of, the other.[65]

Moreover, the transfer from oral to written text, or from one written text to another, never seems to be trivial; it is never taken for granted. The tranfers from oral to written are always reported and analysed. In connection with this, it is meaningful to observe how the compounds of *scribere* are used. In the words *inscribere, exscribere*, *perscribere*, and so on, the root word *scribere*, which expresses the fact of writing, and the prefix, which specifies the conditions of the action, are both full of meaning. In every case the context leads us to understand that they are pregnant with meaning. They refer to situations in which written documents and oral procedures used to play an important role, and in which the connection between oral and written required precautions to be taken. Orality was probably more familiar than writing. But, for documents that were long and complex, such as official documents,

61 Mantovani (2000) 690.

62 Meyer (2004) 254-61.

63 *Dig.* 45.1.134.2.

64 *Cod. Iust.* 4.32.1.

65 Meyer (2004) 260.

writing was essential. The written documents had to be kept and it was necessary to take care of them. So the various means of falsifying written documents deserve to be reviewed, as does the means of getting a good and credible copy of a document. It is easy to understand why Cicero goes into so much detail regarding such topics.

École des Hautes Études en Science Sociales, Paris / CNRS – UMR 8585 Centre G. Glotz

LA JURIDICTION DU GOUVERNEUR PROVINCIAL. RÉFLEXIONS SUR LES *VERRINES* COMME SOURCES POUR L'HISTOIRE DU DROIT

JULIEN DUBOULOZ

Le deuxième et le troisième plaidoyer de la seconde action des *Verrines*, le *de Praetura Siciliensi* et le *de Frumento*, constituent un document d'un très grand intérêt sur la juridiction des gouverneurs provinciaux, à la fin de la période républicaine. Toutefois, l'historien et particulièrement l'historien du droit, se heurte, devant ce témoignage, à deux difficultés: la première est sa nature même de discours d'accusation; la seconde est ce que nous pourrions appeler son caractère clos, dans le sens où nous ne disposons guère de sources suffisamment proches, du point de vue géographique, chronologique et thématique, pour pouvoir les mettre en balance avec les données issues des *Verrines*.

Une telle difficulté est particulièrement sensible quand il s'agit d'envisager comment Verrès administre la justice lors de sa propréture de Sicile, entre 73 et 71 av. J.-C. Cicéron dénonce, en effet, la manière dont le gouverneur abuse de ses pouvoirs judiciaires, pour assurer ses intérêts et ceux de ses complices, à commencer par les fermiers de l'impôt. Verrès aurait, en particulier, dans les contentieux entre contribuables et décimateurs, imposé comme juges des membres de sa suite, sa cohorte, au mépris des règles de la procédure, des normes établies en Sicile par ses prédécesseurs et de la simple équité. Non pas qu'on puisse *a priori* reprocher à Verrès de désigner, comme arbitres des contentieux fiscaux, des citoyens romains sans attache dans la province plutôt que des Romains ayant leurs intérêts en Sicile, mais Cicéron insiste assez sur la basse extraction et la corruption de la suite du préteur, dépourvue de toute impartialité.[1]

Cicéron aborde là un point de procédure qui n'est pas sans implications dans la vie de la cité. En effet, à la fin de la période républicaine, la position censitaire et sociale des juges et le mode de constitution des jurys, dans les provinces aussi bien qu'à Rome, dans la juridiction civile aussi bien que criminelle, constituent un enjeu politique essentiel. Cicéron en témoigne lui-même, dans les *Verrines*, lorsqu'il souligne la position très avantageuse des juges dans la province,[2] mais aussi lorsqu'il met en perspective le procès de Verrès avec le projet de

1 Sur la cohorte de Verrès, *inter alia*, Cic. *Ver.* 3.28-35, 3.54, 3.70, 3.158.

2 Cic. *Ver.* 2.30: 'Dubium nemini est quin omnes omnium pecuniae positae sint in eorum potestate qui iudicia dant, et eorum qui iudicant, quin nemo uestrum possit aedes suas, nemo fundum, nemo bona patria obtinere, si cum haec a quopiam uestrum petita sint, praetor improbus, cui nemo intercedere possit, det quem uelit iudicem, iudex nequam et leuis quod praetor iusserit iudicet.' ('Personne n'ignore que la fortune toute entière de tout un chacun se trouve entre les mains des hommes qui accordent les procès et de ceux qui participent aux jurys, si bien que personne parmi vous ne pourra obtenir sa

réforme des tribunaux pour la *quaestio de repetundis*, dans le contexte du vote de la *lex Aurelia*, en 70 av. J.-C.[3]

La conduite de Verrès dans l'administration de la justice et plus spécifiquement, le fait qu'il ait pu imposer un nouvel organe judiciaire ont été parfois invoqués comme un témoignage des pouvoirs discrétionnaires dont jouit statutairement un gouverneur de province, autour du milieu du Ier siècle av. J.-C. De sorte que la procédure dite formulaire, en vigueur à la fin de la période républicaine, aurait été, dans les provinces, intrinsèquement modifiée pour laisser place à une majeure ingérence du magistrat instructeur. En effet, la procédure formulaire se caractérise, à Rome, notamment par le fait que son déroulement requiert l'accord des parties. Cet accord porte d'abord sur la formule de l'action. Si les prétentions du demandeur doivent prendre place dans le cadre prédéfini des recours juridiques admis, c'est-à-dire des actions dont le magistrat publie la liste à son entrée en charge, les deux parties sont, en théorie, libres de contester la pertinence de l'action donnée par le magistrat. Mais ce consensus des parties, intervenant dans un moment particulier du procès, celui de la *litis contestatio*, porte aussi sur la désignation du ou des juges. Cette étape essentielle constitue le point de passage de la phase *in iure*, phase d'instruction dirigée par le magistrat romain, à la phase *in iudicio*, au moment où le magistrat, par un *iussum iudicandi*, délègue ses pouvoirs judiciaires à un particulier.[4]

Giovanni Pugliese, dont les travaux sur la procédure font autorité, tout en regardant les procès civils provinciaux et en particulier les procès fiscaux évoqués dans les *Verrines*, comme des *iudicia priuata* de type formulaire, considère que les pouvoirs discrétionnaires du gouverneur pouvaient aller jusqu'à nommer des juges contre la volonté des parties, sans pour autant que la validité de la sentence fût attaquable. Se manifeste alors une contradiction dans le discours de Pugliese, qui est symptomatique de la difficulté que rencontre tout romaniste à utiliser les *Verrines* comme source de droit romain. En effet, le juriste italien décrit la conduite de Verrès tantôt comme une illustration de l'arbitraire, voire de l'impunité des gouverneurs, tantôt comme une manifestation de l'étendue *de iure* de leur juridiction, signe avant-coureur de la prépondérance de la *cognitio extra ordinem* à l'époque impériale.[5] Sans doute, c'est mettre sur le même plan l'état de fait et le droit, mais cette contradiction participe légitimement d'une démarche de formalisation et de normalisation, qui conduit les romanistes à envisager en termes de règles ce qui relève avant tout d'une pratique. Par ailleurs, comme nous allons le voir, Cicéron joue lui-même sur cette ambiguïté, que nous chercherons ici à mettre en évidence, plus encore qu'à lever.

maison, un domaine ou les biens de son père si, alors qu'il les réclame devant n'importe lequel d'entre vous, un préteur sans honneur, contre qui personne ne peut opposer d'intercession, donne un juge selon son bon plaisir et si ce juge corrompu et manipulable rend le jugement que lui demandera le préteur.') Le texte original est donné d'après l'édition de A. Klotz, *M. Tulli Ciceronis scripta quae manserunt omnia* (Leipzig 1923); nous ne traduisons que les extraits les plus longs.

3 *Inter alia*, Cic. *Ver.* 3.223. Pour un examen de la situation d'énonciation créée par Cicéron dans les *Verrines*, dans le contexte de la réforme des jurys proposée par Aurelius Cotta pour les procès d'extorsion de fonds, Ferrary (1975).

4 Sur le déroulement du procès formulaire, Pugliese (1947-49) I 220-33.

5 Pugliese (1948) 402-03.

Notre objectif n'est en aucune façon de réhabiliter la conduite de Verrès comme magistrat instructeur[6] et, pour le dire simplement, nous ne nous soucions aucunement de la culpabilité effective de l'accusé. Il est de fait qu'aucune source extérieure aux *Verrines* n'atteste, à notre connaissance, pour la période républicaine, qu'un gouverneur ait jamais nommé des gens de sa cohorte comme juges, ni même qu'il les ait appelés régulièrement à participer à son *consilium* juridique.[7] On peut donc raisonnablement en croire Cicéron: Verrès agissait là, du point de vue de la norme, contre les *instituta* de ses prédécesseurs dans la province et du point de vue des faits, contre l'équité. En revanche, pour qui souhaite lire le *de Frumento* comme un témoignage sur le droit romain,[8] il convient, tout en reconnaissant qu'il entre dans les compétences du promagistrat de codifier et dire le droit dans sa *prouincia*, de mesurer jusqu'à quel point les actes juridiques de Verrès vont contre des règles de procédure positives, mais aussi contre l'évolution générale du droit dans les années 70 av. J.-C.

Nous nous intéresserons ici plus spécifiquement au mode de formation et de désignation, par le magistrat instructeur, des jurys amenés à arbitrer les contentieux relevant du droit fiscal.[9]

Pour interpréter la conduite de Verrès lors de la formation des jurys, à l'occasion de procès fiscaux, il convient alors d'envisager trois questions. Dans un premier temps, il s'agit d'établir si les contentieux sur la perception de l'impôt foncier relèvent de la procédure ordinaire ou d'une catégorie particulière de causes, une manière de 'procès administratif', qui répondrait, même à Rome, à une procédure accordant plus d'initiative au magistrat instructeur dans la désignation des juges. Dans un deuxième temps, il convient de s'assurer si Verrès a, dans la conduite de ces procès fiscaux et de manière générale dans le règlement des contentieux civils, réellement imposé des jurys contre la volonté des parties. Enfin, dans un dernier temps, il s'agit de déterminer si les innovations de Verrès en la matière, pour contraires qu'elles

6 Qu'il soit bien entendu que par 'magistrat', nous entendons évidemment le propréteur ayant reçu le gouvernement d'une *prouincia*. Ce n'est que parce que nous envisageons ici ses compétences juridiques, en particulier dans l'instruction des controverses qui viennent devant lui et dans la désignation des tribunaux compétents, que nous sommes amenés à employer le terme dans le sens français contemporain.

7 Mommsen (1892) I 363-64 opère une distinction entre trois groupes: la *familia* du gouverneur, les membres de sa cohorte, qui certes peuvent assumer des fonctions publiques, mais toujours au service du gouverneur et enfin, les membres du *consilium* du gouverneur. Ce dernier est composé d'anciens magistrats et promagistrats, mais Mommsen suggère aussi, en s'appuyant sur le procès de Sopater (Cic. *Ver.* 2.68-75), que les membres les plus éminents du *conuentus* de la province pouvaient y figurer quasiment de droit. Pour Mellano (1977) 178-79 n. 250, la désignation de récupérateurs dans la cohorte n'était en définitive pas passible de poursuites; de même Genovese (1999) 104-05 et 113-14 se montre enclin à admettre le choix de jurés, au civil et au pénal, dans la *cohors*, sans toutefois apporter aucun autre témoignage de cette pratique.

8 Tel est un des objectifs que s'est fixés le groupe de traduction et commentaire du *de Frumento*, réunissant J. Andreau, J.-L. Ferrary, J. France, S. Pittia, J. Prag, et nous-mêmes, dans le cadre d'un programme de l'UMR 8585 – Centre G. Glotz du CNRS. Nous remercions M. Crawford et A. Lintott pour leurs conseils dans cette recherche sur la juridiction du gouverneur, dont le lecteur voudra bien pardonner qu'elle en soit encore à son commencement.

9 Nous n'envisagerons pas, en revanche, les procès criminels, à propos desquels nous renvoyons à Maggio (1993).

soient à la coutume établie en Sicile et parfois même, dans les faits, à la simple équité, peuvent être regardées comme dérogeant à des règles juridiques positives et aux tendances contemporaines du droit.

I. Les procès fiscaux dans la sphère du droit civil

Quant à la nature même du procès fiscal, les romanistes, en particulier, comme nous l'avons dit Pugliese, considèrent majoritairement que ces causes entrent, durant la période républicaine, dans l'ordre des *iudicia priuata* et sont régies par la procédure formulaire. En cela, Pugliese concorde avec Theodor Mommsen, contre les thèses d'un autre spécialiste de la procédure romaine, Moriz Wlassak, qui jugeait quant à lui que, dans ces controverses où entrait en balance l'intérêt de l'Etat, le magistrat romain ne pouvait manquer de prendre en charge la concession de l'action et la désignation du jury, sans qu'il y eût de place pour l'autodétermination des parties en présence.[10]

Un premier moyen de définir la nature des procès fiscaux[11] est, sans sortir du cadre des *Verrines*, de comparer leur déroulement avec celui de procès de droit civil qui se sont tenus sous la préture sicilienne de Verrès, entre 73 et 71 av. J.-C. Nous prendrons, en particulier, dans la suite, pour exemples deux causes civiles: un procès relevant d'un litige sur une succession entre Heraclius, citoyen de Syracuse et un groupe de concitoyens agissant au nom de la cité et un défi judiciaire (*sponsio*) lancé par un chevalier romain contre un fermier de l'impôt, lui-même romain.[12]

Cicéron rapporte que Verrès avait, en matière de droit fiscal, repris, dans son édit, deux formes de recours juridiques préexistantes. La première instituait, au bénéfice du fermier de l'impôt, un jugement, impliquant compensation au quadruple, contre tout cultivateur qui aurait versé moins que la dîme qui lui était réclamée. L'autre, symétrique, donnait au contribuable qui s'estimait lésé par une imposition supérieure à un dixième, contre le fermier de l'impôt, un jugement impliquant compensation à l'octuple. Un troisième type de recours devant les tribunaux fut donné, probablement en cours de préture, aux fermiers de l'impôt: celui de poursuivre les cultivateurs pour avoir, dans leur déclaration, sous-estimé les surfaces ensemencées, faussant ainsi le calcul de la dîme, ou même pour avoir volontairement négligé de déclarer certaines cultures.[13]

10 Mommsen (1907) I 205-08; Wlassak (1919) 15, sur le rôle du magistrat provincial dans le procès formulaire et Wlassak (1921) 132-33 n. 42, à propos des procès fiscaux dans les *Verrines*; Pugliese (1948) 408-17.

11 L'exemple le plus complet, du point de vue de la désignation du jury est Cic. *Ver.* 3.28-31, mais il s'agit d'un procès imaginé par Cicéron.

12 Respectivement, Cic. *Ver.* 2.35-44 et 3.135-40.

13 Cic. *Ver.* 3.39 et 55. Carcopino (1919) 25 et 139-41 a montré de manière convaincante que ces deux recours juridiques préexistent certainement à l'édit de Verrès et relèvent de la *lex Hieronica*, qui constitue la procédure ordinaire en vigueur sous la domination romaine. Nous renvoyons au long commentaire de ces édits, assorti d'une revue exhaustive de la bibliographie, donné récemment par Genovese (1999). Toutes les interprétations proposées ne sont pas convaincantes au même degré, mais ce n'est pas le lieu ici de les discuter. En revanche, nous recevons sa démonstration (402-04) que le dernier recours juridique est donné dans le cours de la préture de Verrès.

Le lexique employé par Cicéron, dans le cadre des procès fiscaux conduits en Sicile sous la préture de Verrès, aussi bien que des procès civils, emprunte sans conteste à celui de la procédure formulaire. L'introduction de l'instance, dans tous les cas, prend la forme d'un *postulare iudicem aut recuperatores* ou d'un *postulare iudicium.*[14] L'action du préteur, de même, est désignée comme un *dare iudicem aut recuperatores* ou un *dare iudicium.* Ce sont là les termes traditionnels de l'introduction d'instance dans le procès formulaire.[15] Ainsi, dans l'action donnée au fermier de l'impôt romain Apronius contre le cultivateur pérégrin Xénon de Mènes (Menae), pour falsification de sa déclaration, l'expression *si pareret*, 's'il appert que',[16] est caractéristique de la partie de la formule appelée *intentio*, dans laquelle est énoncé le fondement du demandeur à réclamer la constitution d'un tribunal.[17] Cependant, l'argument lexical reste fragile. En effet, certains témoignages, papyrologiques en particulier, attestent que le vocabulaire de la procédure formulaire est encore utilisé, sous l'Empire, dans des procès de droit privé qui ne correspondent plus à un procès *per formulas*, parce que le magistrat romain instructeur est en même temps le juge, selon un type de procédure qui fint par s'imposer sous l'Empire, celui de la *cognitio extra ordinem.*[18]

Au-delà d'un lexique qui peut donc refléter des habitudes de langage, plutôt qu'une application rigoureuse de formules codifiées, il convient alors de rechercher, dans les sources, une preuve plus sûre que les procès fiscaux ne se distinguent pas, dans leur organisation, des

14 Cic. *Ver.* 2.38: 'Aduersarii postulant ut in eam rem iudices dentur'; 3.28: 'Quid tandem postulat arator? nihil nisi ex edicto iudicium in octuplum'; 3.135: 'coepit Scandilius recuperatores aut iudicem postulare'; 3.137: 'Scandilius postulare de conuentu recuperatores'.

15 Cic. *Ver.* 2.33: 'eum iudicem quem commodum erat [...] dabat'; 2.41: 'quinque iudicibus nulla lege, nullo instituto, nulla reiectione, nulla sorte ex libidine istius datis'; 3.35: 'SI VTER VOLET RECVPERATORES DABO'; 3.55: 'Verres in Xenonem iudicium dabat illud suum damnatorium de iugerum professione'; 3.135: 'Recuperatores dicis te daturum'; 3.139: 'negas de conuentu recuperatores daturum'. Un emploi juridique rigoureux du terme *formula* se trouve chez Cic. *Ver.* 3.152, à propos de la première *sponsio* demandée à Apronius: 'QVOD PER VIM ET METVM APSTVLISSET, quam formulam Octauianam et Romae Metellus habuerat et habebat in prouincia'. Carcopino (1919) 144-46 analyse l'ensemble de la procédure dans le contexte des *Verrines.* Pugliese (1948) 413 distingue les expressions *recuperatores/iudicem dare* et *iudicium dare.* La première se trouverait aussi dans des procès relevant de la *cognitio* du magistrat, par ex. dans l'*edictum Augusti ad Cyrenenses* 4.67-70 (*FIRA*^{2} I 409), pour les procès capitaux; la seconde serait réservée aux *iudicia priuata*, comme le montreraient la *lex de Gallia Cisalpina* II xxi 21-24 (*RS* I 466), l'*edictum Augusti de Aquaeductu Venafrano* 65-69 (*FIRA*^{2} I 403) et le *de Litteris Singulis* 5.8 de Valerius Probus, *Grammatici Latini* IV (1864) 274. Mais le témoignage de la *lex Irnitana* 84.23-24 (n. 62 *infra*, pour le texte), incite à la prudence car, dans des causes relevant de la procédure civile et d'une désignation amiable du jury, la *datio* du *iudex* et du *iudicium* se trouvent placées sur le même plan. L'expression *dare iudices* nous semble, en définitive, ne pas refléter nécessairement un mode non consensuel de désigner le jury.

16 Cic. *Ver.* 3.55: 'SI PARERET IVGERA EIVS FVNDI PLVRA ESSE QVAM COLONVS ESSET PROFESSVS', expression que Genovese (1999) 285-86 n. 128 et 312 n. 190 considère, avec le reste de la critique, comme pouvant raisonnablement être rattachée à une procédure formulaire *stricto sensu.*

17 Pour une définition de l'*intentio*, Pugliese (1947-49) II 101-10.

18 Pugliese (1948) 407 et Lemosse (1998) ont montré qu'à l'époque impériale, dans des procès relevant pourtant de la *cognitio extra ordinem* du gouverneur, les demandeurs recourent encore aux *formulae* du droit prétorien.

autres procès de droit privé. C'est dans le mode de constitution des jurys que nous trouvons cette preuve, plus précisément encore dans la désignation des juges nommés *recuperatores*.

Ce n'est pas le lieu ici de faire l'historique des poursuites 'en récupération', d'autant que les romanistes n'ont pu, de manière convaincante, dégager des traits communs à tous les tribunaux de 'récupérateurs', qui se rencontrent aussi bien à Rome que dans les provinces, dans la juridiction civile autant que pénale et criminelle.[19] La critique a longtemps soutenu que ces procès avaient pour dénominateur commun la mise en jeu de l'intérêt de l'Etat, en arguant du fait que la procédure devant les récupérateurs prévoyait un délai bref entre la désignation du jury et la prononciation de la sentence.[20] Cette apparente recherche d'une résolution rapide du contentieux a pu conduire certains romanistes, Wlassak en premier lieu, à conclure que l'institution d'une procédure devant les récupérateurs était le signe que le magistrat prenait en charge la désignation des jurys, pour défendre l'intérêt de la communauté.[21] Comme nous allons le voir, cette acception 'publiciste' du procès devant les récupérateurs, qui se justifie peut-être pour certaines causes de nature criminelle, n'est pas recevable, ou du moins, n'est pas utile pour éclairer l'organisation des procès fiscaux dans les *Verrines*.

Les discours de Cicéron contre Verrès attestent, en effet, l'existence, aussi bien dans les procès privés que dans les procès fiscaux, d'une même procédure en deux temps, pour la désignation de juges qualifiés comme *recuperatores*. Cette procédure est détaillée, dans le *de Frumento*, lorsque Cicéron reconstitue un procès intenté par un cultivateur contre un adjudicataire de l'impôt, qui aurait abusé de son droit en prélevant plus que le dixième de la récolte.[22] Le cultivateur invoque l'édit de Verrès qui donne un jugement, assorti d'une amende à l'octuple, contre les fermiers de l'impôt ayant abusé de leur pouvoir. L'adjudicataire est

19 Citons les synthèses de Pugliese (1947-49) I 196-201, Bongert (1952) et Kelly (1976) 40-70, ainsi que Lintott (1990) pour un point de vue sur l'épigraphie juridique en la matière.

20 Thèse traditionnelle reprise encore par Kelly (1976) 40-70, qui défend l'idée d'une compétence avant tout exécutoire des récupérateurs, peu admissible au regard des textes cicéroniens et de manière plus nuancée, par Lintott (1990). En revanche, les études les plus récentes, comme Johnston (1987) 67-70, en particulier suite à la publication de la *lex Irnitana*, écartent la thèse d'un 'procès récupératoire' comme figure juridique autonome.

21 Wlassak (1891) 324-28.

22 Cic. *Ver.* 3.28-31, dont 28: 'Verum esto: reperietur aliqui fortis et experiens arator, qui cum tantum dederit decumano quantum ille deberi dixerit, iudicio repetat et poenam octupli persequatur: expecto uim edicti, seueritatem praetoris; faueo aratori, cupio octupli damnari Apronium. Quid tandem postulat arator? nihil nisi ex edicto iudicium in octuplum. Quid Apronius? non recusat. Quid praetor? iubet recuperatores reicere. Decurias scribamus. Quas decurias? "De cohorte mea reicies", inquit. Quid? cohors ista quorum hominum est? "Volusi haruspicis et Corneli medici et horum canum quos tribunal meum uides lambere"; nam de conuentu nullum umquam iudicem nec recuperatorem dedit'. ('Soit. Il va se trouver un agriculteur courageux et entreprenant pour verser au décimateur tout ce que ce dernier aura déclaré être dû, puis pour intenter un procès en récupération et le faire condamner à la restitution de l'octuple. J'attends l'efficacité de l'édit, la sévérité de préteur. Je soutiens le cultivateur, je désire qu'Apronius soit condamné à l'octuple. Mais que demande donc le cultivateur? Rien d'autre qu'un procès à l'octuple, conformément à l'édit. Que demande Apronius? Il ne s'y oppose pas. Que fait le préteur? Il ordonne de récuser les récupérateurs. Inscrivons les décuries. Quelles décuries? "C'est parmi les gens de ma cohorte que tu récuseras", dit-il. Mais ta cohorte, de quels hommes se compose-t-elle? "De l'haruspice Volusius, du médecin Cornelius et de ces chiens que tu vois lécher mon tribunal." Car jamais il n'a choisi un seul juge ni un seul récupérateur dans la circonscription judiciaire'.)

censé être Q. Apronius, dont Cicéron fait le complice et le suppôt de Verrès, mais l'ensemble de la reconstitution est une pure fiction, puisque, nous dit Cicéron, jamais un cultivateur n'eut l'audace de demander à Verrès des récupérateurs, quand il savait que ceux-ci seraient sélectionnés dans la cohorte du préteur.[23] Toujours est-il que nous nous trouvons, fictivement, dans la situation d'un cultivateur sicilien qui assigne en justice un adjudicataire de l'impôt détenteur de la citoyenneté romaine. Dans un premier temps, le gouverneur soumet à l'accord des parties l'*album* dans lequel aura lieu la sélection des juges, puis il ouvre aux deux parties la récusation sur cette liste, jusqu'à obtention du nombre de juges prévu dans le jury.[24] Les juges normalement attendus sont non pas des gens de la cohorte de Verrès, mais des hommes sélectionnés dans la circonscription juridique, le *conuentus*.

Or, relatant une controverse survenue entre un particulier et un fermier de l'impôt, mais en dehors du contexte de la perception de la dîme, Cicéron évoque dans des termes identiques la constitution du jury.[25] Il s'agit du défi judiciaire lancé par le chevalier romain Scandilius contre le même fermier de l'impôt, Apronius. En l'espèce, Scandilius provoque Apronius à donner 5000 sesterces, en même temps que sa parole qu'il n'a pas déclaré publiquement que Verrès et lui étaient associés dans la perception de la dîme, c'est-à-dire que le gouverneur percevait des profits illégaux. Dans ce cas aussi, la procédure ordinaire entre deux plaideurs

23 Cic. *Ver.* 3.30: 'Quid est hoc? tot uiri fortes honesti gratiosi, tot Siculi, tot equites Romani ab homine nequissimo ac turpissimo laesi poenam octupli sine ulla dubitatione commissam non persequebantur? Quae causa, quae ratio est? una illa iudices quam uidetis, quod ultro etiam illusos se et irrisos ab iudicio discessuros uidebant. Etenim quod esset iudicium, cum ex Verris turpissimo flagitiosissimoque comitatu tres recuperatorum nomine assedissent adseculae istius [...]?' ('Quoi? Tant d'hommes courageux, honorables, dignes de confiance, tant de Siciliens, tant de chevaliers romains, lésés par un homme qui est le comble de la malhonnêteté et de la dépravation, pouvaient ne pas lui réclamer en justice la condamnation à payer l'octuple, que, incontestablement, il encourait? Quelle explication à cela? Quelle logique? Une seule, juges, et vous la voyez bien: ils sentaient qu'en plus du reste, ils sortiraient du procès bernés et ridiculisés. Oui, que serait un procès dans lequel trois hommes de son entourage – comble de la dépravation et de la débauche – auraient siégé à titre de récupérateurs [...] ?')

24 Processus reconstitué par Genovese (1999) 108-13, qui fait état d'un consensus d'ensemble des romanistes sur cette organisation. Une procédure en deux temps de choix ou de tirage au sort d'une liste dans le collège des jurés, puis de récusation sur cette liste, est la plus courante en matière de désignation de récupérateurs, même si les différents statuts épigraphiques qui sont conservés montrent des variations dans le détail de la procédure. A propos des spécificités de la *lex Irnitana* 88 sur cette question, Lamberti (1993) 177-80 (178 n. 121) fait observer que la possibilité de désignation de récupérateurs, par convention, hors de l'*album* ordinaire, n'est pas mentionnée aux chap. 88-89 de la loi, alors qu'elle est admise pour le *iudex unus* au chap. 84 (n. 62 *infra*, pour le texte). Lamberti interprète cette différence comme le signe du caractère quasi public des procès devant les récupérateurs. Toutefois, il nous semble plus probable que la possibilité d'une désignation amiable ait été envisagée pour toutes les causes dans les dispositions d'ordre général du chap. 84, dans lequel est clairement énoncée la possibilité d'une *addictio recuperatorum*, donc d'une désignation amiable (n. 64 *infra*, sur le sens d'*addictio*).

25 Pour d'autres exemples de *iudicia priuata* devant des récupérateurs, Cic. *Tul.*, daté de 72-71 av. J.-C., et *Caec.*, du début des années 60 av. J.-C., deux procès privés pour voies de fait dans des litiges sur une propriété foncière, ainsi que l'*edictum Augusti de Aquaeductu Venafrano* 65-69 (*FIRA*^{2} I 400-03), pour une cause de droit civil, mais portant sur les intérêts d'une communauté civique.

ayant la citoyenneté romaine prévoit la désignation, par le préteur, de récupérateurs appartenant au *conuentus* de Syracuse et la récusation par les parties.[26]

Ces textes semblent, par ailleurs, témoigner du fait que, dans la procédure telle qu'elle est appliquée en Sicile, l'accord des parties, lors de la *litis contestatio*, est requis moins sur la personne du juge que sur la nature du jury.[27] Ainsi, dans l'affaire de Scandilius, le demandeur, déniant compétence aux récupérateurs proposés par Verrès, tente d'interrompre le processus juridique du défi qu'il a lancé.[28] Sans doute, en l'occurrence, la procédure est-elle un peu particulière, puisqu'il s'agit d'une *sponsio*, pour laquelle le magistrat saisi ne propose pas à proprement parler une formule d'action, mais enregistre seulement le défi judiciaire lancé par un particulier à un autre.[29] Dans ces conditions, plutôt que d'un accord des deux parties sur une formule d'action, il s'agit pour le défendeur d'accepter ou non de prononcer la *sponsio*. Mais on voit aussi les délégués de la cité d'Agyrium, accusés à titre personnel, devant le préteur, d'avoir agi contre un de ses édits, accepter l'instance devant des récupérateurs avant la constitution de la liste nominale sur laquelle ils auront à faire leurs récusations.[30] De même,

26 Cic. *Ver.* 3.135-37, dont 135: 'Recuperatores dicis te daturum. Bene agis; [...] [136 ...] Praeterea conuentus honestus Syracusis, multi equites Romani uiri primarii, ex qua copia recuperatores reici oporteret, qui aliter iudicare nullo modo possent.' ('Tu déclares que tu donneras des récupérateurs. C'est bien; [... 136 ...] En outre, une assemblée honnête à Syracuse, de nombreux chevaliers romains, des hommes de premier rang, parmi lesquels il conviendrait de procéder à la récusation des récupérateurs, qui en aucune façon ne pourraient prononcer un autre jugement.')

27 Pugliese (1947-49) I 225-31 et (1948) 404-05 (404 n. 27) conclut avec prudence que la désignation du juge relevait de la *litis contestatio*, ce qui le conduit à considérer que la désignation du ou des juges requiert le même consensus dans tous les *iudicia*, même devant les récupérateurs. Dès lors, Pugliese se voit contraint par sa conception du procès provincial de supposer que, dans la procédure formulaire appliquée dans les provinces, la formule *iudex esto* n'est qu'une clause de style, qui n'indique plus un réel consensus.

28 Cic. *Ver.* 3.138-39: 'Scandilius uero negat sese apud Artemidorum recuperatorem uerbum esse facturum et tamen auget atque onerat te bonis condicionibus, si tu uti uelis: si ex prouincia Sicilia tota statuas idoneum iudicem aut recuperatorem nullum posse reperiri, postulat abs te ut Romam rem reicias. [...] Negas te Romam reiecturum, negas de conuentu recuperatores daturum, cohortem tuam proponis. Scandilius rem se totam relicturum dicit et suo tempore esse rediturum.' ('Mais Scandilius refuse de dire un seul mot devant un récupérateur comme Artémidore et cependant il te fait la faveur, il t'accable de bonnes conditions, pour peu que tu souhaites en profiter: si tu établis que, dans toute la Sicile, on ne peut trouver un seul juge ou récupérateur qui convienne, il te demande de renvoyer l'affaire à Rome. [...] Tu refuses de renvoyer à Rome, tu refuses de donner des récupérateurs issus de la circonscription, tu donnes à la place ta cohorte. Scandilius déclare qu'il est disposé à abandonner l'ensemble de l'affaire et qu'il reviendra à son heure.') Le médecin Cornelius Artemidorus de Perge, plusieurs fois évoqué dans les *Verrines* comme membre de la cohorte du gouverneur (Cic. *Ver.* 3.28, 3.54, 3.69, 3.117) est mentionné ici à titre d'exemple, non parce qu'il a été choisi comme récupérateur, puisque la procédure de *reiectio* n'a pas encore eu lieu.

29 Sur cette forme particulière de la figure juridique de la *sponsio*, nous renvoyons à Costa (1928) II 55 et Crook (1976) 136 qui montre qu'une telle *sponsio* se distingue des *sponsiones* dites 'préjudicielles', destinées à introduire une instance au titre d'une *actio* définie. Il n'en est pas moins vrai qu'elle aussi doit ouvrir sur un *iudicium*.

30 Cic. *Ver.* 3.68-69: 'Recuperatores se de cohorte sua daturum minabatur. Agyrinenses uiri fortissimi iudicio se passuros esse dicebant. [69] Ingerebat iste Artemidorum Cornelium medicum et Tlepolemum Cornelium pictorem et huiuscemodi recuperatores [...].' ('Il les menaçait de nommer les récupérateurs

enfin, lors des poursuites pour falsification de déclaration fiscale intentées contre le sicilien Xénon de Menae, le défendeur, au moment où il accepte la formule, accepte aussi le jury: 'Ille tametsi recuperatores de cohorte latronum sibi parari uidebat, tamen iudicium se accepturum esse dicebat', expression que Pugliese interprète comme typique de la phase de *litis contestatio* du procès formulaire.[31]

A ce stade de notre réflexion, rien ne permet donc, d'après le seul témoignage des *Verrines* et d'après les expressions employées par Cicéron, d'identifier l'existence d'une procédure propre aux procès fiscaux, dans laquelle le magistrat instructeur jouirait de pouvoirs exceptionnels lors de la désignation des jurys. Notons, à titre de comparaison, qu'une procédure de désignation des *recuperatores* très semblable à celle illustrée dans les *Verrines*, se rencontre dans un autre procès fiscal, antérieur d'environ un demi siècle aux procès évoqués par Cicéron. En effet, la *lex agraria epigraphica*, relative à la perception des contributions foncières sur l'*ager publicus* constitué dans les années 130 av. J.-C., donne aux publicains les moyens juridiques d'obtenir le recouvrement des sommes qui leurs sont dues. Ce passage, si fragmentaire soit-il, est un des rares documents qui permette des comparaisons avec les dispositions de l'édit provincial de Verrès en matière fiscale. La plainte est déposée par le fermier de l'impôt devant un magistrat romain qui, dans le cadre de sa *iurisdictio*,[32] soumet aux parties, sans tirage au sort, une liste de juges de rang sénatorial, probablement au nombre de cinquante, parmi lesquels les deux parties procèdent à une récusation, jusqu'à constituer un jury de onze personnes.[33] Cet exemple, comme celui du *de Frumento*, montre qu'en définitive c'est avant tout de notre point de vue contemporain qu'il est surprenant de voir le rapport juridique entre contribuable et fermier de l'impôt envisagé comme un contentieux entre particuliers, ressortissant strictement au droit privé.[34]

dans sa cohorte. Les Agyriens, des hommes d'un très grand courage, déclaraient qu'ils accepteraient d'aller en jugement. [69] L'accusé leur imposait (comme juges) le médecin Artémidore Cornelius et le peintre Tlépolème Cornelius et des récupérateurs de cette sorte [...].')

31 Cic. *Ver.* 3.55, commenté par Pugliese (1948) 414.

32 Pugliese (1948) 412 indique que l'expression *ius dicere* caractérise l'activité du magistrat instructeur dans les *iudicia priuata*.

33 *Lex agraria epigraphica* 36-38 (*RS* I 117), dont nous simplifions ici les conventions de transcription du texte épigraphique: '[--- sei quid publicanus eius rei causa a quo eorum sibi deberi] dariue oportere de[icet, eis co(n)s(ul) proue co(n)]s(ule) pr(aetor) proue pr(aetore), quo in ious adierint, in diebus (decem) proxsumeis, qu[ibus de ea re ious --- recuperatores ex ci]uibus † L †, quei classis primae sient, (undecim) dato, inde alternos dum[taxat quaternos (?) is quei petet et is] [unde petetur, quos uolent reiciant facito deque ea re iudicare iubeto ---].' Nous traduirions ce texte, en grande partie reconstruit, comme suit: '[Si un publicain] déclare que [quelque chose lui est dû ou] doit lui être versé [à ce titre par un contribuable, que le consul, le proconsul], le préteur ou le propréteur, qui aura été saisi, dans les dix jours [suivants le jour où il aura été saisi à ce titre ...], parmi les citoyens (?) appartenant à la première classe, donne onze [récupérateurs, puis fasse récuser alternativement par le demandeur et le défendeur ceux qu'ils souhaitent], dans une limite de quatre (?) [et les désigne comme juges ...].' Les problèmes d'établissement du texte relativement au nombre de cinquante noms figurant sur la première liste sont envisagés par Lintott (1992) 188 et *RS* I 168-69.

34 Sur ce thème, De Martino (1993) 11-17 se range aux théories de Pugliese (1948) sur la nature privée du procès fiscal.

II. Pouvoirs discrétionnaires du gouverneur et contraintes de la procédure

Dans un second temps, pour bien mesurer l'attitude de Verrès par rapport à la procédure romaine, il convient de déterminer quels exemples attestent réellement la désignation d'un jury, dans les causes civiles et fiscales, malgré ou contre la volonté des parties.

Une interrogation préliminaire doit porter sur la notion même de consensus des parties: dans le déroulement normal de la procédure, il n'est pas certain que les parties pussent, dans les faits, librement refuser les juges que leur proposait le magistrat. Il convient de distinguer, dans ce domaine, la position du demandeur de celle du défendeur. Si le particulier à l'origine de la procédure ne se voit pas proposer la formule ou les juges qu'il considère adaptés à sa situation de droit, il est libre de retirer sa plainte et ne subit que la perte de ce qu'il réclamait; en revanche, le prévenu ne peut pas faire opposition, arguant que le chef d'accusation ne le concerne pas ou que le tribunal devant lequel il va être convoqué n'est pas habilité à statuer sur sa personne, sans s'exposer à de plus lourdes conséquences, celles d'être jugé comme *indefensus*.[35] Le plus souvent le consensus des parties sur la nature du jury devait donc être plus passif qu'actif, s'exprimer dans un consentement formel à la juridiction du magistrat et à la délégation de cette juridiction au *iudex unus* ou aux *iudices*.

La différence d'intérêt entre demandeur et défendeur apparaît très clairement dans le défi judiciaire lancé par Scandilius.[36] Le demandeur se trouve, pour ainsi dire, en position de négociation avec le magistrat, parce que, s'il n'obtient pas le *iudicium*, ses pertes sont très limitées tandis que le défendeur Apronius risque, plus encore qu'une peine financière, une dégradation sociale irrémédiable.[37] Scandilius peut donc refuser la liste de récupérateurs proposée par Verrès, puis demander un renvoi à Rome et enfin, tenter de se retirer, non sans menacer de réitérer le défi devant le successeur de Verrès. Dans la mesure où le renvoi de l'affaire à Rome n'est pas un droit de Scandilius – Cicéron n'aurait pas manqué d'utiliser cet argument – Verrès a sans doute amené le demandeur à tenter d'interrompre le processus juridique, mais jusqu'alors il ne lui a rien imposé. Les suites données par Verrès à cette affaire sont de compréhension difficile. Cicéron expose en effet les trois possibilités qui se présentent à Verrès, non sans en donner une lecture du point de vue de l'éthique, ce qui ne facilite guère notre interprétation.[38] Un point nous semble acquis: dans la mesure où Apronius a accepté la

35 Pugliese (1947-49) I 188-96 insiste alors sur le rôle prépondérant et décisif du magistrat dans la désignation du juge, même en l'absence d'un accord des parties.

36 Cic. *Ver.* 3.135-36.

37 Crook (1976) 132-38 revient sur ces formes de défi dans lesquels entrait en jeu l'honneur de qui recevait le défi.

38 Cic. *Ver.* 3.135-40, dont 139-40: 'Scandilius rem se totam relicturum dicit et suo tempore esse rediturum. Quid? Tu ibi tum quid facis? Scandilium cogis – quid? Sponsionem acceptam facere? Inpudenter tollis expectatum existimationis tuae iudicium; non facis. Quid ergo? Apronio permittis ut quos uelit de cohorte sumat recuperatores? Indignum uni potius ex iniquis sumundi quam utrique ex aequis reiciundi fieri potestatem. Neutrum facis eorum. Quid ergo? Estne aliquid quod improbius fieri possit? Est; cogit enim Scandilium quinque illa milia nummum dare atque adnumerare Apronio.' ('Scandilius déclare qu'il est disposé à abandonner l'ensemble de l'affaire et qu'il reviendra à son heure. Et que fais-tu alors? Que fais-tu? Tu contrains Scandilius. À quoi? À recevoir l'engagement? Sans vergogne, tu supprimes un procès attendu portant sur ta propre réputation: tu n'en fais rien. Et quoi alors? Permettre à Apronius de choisir les récupérateurs qu'il veut dans ta cohorte? Il serait indigne

sponsio, le procès est engagé et Verrès peut légitimement lui donner suite. La première solution est, pensons-nous, envisagée à titre purement rhétorique: contraindre Scandilius à accepter le paiement d'Apronius.[39] Solution impensable, dit Cicéron, car elle reviendrait, pour Verrès, à reconnaître son tort. La deuxième possibilité consisterait à ignorer le rejet du tribunal par le demandeur et à faire se tenir le procès, en laissant au défendeur le choix des jurés.[40] Là aussi, l'amère ironie de Cicéron, son évocation sarcastique d'un Verrès arrêté par le souci de l'*aequitas*, ne permettent pas d'affirmer si la possibilité se présentait réellement ou non. Toutefois, dans la mesure où le défendeur Apronius a accepté la *sponsio*, une telle solution n'est peut-être pas juridiquement intenable, ni d'ailleurs inéquitable, en ce qu'elle donne au défendeur le droit de répondre à une accusation qui pourrait être diffamatoire.[41] La troisième solution, retenue par Verrès, est en définitive de ramener le jugement à sa propre *cognitio*. Elle lui permet, de fait, de condamner Scandilius, contre toute évidence et probablement sans avoir entendu de témoins. Comment comprendre cette attitude du point de vue de la stricte procédure? Etant donné que le défendeur et le demandeur, tous les deux citoyens romains, ne sont pas parvenus à s'accorder sur le jury et que l'engagement a été prononcé, peut-on, du point de vue formel, incriminer le gouverneur pour avoir rendu lui-même une sentence?[42]

De manière plus générale, nous avons recherché, parmi tous les procès civils et pénaux décrits dans le *de Praetura Siciliensi* et dans le *de Frumento,* lesquels s'étaient achevés sur

que soit donnée à l'une des deux parties la possibilité de faire un choix parmi de malhonnêtes gens plutôt qu'aux deux celle de faire une récusation parmi d'honnêtes gens. Tu ne fais ni l'un ni l'autre. Et quoi alors? Il y a donc quelque chose de plus malhonnête encore à faire? Oui. Car il contraint Scandilius à payer et à compter les cinq mille sesterces à Apronius.')

39 Nous proposons à titre hypothétique cette lecture, en rapprochant l'expression *sponsionem acceptam facere* de (*acceptum*) *in rationem* (*re*)*ferre*, dans les tablettes d'Herculanum, dont Gröschler (1997) 199-245 a montré qu'elle indique l'enregistrement dans les comptes d'une entrée, qu'elle liquide une dette ou constitue une créance.

40 Genovese (1999) 109 n. 85 refuse d'admettre qu'Apronius ait pu, dans une procédure régulière, avoir seul le droit de rejeter les récupérateurs et s'en tient à l'hypothèse d'un droit de récusation accordé aux deux parties. Mais *sumere recuperatores*, qui n'est pas à notre connaissance attesté ailleurs, semble être une formule brachylogique de Cicéron: le défendeur étant amené *de facto* mais non *de iure* à procéder seul à la récusation, cela équivaut à un choix.

41 La même difficulté se présente dans le dénouement du procès fictif entre un cultivateur sicilien et l'adjudicataire Apronius (Cic. *Ver.* 3.28-31, n. 22 *supra*), où l'on voit les récupérateurs ne pas se contenter d'acquitter le prévenu, mais tenter de condamner le demandeur: 'Quae cum dixisset, illi uiri optimi de cohorte istius recuperatores non de absoluendo Apronio deliberarent, sed quaererent ecquo modo petitorem ipsum Apronio condemnare possent.' ('Après ces propos, ces personnes de qualité, les récupérateurs de sa cohorte, ne délibéreraient pas sur l'acquittement d'Apronius, mais s'interrogeraient pour savoir comment ils pourraient condamner celui qui précisément l'avait accusé.' Cic. *Ver.* 3.31). Genovese (1999) 140 n. 156 considère que Cicéron n'envisage pas sérieusement que les juges aient pu prononcer une condamnation contre le plaignant, sans proposer toutefois des arguments juridiques, mais seulement d'après l'emploi de l'irréel *quaererent* [...] *possent*, argument non recevable.

42 Andrew Lintott nous suggère que, pour Cicéron, Verrès se rend coupable d'arbitrer lui-même le cas, sans prendre en compte le rejet du tribunal par une des parties (*cf.* Lintott (1976) 212 n. 14).

une sentence rendue par un jury imposé, à proprement parler, contre la volonté d'une des parties.[43]

Au civil, le seul exemple invoqué par Pugliese d'un jury imposé par le préteur,[44] celui de l'affaire d'Heraclius de Syracuse, n'est pas recevable pour différentes raisons. D'une part, il ne relève peut-être pas au sens strict de la procédure formulaire, puisqu'il oppose des pérégrins. En effet, des citoyens de la cité de Syracuse disputent à un concitoyen, Heraclius, un héritage, dont ils prétendent qu'il a été laissé à une institution publique de la cité, sa palestre.[45] Le gouverneur intervient alors non pour donner une formule d'action, mais pour désigner les juges. Le romaniste Leone Mellano a reconstruit l'évolution des prétentions des deux parties: si le défendeur envisage d'abord un règlement au niveau de la cité, les demandeurs réclament du gouverneur qu'il donne un collège juridique, ce que le défendeur ne peut refuser et ce qui ne suscite pas de commentaire chez Cicéron. C'est, en revanche, sur le mode de désignation du jury que se manifeste le désaccord: alors que les demandeurs désirent voir Verrès choisir, *eligere*, un jury de Siciliens provenant des cités de la même circonscription, le défendeur (et Cicéron plus tard) argue que la *lex Rupilia* prévoit un tirage au sort, une *sortitio*.[46] Ce faisant,

43 Nous avons recensé: Cic. *Diu. Caec.* 56 ; *Ver.* 3.28-31 (fiction de procès); 3.54; 3.55; 3.67-71: affaire de la cité d'Agyrium dont les légats acceptent la formule et les récupérateurs iniques de Verrès, puis sont amenés par la menace à conclure une convention avec lui; 3.110-17; 3.135-40; 5.141-42, affaire de *sponsio* demandée par le gouverneur lui-même à un *negotiator*, C. Servilius qui, après avoir refusé les récupérateurs de Verrès, est battu à mort par ses licteurs. Dans l'affaire de Sopater d'Halycies (Halicyae) (Cic. *Ver.* 2.68-75), certes le prévenu, jugé par les membres de la cohorte, demande jusqu'à sa condamnation le rétablissement du *consilium* ordinaire, mais la cause est capitale, non civile.

44 Pugliese (1947-49) I 228-29 et (1948) 403.

45 Cic. *Ver.* 2.35-44, dont 38: 'Heraclius cum aduocatis adit et postulat ut sibi cum palaestritis, hoc est cum populo Syracusano, aequo iure disceptare liceat. Aduersarii postulant ut in eam rem iudices dentur ex iis ciuitatibus quae in id forum conuenirent, electi qui Verri uiderentur, Heraclius contra ut iudices ex lege Rupilia dentur, ut ab institutis superiorum, ab auctoritate senatus, ab iure omnium Siculorum ne recedatur. [39 ...] Cum id quod omnes intellegebant, diceret Heraclius, certum ius esse Siculis, inter se quo iure certarent, legem esse Rupiliam, quam P. Rupilius consul de decem legatorum sententia dedisset; hanc omnes semper in Sicilia consules praetoresque seruasse: negauit se iudices e lege Rupilia sortiturum, quinque iudices quos commodum ipsi fuit dedit. [... 44] Profecto enim negare non potes te ex lege Rupilia sortiri iudices debuisse, cum praesertim Heraclius id postularet.' ('Heraclius se présente avec ses avocats et demande qu'il lui soit permis de plaider contre les gens de la palestre, c'est-à-dire contre la communauté de Syracuse, selon le droit ordinaire. La partie adverse demande que, pour cette affaire, Verrès nomme des juges provenant des cités qui se réunissaient sur ce même forum, en choisissant ceux qu'il désire; Heraclius, au contraire, que des juges soient donnés aux termes de la Loi Rupilia, dans le respect des institutions des anciens, de l'autorité du Sénat et de tous les droits des Siciliens. [39 ...] Alors que Heraclius disait – et que personne n'ignorait – qu'il existe un droit défini pour les Siciliens, qui régit les contentieux qui les opposent, qu'il existe une Loi Rupilia, donnée par le consul P. Rupilius en vertu de l'avis de dix légats du Sénat, que cette loi a été toujours observée en Sicile par tous les consuls et les préteurs: Verrès, refusant de procéder à un tirage au sort en vertu de la Loi Rupilia, nomma cinq juges qui l'arrangeaient. [... 44] Assurément, tu ne peux nier que tu aurais dû, d'après la Loi Rupilia, procéder au tirage au sort des juges, surtout quand Heraclius te le demandait.')

46 Pour un commentaire de l'affaire, Pugliese (1948) 402, sur les albums de juges pérégrins dans les provinces; Martini (1969) 20-25, Mellano (1977) 28-52 (36-52), Maggio (1993) 251-55, à propos de la question de la portée des dispositions de la *lex Rupilia* en matière de droit criminel et Platschek (2001) 244 lequel considère que Verrès ne commet pas d'abus en retirant le cas à la juridiction locale. Mellano (1977) 29 semble accepter qu'il s'agisse d'un procès formulaire.

le prévenu accepte que l'affaire ne soit plus traitée selon le droit en vigueur à Syracuse, comme cela est prévu dans l'édit même du préteur, d'après ce qui est dit dans un passage du *de Praetura Siciliensi* sur lequel nous reviendrons, mais qu'elle passe sous la juridiction du préteur.[47] Sans doute, dans un premier temps, Verrès peut-il sembler contrevenir à la procédure en vigueur en imposant cinq juges. Cependant, d'une part, la situation est, de toutes façons, particulière, parce que le défendeur est en état de fuite et d'autre part, Verrès prend soin, au dernier moment, de désigner des juges selon la procédure normale fixée par la *lex Rupilia*.[48] De sorte que, du point de vue strict des règles de la procédure, il n'y a pas à proprement parler d'abus. Au contraire, on voit le gouverneur faire machines arrière en raison de l'impopularité d'une prise de position qui va contre la coutume.

Pour ce qui est des procès fiscaux, il n'y a guère plus d'évidence.

Un seul procès peut être invoqué de manière à peu près sûre, même s'il n'est pas fait mention de protestations du défendeur contre l'intervention de la cohorte de Verrès et s'il subsiste quelque doute sur le fait qu'il se soit présenté au jugement, puisque Cicéron indique, en passant, qu'il avait fui à Rome. C'est, à dire vrai, le seul exemple du *de Frumento* pour lequel il est explicitement indiqué que les récupérateurs désignés *de cohorte* aient rendu un verdict. Poursuivi pour n'avoir pas déclaré son activité de cultivateur, Nymphon de Centuripae se voit imposer par Verrès un règlement du contentieux devant des récupérateurs qui confisquent, à titre de peine, au bénéfice du fermier de l'impôt lésé, l'ensemble de la récolte, encore sur l'aire.[49]

Dans le procès de Xénon de Menae, tombant sous le même chef d'accusation, l'incrimination de Cicéron repose sur des pratiques abusives, non sur la contravention à des règles de

47 Cic. *Ver.* 2.32 (n. 58 *infra* pour le texte).

48 Cic. *Ver.* 2.42: 'Interea sane perturbatus et ipse et eius amici et consiliarii moleste ferre coeperunt Heraclium profugisse; putabant absentis damnationem praesertim tantae pecuniae multo inuidiosiorem fore, quam si praesens damnatus esset. Eo accedebat, quod iudices ex lege Rupilia dati non erant; multo etiam rem turpiorem et iniquiorem uisum iri intellegebant. Itaque hoc dum corrigere uolt, apertior eius cupiditas improbitasque facta est. Nam illis quinque iudicibus uti se negat; iubet, id quod initio lege Rupilia fieri oportuerat, citari Heraclium et eos qui dicam scripserant; ait se iudices ex lege uelle sortiri. [...] Educit ex urna tris; his ut absentem Heraclium condemnent imperat, itaque condemnant.' ('Cependant, Verrès était dans la plus grande agitation; lui-même, ses amis et ses conseillers commencèrent à s'inquiéter de la fuite d'Héraclius; ils pensaient qu'une condamnation en son absence, surtout pour une somme si importante, serait bien plus odieuse que s'il était condamné en sa présence. S'ajoutait à cela que les juges n'avaient pas été nommés conformément à la Loi Rupilia; ils voyaient bien que l'affaire n'en paraîtrait que plus injuste et plus inique encore. C'est ainsi que, voulant corriger cela, il ne fit que rendre plus manifestes sa cupidité et sa malhonnêteté. Il déclare, en effet, ne pas vouloir recourir à ces cinq juges; il fait citer Héraclius, ainsi que ceux qui lui avaient notifié par écrit sa mise en accusation – ce qu'il fallait faire dès le début, conformément à la Loi Rupilia – il déclare vouloir procéder à un tirage au sort, conformément à la loi. [...] Il tire trois noms de l'urne; il ordonne à ces juges de condamner Heraclius en son absence: ils s'exécutent.')

49 Cic. *Ver.* 3.53-54, dont 54: 'Nympho cum se uellet aequo iudicio defendere, dat iste uiros optimos recuperatores [...]. Nympho antequam plane constitit, condemnatur. Quanti fortasse quaeritis. Nulla erat edicti poena certa: frumenti eius omnis quod in areis esset.' ('Comme Nymphon voulait se défendre selon la procédure ordinaire, l'accusé désigne comme récupérateurs des hommes parfaitement honnêtes [...]. Nymphon est condamné avant même l'établissement des faits. A combien? demandez-vous peut-être. Il n'y avait pas de peine fixée par l'édit: à verser tout le froment qui était sur les aires.')

droit positif. Ce sont, en effet, des menaces physiques qui parviennent à dissuader Xénon de Menae de s'obstiner à accepter le procès en falsification de déclaration fiscale qui lui est intenté, alors même qu'il est poursuivi pour avoir déclaré la mise en culture de terrains dont il affirme n'être ni le propriétaire ni même l'exploitant.[50] Verrès n'en sort en rien réhabilité: il est évidemment indiscutable qu'il a recouru à la violence pour dissuader les Siciliens de se lancer dans des procès ou bien pour les arrêter, quand il les voyait sur le point d'accepter un jugement dont la conclusion leur aurait certes causé des torts financiers, mais n'en aurait pas moins porté préjudice à la réputation du gouverneur. Toujours est-il qu'à tout prendre Verrès apparaît, dans ce dernier exemple, pris par la procédure qu'il a proposée aux fermiers et contraint de recourir à des voies de fait pour y échapper. Il est de fait que, devant la menace, Xénon de Menae en vient à conclure une convention – léonine, certes – avec le fermier, sans qu'il soit plus question d'une sentence dans le procès qui lui est intenté.[51]

Au demeurant – ce point nous semble fondamental – de l'aveu même de Cicéron, non seulement, les cultivateurs renoncèrent à défendre leurs droits en justice mais encore, le plus souvent c'est par des violences physiques que les fermiers de l'impôt, avec ou sans l'intervention du préteur, parvinrent à leurs fins. Dès lors, toute l'argumentation proposée par l'orateur sur le détournement et la violation du droit fiscal apparaît, à l'examen, reposer soit sur des exemples fictifs, soit sur des cas de poursuites réellement intentées mais qui, à les observer de près, n'aboutissent pratiquement jamais à une sentence en bonne et due forme. Ces exemples témoignent sans aucun doute d'un usage scandaleux du droit, mais d'un usage indirect, comme moyen de pression. Une rapide revue de la casuistique développée dans les *Verrines*, que nous nous réservons d'examiner plus systématiquement dans un autre lieu, suggère donc l'hypothèse suivante: le fait même que Verrès en vienne à interrompre les règlements en justice des contentieux par la menace ou l'exercice de violences indique que, s'il est libre de constituer un organe judiciaire nouveau, il ne peut pas réellement l'imposer et ne peut pas mépriser complètement les règles de la procédure telles qu'elles sont codifiées dans son édit.

III. L'autonomie juridique des cités siciliennes et les formes de l'appel au préteur

A ce point, c'est vers la rhétorique de Cicéron, vers sa construction du discours d'accusation qu'il convient de se tourner. Car si l'orateur développe des points de procédure très précis,

50 Genovese (1999) 288-89 considère que, du point de vue juridique, la responsabilité solidaire du prévenu sur la déclaration de son locataire et pour des biens de sa femme ne serait pas indéfendable.

51 Cic. *Ver.* 3.55: 'Ille tametsi recuperatores de cohorte latronum sibi parari uidebat, tamen iudicium se accepturum esse dicebat. Tum iste magna uoce Veneriis imperat ut Xeno audiret, dum res iudicetur, hominem adseruent; cum iudicata sit, ad se ut adducant. Et illud simul ait se non putare illum, si propter diuitias poenam damnationis contemneret, etiam uirgas contempturum. Hac ille ui et hoc metu adductus tantum decumanis dedit quantum iste imperauit.' ('Xénon, quoiqu'il vît que les récupérateurs qu'on lui préparait étaient des hommes venus de cette troupe de bandits, cependant, déclarait qu'il accepterait la procédure. Alors, Verrès ordonne aux esclaves de Vénus, suffisamment fort pour que Xénon pût l'entendre, de s'assurer de sa personne pendant la durée du procès. Dès que le jugement aurait été rendu, qu'ils le conduisent devant lui. Et en même temps, il dit que, si du fait de ses richesses, Xénon tenait pour rien une peine d'amende, à son avis, il ne tiendrait pas pour rien les verges. Xénon, ébranlé par cette menace de violence, paya aux décimateurs autant que Verrès le lui ordonna.')

sciemment il les traite dans une dimension morale, au point de pouvoir incriminer Verrès sur ses intentions, plus encore que sur sa pratique.

Qu'il nous soit permis de prendre ici un seul exemple, qui a trait justement à la désignation des jurys dans les procès fiscaux. Cicéron commente, en effet, une clause placée par Verrès dans le dispositif conclusif de l'édit instituant les deux jugements en récupération dont nous avons déjà parlé. L'orateur cite le texte même de l'édit, dans lequel Verrès déclare *si uter uolet, recuperatores dabo* ('à la demande de l'une ou l'autre partie, je donnerai des récupérateurs').[52] Cicéron propose un commentaire très amer de cette clause, arguant que les récupérateurs, issus de la cohorte de Verrès, auraient été tout acquis aux fermiers de l'impôt, complices de Verrès dans ses exactions, ce qui aurait *de facto* dissuadé les contribuables lésés de faire appel au préteur. A l'en croire, cette clause n'a donc jamais été invoquée sous la préture de Verrès. Dès lors, l'argument de Cicéron ne saurait avoir de réel poids juridique que si l'orateur parvenait à convaincre que proposer cette clause était en soi, du point de vue de la procédure, répréhensible.

La critique la plus récente, à commencer Mellano, repris et nuancé par Mario Genovese,[53] dans un récent commentaire de l'oeuvre juridique de Verrès, a mis en perspective les enjeux de cette clause *si uter uolet recuperatores dabo* avec le §32 du *de Praetura Siciliensi*, passage essentiel dans lequel Cicéron met systématiquement en regard la procédure reconnue en Sicile pour la désignation des jurys avec la pratique imposée par Verrès,[54] pour montrer que l'alternative portait sur une résolution au niveau local du litige ou bien la désignation d'un tribunal par le gouverneur.[55] Cette lecture amène à renoncer définitivement à l'ancienne

52 Cic. *Ver.* 3.35: 'Illa uero praeclara est clausula edicti, quod omnium controuersiarum quae essent inter aratorem et decumanum, si uter uelit, edicit se recuperatores daturum. Primum quae potest esse controuersia, cum is qui petere debet aufert, et cum is non quantum debetur, sed quantum commodum est aufert, ille autem unde ablatum est iudicio suum recuperare nullo modo potest? Deinde in hoc homo luteus etiam callidus ac ueterator esse uult quod ita scribit: SI VTER VOLET, RECVPERATORES DABO. Quam lepide se furari putat! Vtrique facit potestatem, sed utrum ita scripserit "si uter uolet" an "si decumanus uolet" nihil interest; arator enim tuos istos recuperatores numquam uolet.' ('Il y a dans ton édit une conclusion extraordinaire: dans toutes les controverses qui viendront à exister entre un cultivateur et un décimateur, si l'une des parties le veut, il décrète qu'il désignera des récupérateurs. D'abord, quelle controverse peut-il y avoir quand celui qui doit être le demandeur prélève d'autorité non pas autant qu'il est exigible, mais autant qu'il lui est agréable, tandis que celui qui a subi le prélèvement ne peut en aucune manière rentrer dans son bien en exerçant une action judiciaire? Et ensuite, cet individu abject veut passer pour un homme madré et un vieux routier en écrivant: "si l'une des parties le veut, je désignerai des récupérateurs." Il se croit un voleur distingué! Il a donné ce pouvoir aux deux, mais qu'il ait écrit "si l'une des parties le veut" ou "si le décimateur le veut", quelle différence? L'agriculteur, en effet, ne voudra jamais de ces récupérateurs qui te sont dévoués.') La littérature sur la clause *si uter uolet recuperatores dabo* est utilement synthétisée par Genovese (1999) 170-79.

53 Genovese (1999) 153-93.

54 Cic. *Ver.* 2.32-34. Nous renvoyons au long commentaire de Genovese (1999) 74-89, pour une présentation de l'état de la question sur ce texte fondamental, mais complexe.

55 Mellano (1977) 133-37 et 153-57, spécifiquement à propos de la clause *si uter uolet*; l'auteur défend, avec une argumentation parfois un peu lâche, la thèse que l'autonomie des Siciliens, assurée par la *lex Hieronica*, ne porte pas seulement sur les modes de perception, mais aussi sur la procédure de contentieux, thèse qui est déjà, dans une certaine mesure, celle de Carcopino (1919) 35 et que reprend en partie Genovese (1999) 192-94.

interprétation, selon laquelle la clause donnait aux parties un choix entre la désignation d'un *iudex unus* et celle de récupérateurs.[56] Cette alternative est certes attestée dans le *de Frumento* pour des controverses de droit civil et pourrait exister pour des procès fiscaux, mais elle ne rend pas compte de l'enjeu évident de cette clause, l'intervention directe du gouverneur dans la composition d'un jury.[57]

De fait, comme l'expose Cicéron dans le *de Praetura Siciliensi*, le règlement général de la province prévoyait qu'en cas de controverse entre pérégrins, on s'en reportât à des normes et à des organes judiciaires pérégrins. Mais, alors que les contentieux internes aux cités étaient normalement résolus sans appel au gouverneur, ce dernier intervenait, dans diverses circonstances, pour désigner des juges siciliens. C'était le cas, notamment, quand le litige opposait deux pérégrins n'appartenant pas à la même communauté ou encore, dans toutes les causes opposant un Romain et un Sicilien, quand le pérégrin était en position de défendeur.[58]

56 Thèse défendue, entre autres, par Degenkolb (1861) 29, puis Wlassak (1891) 321-23 et encore Pugliese (1947-49) I 188-89, mais justement rejetée par Schmidlin (1964) 211, comme l'avait déjà fait Carcopino (1919) 147-48. Tout à sa démonstration et à la réfutation de Degenkolb (1861) 23-26, Carcopino (1919) 147-56 (149-52), comme après lui Schmidlin, en vient cependant à minimiser le caractère d'alternative de la clause: pour lui, elle permettrait simplement aux deux parties l'introduction de l'instance devant le préteur.

57 Il semble que cette alternative existe pour la *sponsio* demandée par Scandilius, Cic. *Ver.* 3.135: 'coepit Scandilius recuperatores aut iudicem postulare'. Pugliese (1947-49) I 188 utilise cet exemple pour défendre la thèse qu'il n'existe pas de différence substantielle entre procès devant le juge unique et devant les récupérateurs.

58 Cic. *Ver.* 2.32-34: 'Verum ut totum genus amplectamini iudiciorum, prius iura Siculorum, deinde istius instituta cognoscite. Siculi hoc iure sunt ut quod ciuis cum ciue agat, domi certet suis legibus, quod Siculus cum Siculo non eiusdem ciuitatis, ut de eo praetor iudices ex P. Rupili decreto, quod is de decem legatorum sententia statuit, quam illi legem Rupiliam uocant, sortiatur; quod priuatus a populo petit aut populus a priuato, senatus ex aliqua ciuitate qui iudicet datur, cum alternae ciuitates reiectae sunt; quod ciuis Romanus a Siculo petit, Siculus iudex, quod Siculus a ciui Romano, ciuis Romanus datur; ceterarum rerum selecti iudices ex ciuium Romanorum conuentu proponi solent. Inter aratores et decumanos lege frumentaria quam Hieronicam appellant iudicia fiunt. [33] Haec omnia isto praetore non modo perturbata, sed plane et Siculis et ciuibus Romanis erepta sunt. Primum suae leges. Quod ciuis cum ciui ageret, aut eum iudicem quem commodum erat, praeconem haruspicem medicum suum dabat, aut si legibus erat iudicium constitutum et ad ciuem suum iudicem uenerant, libere ciui iudicare non licebat. Edictum enim hominis cognoscite, quo edicto omnia iudicia redegerat in suam potestatem: SI QVI PERPERAM IVDICASSET, SE COGNITVRVM; CVM COGNOSSET, ANIMADVERSVRVM. Idque cum faciebat, nemo dubitabat quin cum iudex alium de suo iudicio putaret iudicaturum seque in eo capitis periculum aditurum, uoluntatem spectaret eius quem statim de capite suo putaret iudicaturum. [34] Selecti ex conuentu aut propositi ex negotiatoribus iudices nulli; haec copia quam dico iudicum, cohors non Q. Scaeuolae qui tamen de cohorte sua dare non solebat, sed C. Verris. Cuius modi cohortem putatis hoc principe fuisse? Sicubi uidetis edictum: SI QVID PERPERAM IVDICARIT SENATVS, eum quoque ostendam, si quando sit datus, coactu istius quod non senserit iudicasse. Ex lege Rupilia sortitio nulla, nisi cum nihil intererat istius; lege Hieronica iudicia plurimarum controuersiarum sublata uno nomine omnia; de conuentu ac negotiatoribus nulli iudices.' ('[32] Mais, pour envisager l'ensemble des types de procès, apprenez d'abord quels sont les droits reconnus aux Siciliens, puis ce qu'il a mis en pratique lui-même. Voici le droit en vigueur chez les Siciliens: quand un citoyen agit en justice contre un concitoyen, il le poursuit dans leur cité et selon leur droit propre; quand un Sicilien agit contre un Sicilien n'appartenant pas à la même cité, le préteur tire au sort des juges, en vertu du décret pris par P. Rupilius, que ce dernier a établi sur l'avis de dix légats du Sénat et que les Siciliens appellent la Loi Rupilia; quand un particulier se pourvoit en justice contre une communauté civique, ou une

Même si Cicéron, dans ce même passage du *de Praetura Siciliensi*, présente la procédure relative au contentieux sur les dîmes comme indépendante, on peut faire l'hypothèse que, du moins pour ce qui est de l'alternative entre résolution locale et appel au gouverneur, elle obéissait normalement aux même règles que la procédure civile.[59] Cela amènerait à supposer que ces contentieux pouvaient, quand le cultivateur et le décimateur étaient des pérégrins, se résoudre dans le droit grec et que la citoyenneté des juges était ordinairement celle du défendeur, dans les affaires opposant Romains et Siciliens. Cependant, le seul témoignage du *de Frumento* ne nous semble pas permette de trancher cette question. En effet, le fait que Verrès ait invoqué les mauvaises dispositions des cultivateurs locaux vis-à-vis des fermiers de l'impôt pour les écarter des jurys peut s'appliquer aussi bien à des propriétaires terriens siciliens que romains.[60]

Pour interpréter cette clause *si uter uolet recuperatores dabo*, deux documents épigraphiques, présentant une clause similaire, offrent un point de confrontation, à condition de raisonner tout autant sur les différences que sur les similitudes qu'ils présentent avec l'édit de Verrès. Le premier document est le quatrième édit donné par Auguste pour la Cyrénaïque, en 7-6 av. J.-C., établissant, au civil et au pénal, une distinction entre les causes qui seront

communauté contre un particulier, le sénat d'une cité est donné comme juge, quand les cités des deux parties ont été récusées; quand un citoyen romain se pourvoit contre un Sicilien, c'est un juge sicilien qui est donné et quand un Sicilien se pourvoit contre un citoyen romain, c'est un juge romain; pour les autres causes, il est d'usage de proposer des juges sélectionnés dans la circonscription des citoyens romains. Entre les cultivateurs et les fermiers de la dîme, c'est en vertu d'une loi frumentaire qu'ils appellent la Loi d'Hiéron que les procès sont organisés. [33] Durant la préture de l'accusé, toute cette organisation n'a pas seulement été bouleversée, les Siciliens mais aussi les citoyens Romains en ont été entièrement dépossédés. D'abord, leur droit propre: quand un citoyen agissait en justice contre un concitoyen, ou bien Verrès donnait un juge selon son intérêt, son héraut, son haruspice, son médecin, ou bien, si le procès avait été organisé selon leur droit propre et si les parties venaient devant un juge qui fût leur concitoyen, il n'était pas permis au juge de rendre librement sa sentence. Connaissez, en effet, l'édit de cet individu, édit qui lui permit de ramener tous les procés sous son autorité: DANS LE CAS OÙ QUELQU'UN AURA PRONONCÉ UN JUGEMENT INCORRECT, LUI-MÊME INSTRUIRA L'AFFAIRE; UNE FOIS INSTRUITE L'AFFAIRE, IL PRENDRA DES MESURES. Et quand il agissait de la sorte, personne ne doutait qu'un juge, quand il savait qu'un autre allait rendre une sentence sur sa propre sentence et qu'il allait en cela encourir une peine capitale, ce juge prenait en considération la volonté de celui dont il savait qu'il allait rendre aussitôt après une sentence sur sa personne civile. [34] De juges sélectionnés dans la circonscription ou proposés parmi les hommes d'affaires, point. Mais ce corps des juges, si je puis dire: une cohorte, qui n'est pas celle de Q. Scaevola, lequel d'ailleurs n'avait pas l'usage de donner des juges de sa cohorte, mais celle de C. Verrès. De quel genre était la cohorte, à votre avis, quand cet individu en était la tête? De même, vous voyez l'édit DANS LE CAS OÙ UN SÉNAT AURA PRONONCÉ UN JUGEMENT INCORRECT et je montrerai que, dans les cas où il a été donné, le sénat en question s'est vu contraint par lui de rendre une sentence contre son avis. De tirage au sort en vertu de la Loi Rupilia, point, sauf quand l'intérêt de cet individu n'était pas en jeu; les procès organisés en vertu de la Loi d'Hiéron à propos de nombreuses controverses, tous supprimés du même coup; de juges issus de la circonscription ou du groupe des hommes d'affaires, point.')

59 Genovese (1999) 316-26 rappelle que la publication, par Verrès, de l'édit *ut arator decumano quo uellet decumanus uadimonium promitteret*, en 71 av. J.-C. (Cic. *Ver.* 3.38) vint, probablement pour les seules causes frumentaires, enlever aux défendeurs le droit de plaider devant leur tribunal ordinaire.

60 Cic. *Ver.* 3.28: 'iniquos decumanis esse aiebat omnis qui ullam agri glebam possiderent.' Carcopino, (1919) 148-54 argumente en faveur des jurés exclusivement citoyens romains et Genovese (1999) 88-114 (88-99) prolonge cette théorie.

arbitrées par des juges pérégrins et celles pour lesquelles le gouverneur de la province désignera un jury de citoyens romains.[61] Le second est le chap. 84 de la *lex Irnitana*, d'époque flavienne, qui distingue les causes qui relèvent de la compétence des magistrats du municipe de celles qui, en raison de leur nature ou du montant des sommes en jeu, sont renvoyées à la *cognitio* du gouverneur de Bétique (Baetica).[62] Tentons une lecture parallèle de ces deux textes et leur mise en perspective avec la clause de l'édit *si uter uolet*.[63]

L'édit de Cyrène prescrit que, pour toutes les causes non criminelles, une alternative est créée entre un jury de pérégrins et un jury de citoyens romains: à la demande du défendeur, le gouverneur transférera vers un tribunal romain les causes qui ordinairement seraient du

61 *Edictum Augusti ad Cyrenenses* 4.64-68, *FIRA*^{2} I 409, transcription latine de G. Oliverio, revue par V. Arangio-Ruiz: 'Quaecumque controuersiae erunt inter Graecos in Cyrenaica prouincia exceptis reis capitis, de quibus qui prouinciam obtinebit ipse cognoscere statuere uel consilium iudicum dare debet, de ceteris rebus omnibus Graecos iudices dari placet, nisi is unde petitur quiue accusatur ciues Romanos iudices habere uelit. Inter eos uero quibus hoc edicto meo Graeci iudices dati erunt, iudicem dari non placet ex illa ciuitate neminem, ex qua actor accusatorue erit aut ex qua ille unde petitur quiue accusatur.' Nous proposons de ce texte la traduction suivante, d'après celle de F. de Visscher (1965) 21-22: 'Pour toutes les controverses qui surviendront entre Grecs dans la province de Cyrénaïque, à l'exception des procès capitaux, pour lesquels celui qui obtiendra la province devra exercer sa cognition et statuer en personne ou bien désigner un conseil de juges, pour toutes les autres controverses, il convient de désigner des Grecs comme juges, à moins que celui qui est poursuivi ou qui est accusé ne veuille avoir des citoyens romains comme juges. Cependant, entre deux parties pour lesquelles, en vertu de mon présent édit, des Grecs auront été désignés comme juges, personne ne peut être désigné comme juge qui appartienne à la cité dont est issu celui qui agit en justice ou qui porte une accusation ou bien à la cité dont est issu celui qui est poursuivi ou qui est accusé.'

62 *Lex Irnitana* 84.1-4: '<LXXXIV> / R(ubrica). Quarum rerum et ad quantam pecuniam in eo municipio i(uris) d(ictio) sit. / Qui eius municipi municipes incolaeue erunt, q(ua) d(e) r(e) ii inter se suo alte/riu[s]ue nomin<e> qui municeps incola((e))ue sit priuatim intra fines eius / municipi agere petere persequi uolent, quae res HS (sestertium) 8 (mille) / minorisue erit ...'; 84.17-25: 'De is re[bus etia]m, si uterque inter eos quos ambige((re))tur / uolet, de ceteris quo[que o]mnibus de quibus priuatim age/tur neque in iis prae[iudici]um de capite libero futurum / erit, et omnium rerum [quoqu]e de uadimonio promittendo in eum / [locum in] quo is erit qui e[i] prouinciae erit futurusue esse ui/debitur eo die in quem ut uadimonium promittatur postula/bitur, IIuir(i), qui ibi i(ure) d(icundo) praeerit, iuris dictio, iudicis arbitri / recuperatorum, ex iis qui ibi propositi erunt, iudici datio / addictio ...', dans l'édition de Lamberti (1993) 348-50, dont nous simplifions ici les conventions de transcription du texte épigraphique. Nous proposons la traduction suivante, d'après P. Le Roux, *AE* (1985) 133-34 et Jacques (1990) 141-42: 'Rubrique 84. Quelles affaires peuvent être jugées dans ce municipe et dans quelles limites financières. Ceux qui seront citoyens ou résidents de ce municipe, qui voudront, de façon privée, dans les limites de ce municipe, engager une action, réclamer quelque chose ou poursuivre quelqu'un, en leur propre nom ou au nom de quelqu'un d'autre, citoyen ou résident de ce municipe, du moment que la cause engagera 1000 sesterces ou moins ... et même dans les (autres) affaires, à condition que les deux parties soient d'accord, ainsi que dans toutes les affaires pour lesquelles sont engagées des actions privées et dans lesquelles il n'y aura pas eu de question préjudicielle concernant une personne libre et de manière générale, pour toutes les engagements à comparaître dans l'endroit où celui qui gouverne cette province se trouvera ou sera attendu le jour pour lequel la requête d'engagement à comparaître sera présentée: le *duumuir* en charge de la justice aura la juridiction et le droit de nommer et d'assigner un juge, un arbitre ou des récupérateurs, parmi ceux dont les noms seront proposés ici ... .'

63 Le Roux (1991) 100-02 a déjà souligné les parallèles possibles et les décalages entre les statuts de Cyrène et de Bétique. Genovese (1999) 192-93 n. 278, cherchant des parallèles à la clause *si uter uolet*, prend en compte la *lex Irnitana*, 84-86, mais néglige le témoignage de l'édit de Cyrène.

ressort d'un tribunal local. La *lex Irnitana* institue, quant à elle, une alternative entre règlement local des causes et appel à la juridiction du gouverneur: presque toutes les causes qui devraient ordinairement venir devant le gouverneur peuvent être tranchées au niveau du municipe, à condition que les deux parties le demandent conjointement. La différence est très significative: à Cyrène, pour échapper au tribunal ordinaire, la volonté d'une des deux parties est suffisante, tandis qu'à Irni, dans les affaires d'une certaine importance, un consensus des deux intéressés est requis pour leur maintien devant le tribunal local.[64]

Mais cette distinction s'explique sans difficulté par la nature de l'enjeu. Au chap. 84 de la *lex Irnitana*, le passage d'une affaire de la juridiction du gouverneur au tribunal municipal ne se comprend que de manière exceptionnelle, comme le choix amiable du ressort 'inférieur' et l'accord des deux parties doit garantir qu'elles reconnaissent à leurs concitoyens la capacité d'arbitrer le litige qui les oppose de manière équitable et impartiale. Dans l'édit de Cyrène, le gouverneur se voit *a priori* contraint par l'édit impérial à renvoyer, de manière ordinaire, aux tribunaux pérégrins, même si la possibilité est laissée au défendeur pérégrin d'obtenir un tribunal de citoyens romains.[65] Dès lors, d'après Fernand de Visscher, l'édit illustrerait non pas le vaste domaine d'application de la *cognitio* du préteur dans la province, mais, au contraire, une forme de régulation, par Rome, de sa propre autorité, au bénéfice de l'autonomie des Grecs. Cependant, il serait impensable que les cités aient perdu toute autonomie juridique et la majorité des causes entre citoyens d'une même cité devaient être réglées *domi*, sans intervention aucune de l'autorité romaine.[66] Les causes envisagées dans l'édit d'Auguste ne seraient donc pas toutes les causes civiles et pénales survenant dans la province, mais seulement celles qui viendraient devant le gouverneur à la suite d'une requête spontanée de désignation d'un tiers comme arbitre, dans une tradition qui trouverait son origine dans les rapports entre les cités grecques et les souverains hellénistiques.[67] Tout en donnant raison à de Visscher sur l'existence d'une juridiction autonome des cités et sur l'idée

64 *Lex Irnitana* 84.17. Par ailleurs, M. Crawford, dans son commentaire (*RS* I 324) du *fragmentum Atestinum* 14-15: 'Quod priuatim ambig<er>etur, iuris dict[i]/o iudicis arbitri recuperatorum datio addictiou[e fuit] / quantaeque rei pequniaeue fuit', interprète l'expression *dare addicere*, dans l'acte de désignation des juges, au chap. 84.23-26 de la *lex Irnitana*, comme 'donner et confirmer', sans le cadre d'une procédure amiable, par opposition au simple *dare*, qui signifie un juge désigné. Dans sa reprise du dossier épigraphique relatif aux partages de juridiction entre communautés locales et autorité centrale, Laffi (1988) 148-49 considère que les dérogations conventionnelles aux limites de compétence, si elles peuvent être tacites, sont de toute façon l'objet d'un accord des deux parties.

65 La formule *Graecos iudices dari placet* de l'*Edictum* 4.67 (n. 61 *supra*) est interprétée aussi bien par de Visscher (1965) 129 et (1964) 323 et 325-28, que par Le Roux (1991) 101 dans le sens d'une *datio iudicis* ou *iudicum* par le gouverneur lui-même. De Visscher (1965) 129-30 considère que la procédure en question, dans le quatrième édit de Cyrène, ne peut être assimilée à la *cognitio* du préteur et plus précisément à sa phase *in iudicio*: pour lui, le gouverneur ne se prononce ici que parce que son arbitrage a été expressément demandé.

66 Argumentation développée par de Visscher (1965) 122-28, mettant en oeuvre notamment le témoignage de Cicéron sur la Sicile, *contra* Platschek (2001) 249.

67 Martini (1969) 11-48 (19-26) et de Visscher (1965) 126-27 concordent pour voir l'origine de cette intervention du gouverneur romain pour la désignation de juges entre pérégrins dans le rôle d'arbitre joué auparavant par le monarque hellénistique, à la demande de cités de Grèce et d'Asie Mineure. Heuss (1963) 69-90 présente le dossier correspondant d'inscriptions de la période hellénistique.

d'un appel au préteur, il convient toutefois de nuancer son acception trop irénique de l'édit d'Auguste. Tout pérégrin poursuivi par des concitoyens était libre d'en appeler à un tribunal de *ciues Romani*, partant de demander l'application de normes juridiques romaines ou du moins romanisées.[68] L'édit ne saurait donc, comme le dit de Visscher, avoir limité la 'pratique particulièrement choquante', selon laquelle, quand on en appelait à lui, 'le gouverneur désignait fréquemment comme juges des citoyens romains'.[69] Dans les faits, il encadrait cette pratique, la formalisait juridiquement, en en faisant une prérogative de la défense.

Il faut donc distinguer trois types de procès à Cyrène, à s'en tenir aux seules causes impliquant exclusivement des pérégrins: des procès entièrement traités au niveau local; des procès entre pérégrins pour lesquels l'intervention du gouverneur était requise dans la désignation de jurés pérégrins; et enfin des procès devant les tribunaux romains. Le gouverneur pouvait alors se limiter à la désignation d'un jury de citoyens romains, à la demande de la défense, ou bien, comme c'est le cas pour les procès criminels entraînant une peine capitale, exercer lui-même sa *cognitio*. Sans chercher en aucune façon à minimiser les spécificités respectives, nous pensons que cette distribution entre tribunaux locaux et romains peut permettre de comprendre l'organisation de la justice en Sicile sous la domination romaine, y compris en matière fiscale.[70]

Dans cette perspective, il n'est pas possible d'émettre un jugement *a priori* sur le caractère équitable ou non de la clause *si uter uolet recuperatores dabo* de l'édit de Verrès, pas plus que l'on ne peut juger la clause voisine dans les édits d'Auguste pour la Cyrénaïque. Elle permettait probablement qu'en cas de contentieux fiscal, une des parties pût demander au préteur la désignation d'un tribunal de citoyens romains.[71] On peut, sans doute, supposer que tout Sicilien d'un rang élevé devait volontiers l'invoquer, à commencer par les adjudicataires pérégrins des contributions romaines, qui auraient été poursuivis pour des abus lors de la perception de la dîme. Cependant, il n'était pas dans l'intérêt de l'autorité romaine de donner systématiquement raison aux adjudicataires, en cas d'abus patent. De fait, Cicéron n'attaque pas cette clause sur le fond, mais s'applique, au contraire, à montrer comment, sous les dehors d'une disposition équitable, elle est subvertie dans les faits par Verrès, en raison de la nature

68 Dans le même ordre d'idée, Cic. *Ver.* 2.31 évoque l'application, par Verrès, à des pérégrins, de formes de procédure réservées aux Romains et inversement, passage commenté par Genovese (1999) 76-78 n. 6, qui opte pour une interprétation comme *fictio ciuitatis* non formalisée.

69 De Visscher (1965) 130.

70 Nous nous éloignons ici de Carcopino (1919) 150-52, qui jugeait impensable que l'autorité romaine pût abandonner à des tribunaux pérégrins la résolution de controverses sur l'impôt foncier.

71 A dire vrai, rien, dans le texte des *Verrines*, ne permet d'affirmer que ces *recuperatores* sont nécessairement des citoyens romains. Il n'est peut-être pas impossible que ce terme ait pu désigner aussi des juges pérégrins, auquel cas la clause aurait prévu seulement l'appel au préteur et des dispositions successives auraient éventuellement prévu un partage des causes entre jurés pérégrins et romains. Genovese (1999) 371-92 va jusqu'à supposer que la clause *si uter uolet*, de même que les deux jugements à l'octuple et au quadruple, n'auraient concerné *de iure* que des cultivateurs pérégrins, mais sa démonstration se fonde essentiellement sur un argument *e silentio*.

des récupérateurs qu'il se propose de donner.[72] Toujours est-il cependant que, du point de vue de la procédure, une telle disposition ne paraît pas entièrement étrangère avec la pratique du droit provincial, au point qu'on peut se demander si elle ne figurait pas déjà dans les édits donnés pour la Sicile avant la préture de Verrès.[73] Il apparaît, en tous cas, que l'art de Cicéron est d'appuyer sur des arguments juridiques, faisant appel à des développements techniques sur la procédure, une accusation dont les fondements sont avant tout de nature morale.

*IV. Réflexions conclusives sur l'*imperium *du magistrat romain*

En définitive, d'un point de vue de méthode, une lecture des *Verrines* comme source pour le droit romain, doit peut-être s'interroger d'abord sur ce qu'elles révèlent de la construction d'un discours d'accusation dans un procès pour extorsion de fonds et de la place accordée, dans l'argumentation, aux abus de pouvoirs judiciaires de l'accusé. Dans cette perspective, il apparaît que Cicéron présente la procédure romaine comme un instrument souple, permettant au gouverneur de définir et de tenir un équilibre, sans doute généralement plus subtil que ne veut le dire Cicéron à propos de Verrès, entre les intérêts du peuple romain, ceux des provinciaux, ceux des Romains installés dans la province et les siens propres. On comprend alors, d'une part, que Cicéron oriente systématiquement son traitement de la question vers l'éthique, mais aussi, d'autre part, que les arguments juridiques aient une telle place dans la construction de la personnalité de l'accusé. Le discours d'accusation, conçu comme un portait à charge, restitue une image du gouverneur dans son administration de la justice.

Plusieurs facteurs, relevant du droit administratif, expliquent cette stratégie rhétorique, en ce qu'ils donnent l'idée du caractère fortement personnel de la juridiction des magistrats. Durant la pleine période impériale, époque de majeure codification du droit et certainement de moindre autonomie des gouverneurs provinciaux, Gaius attire encore l'attention sur l'autonomie reconnue aux promagistrats dans l'instruction des procès. Ainsi, dans ses *Institutes*,[74] Gaius identifie une catégorie de causes, celle des *iudicia imperio continentia*, reposant sur *l'imperium* du magistrat. Relèvent de cette catégorie l'ensemble des *iudicia* qui se déroulent au-delà du premier mille autour de Rome, *a fortiori* les procès provinciaux et tous les *iudicia recuperatoria*, même ceux tenus à Rome.[75] Une telle construction doctrinale se traduit de manière très concrète dans la procédure, mais aussi dans une forme de lien personnel entre ces causes et le magistrat qui les instruit. De fait, la règle qui veut que tous les procès de ce type en cours d'instruction s'interrompent quand vient à échéance l'*imperium* du magistrat justifie la brièveté reconnue de la procédure devant les récupérateurs.

72 Par ailleurs, à en croire Cicéron (*Ver.* 2.33-34), Verrès s'était ménagé la possibilité d'appeler à lui des causes arbitrées entre pérégrins par le conseil d'une cité sicilienne désignée comme arbitre, en attaquant sur le fond le jugement rendu, édit commenté par Genovese (1999) 199-202.

73 En revanche, après Mellano (1977) 147 n. 62 et 157, Genovese (1999) 182-83 (n. 258-59) et 229-35 considère que la clause *si uter uolet* est introduite par Verrès. A la vérité, le texte ne permet pas de trancher.

74 Gaius *Inst.* 4.105.

75 On notera, dans l'*edictum de Aquaeductu Venafrano* 65-69 (*FIRA*^{2} I 402-03), que les dispositions finales établissant une procédure de *recuperatorum reiectio* se réfèrent à la *lex Iulia de iudiciis priuatis*; le procès n'en repose pas moins sur l'*imperium* du préteur pérégrin.

Inversement, une fois prononcée la sentence, dans les provinces, les parties ne disposent pas, contre l'*imperium* d'un magistrat, de l'appel à l'*intercessio* d'un autre. L. Calpurnius Piso, collègue de Verrès dans sa préture urbaine, interposa son veto à un certain nombre des jugements que ce dernier avait rendus, dans des affaires relevant du droit des successions. Verrès avait alors introduit des clauses nouvelles dans son *edictum urbanum*, en prévision des causes qui viendraient devant lui et au bénéfice de celle des parties qui avait acheté sa sentence. Aux dires de Cicéron, personne ne pouvait jouer le même rôle contre Verrès en Sicile.[76] Il reste que L. Caecilius Metellus, successeur de Verrès dans la province, cassa un certain nombre de ses décisions de justice, comme Verrès était revenu sur certains arrêts de son prédécesseur.[77] Il ne s'agit pas d'une *intercessio* au sens strict du droit public, mais une telle intervention, que Cicéron ne peut pas condamner, produit probablement les mêmes effets, c'est-à-dire probablement la *restitutio in integrum* au bénéfice des parties lésées.

Un même caractère fortement personnel semble revêtir, plus encore que la juridiction, l'activité normative même du promagistrat. Ce que les Siciliens appelaient, par abus de langage, nous dit Cicéron, la *lex Rupilia* n'était probablement, comme l'a montré Michael Crawford, rien d'autre qu'un *decretum* du gouverneur de 131 av. J.-C., ayant trait à des questions de procédure impliquant des pérégrins.[78] Il n'est pas sans signification que les dispositions de cette '*lex*' *Rupilia*, selon lesquelles des Siciliens d'une même cité pouvaient se pourvoir devant un juge local, se trouvaient reprises dans l'édit de Verrès.[79] Dans l'édit publié à chaque prise de charge, aussi bien le droit local des cités que les normes romaines de toute origine recevaient alors, en quelque sorte, la légitimation de l'*imperium* du promagistrat en charge.[80] Cette confirmation devait aller de soi dans les faits, mais elle n'en semble pas moins avoir été nécessaire du point de vue du droit. Dans le même sens, des témoignages épigraphiques de peu antérieurs aux *Verrines* font état que la *sanctio* de certaines dispositions législatives, émanant en particulier du Sénat, prévoyait que l'on fît prêter serment aux magistrats en charge et à leurs successeurs de les faire appliquer.[81] Bien plus, le caractère contraignant de son propre édit sur le magistrat fait l'objet de discussions et d'une tentative de réglementation dans les années 70 av. J.-C. En effet, en 67 av. J.-C., le tribun C. Cornelius parvint à faire voter un plébiscite qui contraignait les préteurs à se conformer à leur propre édit.[82] La nécessité d'une telle disposition normative témoigne à elle seule d'une grande

76 Cic. *Ver.* 1.119, 2.30.

77 Cic. *Ver.* 2.63, 2.68, 2.81.

78 Crawford (1990) 112-13 et 119-20. Pour une reprise de la bibliographie sur le contenu et le statut de la *lex Rupilia*, Genovese (1990) 79-81 n. 10.

79 Cic. *Ver.* 2.90.

80 Cette intégration de l'édit du préteur dans le système juridique romain correspond à la reconstitution de Carcopino (1919) 73-74 et 125-26.

81 Pour une analyse de ce phénomène, *RS* I 23, et les exemples de la *lex latina tabulae Bantinae* 23-26 (*RS* I 200), loi de majesté des années 130-110 av. J.-C., et de la *lex de prouinciis praetoriis*, Delphes C 10-15 (*RS* I 251 pour le texte et 267-68 pour le commentaire, ainsi que Giuffrè (1977) 136-37 pour une traduction). Il s'agit d'une loi de répartition et d'un règlement des provinces de Cilicie et de Macédoine pour 100 av. J.-C.

82 *Lex Cornelia de iurisdictione*, Rotondi (1912) 371.

mutabilité de la norme émise par les magistrats. Cependant, d'une part, la *lex Cornelia* ne semble pas avoir porté explicitement sur les compétences des gouverneurs provinciaux; d'autre part, elle n'interdisait pas au préteur d'introduire des innovations au moment de la publication de son édit et enfin elle ne limitait pas sa capacité de publier des normes substantielles ou procédurales durant sa charge même, sous forme de *decreta*.[83]

Une approche strictement juridique pourrait sans doute inciter à évaluer la conduite de Verrès dans son administration de la justice comme une conduite qui joue avec les limites de ses possibilités d'intervention, qui subvertit les règles de la procédure sans réellement les bafouer. Au contraire, notre brève enquête sur les *Verrines* nous semble témoigner du fait que le gouverneur en vient à recourir aux menaces et à la violence pour interrompre des procédures engagées. La désignation comme collège judiciaire de sa propre cohorte apparaît alors destinée à décourager les plaignants sans sortir des formes du droit. Il ne faut pas, pour autant, sous-estimer la valeur juridique, mais dans une coloration plus politique, plus morale aussi, des accusations portées par Cicéron contre Verrès: le mépris des *instituta*, la rupture des liens de *fides* et d'*amicitia* avec les alliés, l'abus d'une position de pouvoir. Autant d'aspects qui infléchissent le procès *de repetundis*, dont les enjeux sont juridiquement seulement financiers, vers une cause pénale, dans laquelle est mise en jeu la personnalité civile du gouverneur, menacé d'*infamia*.

Du point de vue de la méthode, se dessine de la sorte une approche de la dimension juridique des *Verrines* comme sources sur les normes et les procédures en vigueur dans la province. Il s'agit moins de remonter à un état originel et supposé équitable du droit avant Verrès que de restituer un usage de la thématique juridique par Cicéron dans la construction du discours d'accusation.

Université Aix-Marseille I / CNRS – UMR 8585 Centre G. Glotz

83 A propos de l'activité législative des magistrats, Mancuso (1997) 379-86, 398 insiste sur la très grande autonomie des *decreta* du magistrat, d'après la documentation cicéronienne.

APRONIUS IN THE AGORA: SICILIAN CIVIL ARCHITECTURE AND THE *LEX HIERONICA*

MALCOLM BELL III

The *Verrines* give us occasional glimpses of the physical settings for some of the procedures of the *lex Hieronica*.[1] The town of Aetna in eastern Sicily offers one example.[2] The corrupt *decumanus* Q. Apronius has won the contract for collecting the grain tithe at Aetna, and he and his staff party in the agora to the accompaniment of music and song. A wild olive tree grows in the public square, and from its branches Apronius strings up an unhappy farmer who has come from the neighbouring city of Centuripae to protest the exactions of the *decumanus*.[3] Apronius summons a magistrate or magistrates from civic offices that are likely to have been nearby.[4] Of particular importance to his work as collector of the tithes would have been the different sorts of *litterae publicae* documenting the procedures of the tax law and requiring a secure storage place. As public documents it seems probable that they were kept in the offices of the magistrate (or magistrates) in proximity to the agora.

The public space of the agora was the normal centre of civic administration, in which we are most likely to find surviving physical evidence for the procedures of the *lex Hieronica*, as it was applied before and after the Roman conquest. This is the case at Morgantina, as I shall attempt to demonstrate. The *Verrines* make clear the importance of this central space for the work of the *decumanus*. By controlling the agora, a figure like Apronius could, in effect, command the town, as he seems to have done at Aetna. Cicero tells us that this was Apronius's standard practice, for he led his staff from place to place, ordering that *triclinia* be set up and banquets served in the agora.[5] Among the central Sicilian cities where Apronius

1 I am indebted to Jonathan Prag and Claudio Parisi Presicce for helpful suggestions.

2 On Apronius's visit to Aetna, Cic. *Ver.* 3.57, 3.61, 3.105.

3 Apronius also exercises in the palaestra at Aetna, which was probably located on the town's periphery, Cic. *Ver.* 3.61. On Sicilian gymnasia, Ferruti (2004).

4 At Cic. *Ver.* 3.105 modern editors have preferred 'vocasse at se magistratus', following the best manuscript of the *de Frumento* (Florence, Laur. Conv. Soppr. 79 = O); on the manuscript tradition of the Verrines, Reynolds (1983) 68-73. The singular *magistratum* occurs in lesser manuscripts; were it correct, the official in question might be identified with the *magistratus Siculus* referred to elsewhere (on this figure, Carcopino (1919) 33-35).

5 In one or more years of Verres' praetorship, Apronius is known to have collected tithes at Leontini, Catina, Herbita, Agyrium, Imachara, and Henna; on his practices, Cic. *Ver.* 3.65. Carcopino (1919) 270 describes these well: 'Revêtu, contrairement à l'usage, des fonctions de *praefectus*, entouré d'appariteurs, comme à Agyrium, suivi d'une bande armée comme à Herbita, escorté par une garde d'esclaves de Vénus Erycine, come à Aetna, reçu dans les cités où il passe comme un maître ou comme l'envoyé du maître, le décimateur n'a aucune audace à tout oser.'

collected tithes was Henna. It is tempting to suppose that he also did so at Morgantina, whose territory lay immediately to the east of Henna.[6] Although Cicero makes no reference to tax collection at Morgantina (or Murgentia, as he names the city), he nonetheless provides useful information for interpreting buildings in and around the city's agora, which has been extensively excavated during the past half century.

The agora at Morgantina was given its definitive form in the third century BC and thus offers evidence for the functioning of the original Greek phase of Hieron's law (Figure 1).[7] After the Roman conquest the public space continued in use, although its buildings and monuments increasingly fell into disrepair. In the later period it was probably not unlike the urban centre of the ancient and once prosperous city of Leontini, which Cicero calls 'misera [...] atque inanis'.[8] Other, older *poleis* like Megara Hyblaea, Camarina, and Selinus were no longer defined juridically as cities, their former territories evidently absorbed into those of their neighbours.[9] While some cities sank into obscurity, kept alive partly or perhaps even primarily by the city- and territory-based form of the tax law, which required local magistrates and archives, other places prospered greatly. Halaesa and Soluntum on the north coast possessed agoras that were handsomely embellished in the second or early first century BC with L-shaped stoas and other public buildings; both of these urban spaces would have formed elegant settings for the June banquets of an Apronius.[10] The late Hellenistic prosperity of Halaesa and Soluntum may be owed in good part to their location on the sea, for as ports they could be used for the export of cereals to Rome.[11] The inland city of Ietas in western Sicily bridged the early and late Hellenistic periods with an agora containing buildings dating both to the third and second centuries; some of these are likely to have served the ends of the Roman tax law.[12] Agrigentum, Acrae, and Segesta also spanned the two eras.[13] Other public spaces in Hellenistic Sicily are little known.[14]

6 Cicero twice notes the poor condition of the *ager Murgentinus* (*Ver.* 3.47, 3.103) and describes Verres' mistreatment at Syracuse of Polemarchus, a local farmer (*Ver.* 3.56).

7 On the agora at Morgantina, see Bell (1988) 338-40; Bell (2005) 166; Bell (in press).

8 Cic. *Ver.* 2.160.

9 Presumably the territory of Megara went to Syracuse, that of Camarina to Gela, and that of Selinus to Lilybaeum. There may have been a small population at Camarina: Pelagatti (1976) 128.

10 Halaesa: Carettoni (1961) 285-96; Wilson (2000) 145-47. Soluntum: Adriani *et al.* (1971); von Sydow (1984) cat. no. 40 and *passim*; Wilson (2000) 140-44. The prosperity of these cities does not appear to have been based on agriculture.

11 Halaesa as a coastal destination of grain for export, Cic. *Ver.* 3.193.

12 Ietas: Daehn (1991); Isler (2002) 113 Abb. 1; Isler (2004) 6 fig. 1; Isler (2005) 165.

13 The political agora of Agrigentum must have been located in the centre of the city in the area of the *ekklesiasterion* and the *bouleuterion*; Fiorentini (1990) 15; Fiorentini (2005) 61-63. For Acrae: Bernabò Brea (1956) 26-27. For Segesta: Vaggioli (1997); Ampolo and Parra (2005) 167-68.

14 The missing link in this picture is, of course, the agora of Syracuse, about which almost nothing certain is known on the ground; for a recent view, Campagna (2004) 157-61. For the agora at Tauromenium, Campagna (2004) 163 n. 44.

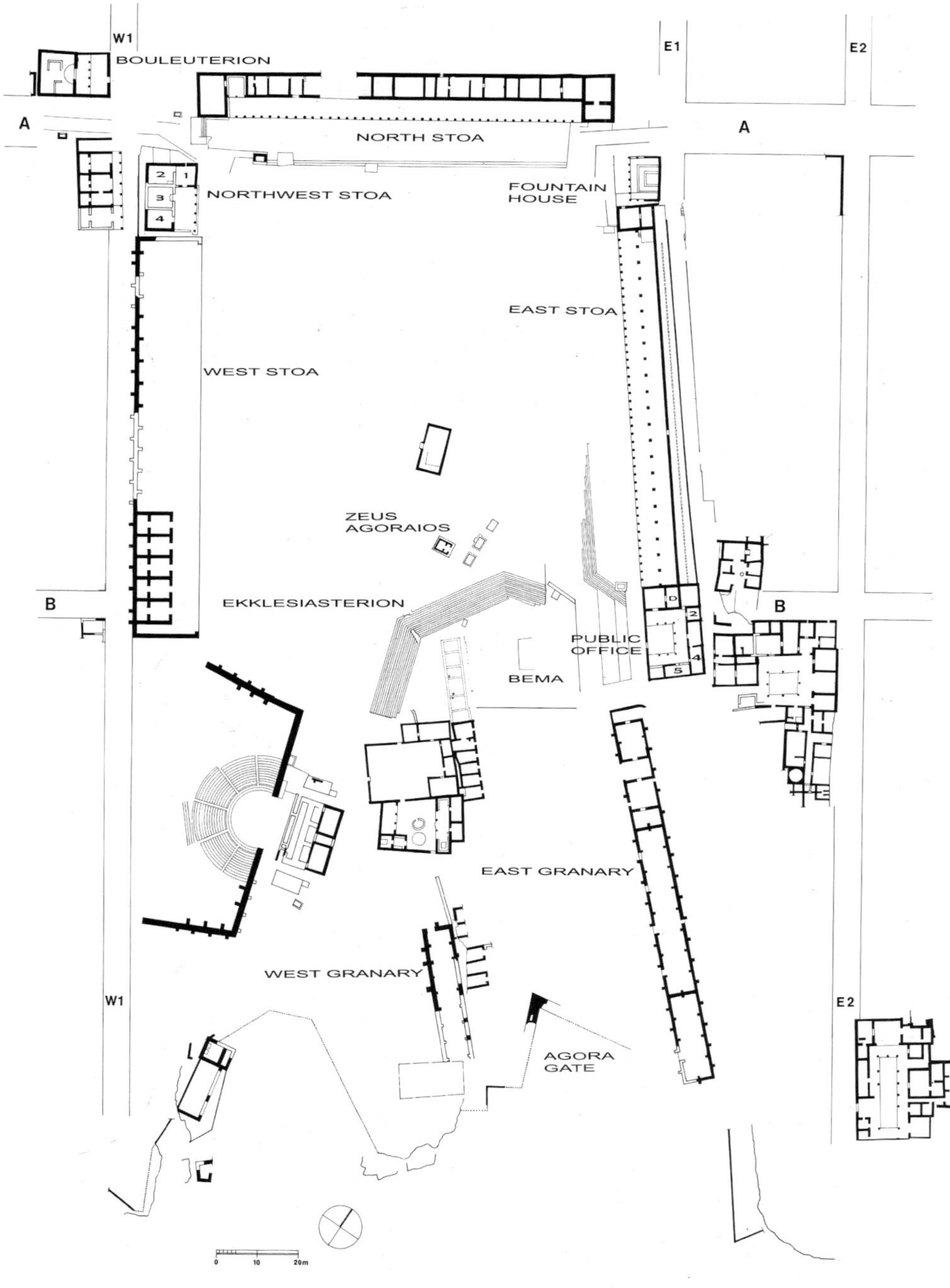

Figure 1. Plan of the agora at Morgantina, third century BC.

Although no written source tells us that Morgantina was a part of the early Hellenistic Syracusan kingdom and thus subject to Hieron's tax code, there are several reasons to believe that this was so, and it may be well to review them. 1) The city provided crucial support for Agathocles in his successful bid for power at Syracuse in 317 BC.[15] The local mint, which had been active just before this time, now ceased operation and remained closed until the end of the Hieronian period. For more than a century Syracusan coins served as the local currency.[16] The cessation of local coinage throughout the era of the city's greatest prosperity indicates a significant yielding of local autonomy.[17] 2) Morgantina appears to have followed Hieron in his long alliance with Rome, and when Hieronymus broke the alliance after his grandfather's death in 215 BC, Morgantina did so too.[18] 3) The extensive construction effort that both provided the city with its fortifications and totally transformed the agora (see Figure 1) is securely dated to the Hieronian period; for this building program to have been conceived and carried out, it is likely that outside investment was needed. Syracuse is much the most probable source for this.[19] 4) The material culture of Morgantina in the third century BC is Syracusan in character. Close parallels exist in building types, sculpture, terracotta figurines, and such household furnishings as ceramics, silver plate, and domestic *arulae*.[20] This combined evidence has convinced us that Morgantina lay within the western boundary of Hieron's kingdom.[21] If we accept this reading, Morgantina can serve as an example of a city subject to Hieron's legal and economic system: that is, to the original version of the *lex Hieronica*.

15 Diod. Sic. 19.6.2-3.

16 As is shown in Buttrey *et al.* (1989), approximately 3065 Syracusan coins dating between *c.* 317 and 215 BC (not including coins of Pyrrhus) have been found at Morgantina in the U.S. excavations from 1955-1981; roughly 74% of these are Hieronian.

17 On the closing of mints in Asia Minor following the establishment of Pergamene rule in 188 BC, Allen (1983) 109-13. On the closing of mints by the Ptolemies, Rostovtzeff (1941) III 1417; the exceptions to Ptolemaic policy (*e.g.* Ephesus, Lebedus, Miletus) are analogous in Hieronian Sicily to Tauromenium, which continued to coin.

18 Livy 24.36.10, 24.38.3, 24.39.10.

19 On Hieron's building policy: von Sydow (1984) 340-45; Bell (1999); Campagna (2004); Ferruti (2004); Karlsson (1993).

20 For building types: Bell (1993) 334-36. Terracotta figurines: Bell (1981) chapters 2 and 3. *Arulae*: Bell (1986-87) esp. 122 n. 31. Silver plate: Bell (2000) esp. 40 n. 13 (parallels for vessel forms and decorative schemes represented in the silver treasure from Morgantina now in New York).

21 The western flank of the Syracusan kingdom may then have consisted of the wheat-growing territories of Agyrium to the north, Assorus and Morgantina in the centre, and, to the south, Herbessus (Montagna di Marzo). The coastal side is defined by the cities mentioned by Diodorus (23.4.1): Leontini, Megara, Helorus, and Netum, with Acrae in the interior. Of the cities on Diodorus's list only Leontini was a major producer of wheat. More extensive cereal-growing lands under Syracusan rule better explain the need both for the *lex Hieronica* and the fortified granaries on Ortygia (Livy 24.21.12). The fullest recent discussion of the boundaries of the kingdom is Karlsson (1993) 41-45 (accepting Morgantina); see also Campagna (2004) 155-56 n. 14 (questioning Morgantina). The convincing identification of Herbessus with the city at Montagna di Marzo is owed to Manganaro (1999) 7-33. Accepting Herbessus as part of the kingdom of Hieron, de Sensi Sestito (1997) 116; rejecting Herbessus, Manganaro (1999) 16.

After the Roman capture of the city in 211 BC the local situation changed radically. Although Morgantina survived the Roman conquest in a material sense, the Morgantini did not, and they now disappear from the scene. Livy tells us that in 210 BC the city and its territory were handed over to a troop of Spanish mercenaries, and we must assume that the former inhabitants were sold into slavery or did not otherwise survive.[22] After 210 BC the extent of the area occupied by housing was much reduced. In the third century we have guessed that the total intramural population exceeded 6000.[23] The inhabited area then reached its maximum extent. A recent estimate puts the population in the following century at *c.* 2000.[24] Large portions of the city appear to have been abandoned, as were all of the neighbourhood sanctuaries of Demeter and Persephone, including those in the quarters that were reoccupied by the Hispani.[25]

Morgantina's status *vis à vis* Rome was now presumably that of a *ciuitas decumana*. We can assume that the *ager Murgentinus* continued to produce at past levels, although there appears to have been a decline in the number of small holdings. The field survey conducted by Stephen M. Thompson in 1992-94 has shown that the number of rural sites in the territory decreased significantly between the third and second centuries; the few major sites were now located in river valleys, which would also have served as communication routes leading eastward to the coast.[26] The general picture is one of consolidation of land-holdings, and there is no sign here of any large, semi-urban agricultural settlement of the sort hypothesized by Roger Wilson.[27]

This last phase of Morgantina's history as a city came to an abrupt end in the third quarter of the first century BC. Stone has argued that in the contest between Sextus Pompey and Octavian, the city took the side of the former. The sudden steep decline in population and prosperity after *c.* 30 BC would then be owed to its harsh punishment by the latter.[28] Although a remnant of the population eked out an existence into the first years of the common era, Strabo's statement that 'Morgantina was a city but exists no longer' is essentially correct.[29]

In its buildings and spaces the agora at Morgantina thus appears to document some of the conditions of the original code of Hieron, and, because it continues in use down to the time of Cicero and just beyond, it also exemplifies a setting for the procedures of the Roman

22 Livy 26.21.17. The discovery at Morgantina of many buried or hidden coin hoards and other objects of value dating to the time of the Second Punic War clearly suggests that their owners were never able to regain them, and so must have perished or been enslaved.

23 The projected population of *c.* 6000 is based on the available number of house lots (*c.* 1200) and a household size of *c.* five persons (not counting slaves); for household size: Gallant (1991) 11-33. See also the comparable estimates for Olynthus: Cahill (2002) 40-41.

24 Stone (2002) 149.

25 On the abandonment of the North and South Sanctuaries after 211 BC: White (1964).

26 Thompson (1999) 444-57.

27 Wilson (1990) 23, 155.

28 Stone (2002). The excavated coins support Stone's view: between 1955 and 1981, 219 coins of Sextus Pompey were found, as compared to 43 for the entire reign of Augustus (Buttrey *et al.* (1989) 126-29).

29 Strabo 6.2.4.

version of the law, serving as a stage for the activities of men like Apronius. At the start of Hieron's long reign the agora was mostly a huge *tabula rasa* of some 30,000 m^2, its boundaries originally laid out more than a century earlier.[30] Development finally came in the second quarter of the third century, when a carefully devised monumental plan was adopted, evidently at a single moment (Figure 1).[31] The largest building, a two-storey stoa of Pergamene type, was still unfinished in 211 BC when the city was captured by Marcellus's successor M. Cornelius Cethegus. Construction was never resumed.[32] It seems likely that adoption of the monumental plan was a consequence of Syracusan investment in the city, perhaps following upon Hieron's settlement with Rome in 262 BC. The initial phase of construction in the agora can be dated to 260-240 BC; in the ensuing period, down to the death of the king in 215 BC, there were several modifications to the original scheme, the basic lines of which continued to be followed. The changes must reflect a growing population. Two of them, as will be seen, seem to document a local response to Hieron's taxation law.

The building program shows first that Morgantina possessed several otherwise unattested civic institutions. The *bouleuterion* in the north-west corner of the public space and the *ekklesiasterion* in the centre indicate the existence of council and assembly.[33] Other political institutions include a court, or *dikasterion*, at the north end of the East Stoa, shown by the presence of a *bema* and adjacent chambers; and a space (*archeia*?) for the display of public documents, in room 4 of the North-West Stoa. Three sets of paired holes, and three single holes, in the fine white stucco surface of the west wall of room 4 can be interpreted as having served for the mounting and display of rectangular bronze tablets (Figure 2).[34] The holes were packed with pieces of bronze wire to provide purchase for the nails attaching the tablets to the wall. The tablets must have been melted down after 211 BC by the Hispani, who are unlikely to have had any interest in Greek public documents beyond their intrinsic value as metal. Two

30 The agora at Morgantina is one of the largest known in Sicily, in area exceeded apparently only by the recently discovered agora of Selinus. For the early agora at Morgantina, see Bell (in press).

31 Bell (1993) 328-31.

32 For the West Stoa, Bell (1988) 338.

33 Civic inscriptions from Agrigentum, Entella, and Nakone show that the citizen assembly in these Doric-speaking cities was called the ἁλία, and this is likely also to have been the case at Morgantina (on these inscriptions see the following note). The conventional term *ekklesiasterion* has been retained to designate the actual meeting place.

34 The distances between the paired holes are as follows: a) 0.135 m, b) 0.227 m, and c) 0.23 m. Tablet c) at Morgantina may have been similar in design and proportions to the rectangular bronze tablet Nakone A (Ampolo = *SEG* 30.1119), which was intended to be attached to a wall in the temple of Zeus Olympios by two nails, the holes for which are located at the top of the tablet *c*. 0.20-0.21 m apart: Ampolo, Magnetto, and Porciani (2001) esp. 5; also Ampolo *et al.* (2001) 26 (photograph of Nakone A). The two nail-holes for Morgantina b) are not quite level, like the holes in Entella tablets A3 (= *SEG* 35.999) and C3 (= *SEG* 30.1118). Six of the Entella tablets with triangular 'pediments' were instead attached with three nails, one in the pediment and two at the bottom; the same holds for at least one of the Corcyra tablets (*IG* IX i 686). Other tablets with pediments were attached with four nails (*IG* IX i 682, from Corcyra; Entella B1 = *SEG* 30.1120). On bronze tablets: Manganaro (1963). A similar wall with holes, possibly for tablets, is found in the Hestiaterion at Palike: Maniscalco and McConnell (2003) 173 with fig. 22. An external wall in the 'forum' at Assisi has holes for tablets ranging in size from 0.25 by 0.20 m. to 1.30 by 0.70 m: Gros and Theodorescu (1985) figs 2 and 4.

Figure 2. West wall of room 4, North-West Stoa, with nail-holes and tablets in outline.

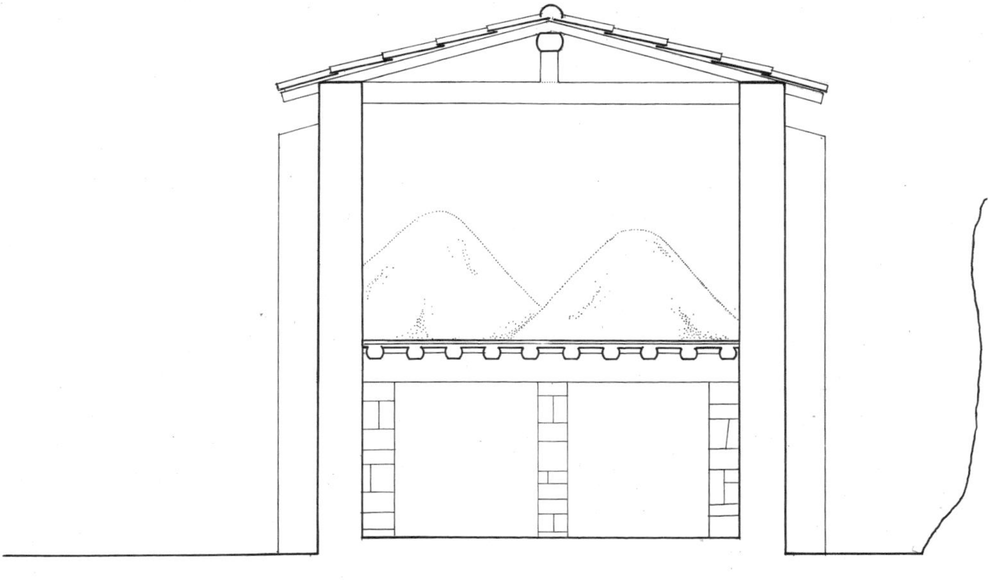

Figure 3. Reconstructed section through East Granary (drawing by J. Mygatt).

surviving beam sockets in the south wall of the same room suggest the installation of heavy wooden cabinets, possibly for the storage of other records. A bronze compass was found in this room.

Three public buildings can be interpreted as manifestations of local compliance with Hieron's agrarian law. The lower agora was dominated by two parallel granaries of similar design: long, narrow structures with walls strengthened by internal and external buttresses (Figures 1, 3).[35] The older and smaller building, which may be pre-Hieronian, lies to the west. Across the lower agora, just inside the city gate, is the larger and better built East Granary, which belongs to the initial phase of the Hieronian program. My colleague Paul W. Deussen is preparing the final report. At first the East Granary consisted of the two large southern rooms, one twice the size of the other. Later in the century four smaller rooms were added at the north end.[36] The larger rooms were probably used for storage of different cereals, presumably barley and wheat. The smaller rooms may have been needed for the other agricultural products that were also taxed, such as beans, or have served administrative purposes.[37]

The presence of two granaries with rooms that may have been used for specialized storage also suggests the possibility that certain categories or quantities of the stored grain had different destinations, some intended for Hieron's massive granaries on Ortygia, which are mentioned by Livy, some for local use.[38] From Livy we also know that a 'great quantity of grain' was stored at Morgantina in 213 BC for provisioning Roman troops.[39] However, the initial purpose of the granaries at Morgantina, as of analogous buildings elsewhere in the kingdom, must have been to provide secure storage for the cereals and other produce either owed to Hieron or acquired by the city through the procedures of the tax code. As Erik Sjöqvist and Paul Deussen have seen, the granaries offer important, if only partially understood, evidence for the functioning of the original taxation law at the local level.

Immediately north of the East Granary, overlooking the *ekklesiasterion*, is the peristyle building we have called a Public Office, which resembles similar structures adjacent to the Hellenistic agoras of Ietas in western Sicily and Cassope in Epirus (Figure 4).[40] Archaeological probes carried out in the summer of 2004 showed that the Public Office was constructed in the second half of the third century BC. The building can thus be assigned to the second phase of the Hieronian program. It took over the two existing rooms at the south

35 Deussen (1994); Sjöqvist (1960) 131; Bell (1988) 321-24.

36 The careful orientation of the southern rooms argues that the northern addition was planned from the start.

37 Fava beans (κύαμοι) and millet (μελίνη) are mentioned in the Tauromenium account tablets (*SEG* 38 (1988) 973): Fantasia (1999) esp. 253-56; on millet: Nenci (1989).

38 Livy 24.21.12. Cities could hold the contract for the collection of their own tithe (Cic. *Ver.* 3.99, Thermae Himerenses intending to bid on its tithes); in such cases the percentage retained by the *decumanus*, paid in kind, would have required adequate public storage.

39 Livy 24.39.10, 'magna uis frumenti commeatusque'.

40 No evidence supports the original designation of this building as a *prytaneion*; doubting the early identification: Miller (1978) 116-17, 126-27. For Ietas: Isler (1994) 33-35. For Cassope: Hoepfner and Schwandner (1986) 98-101.

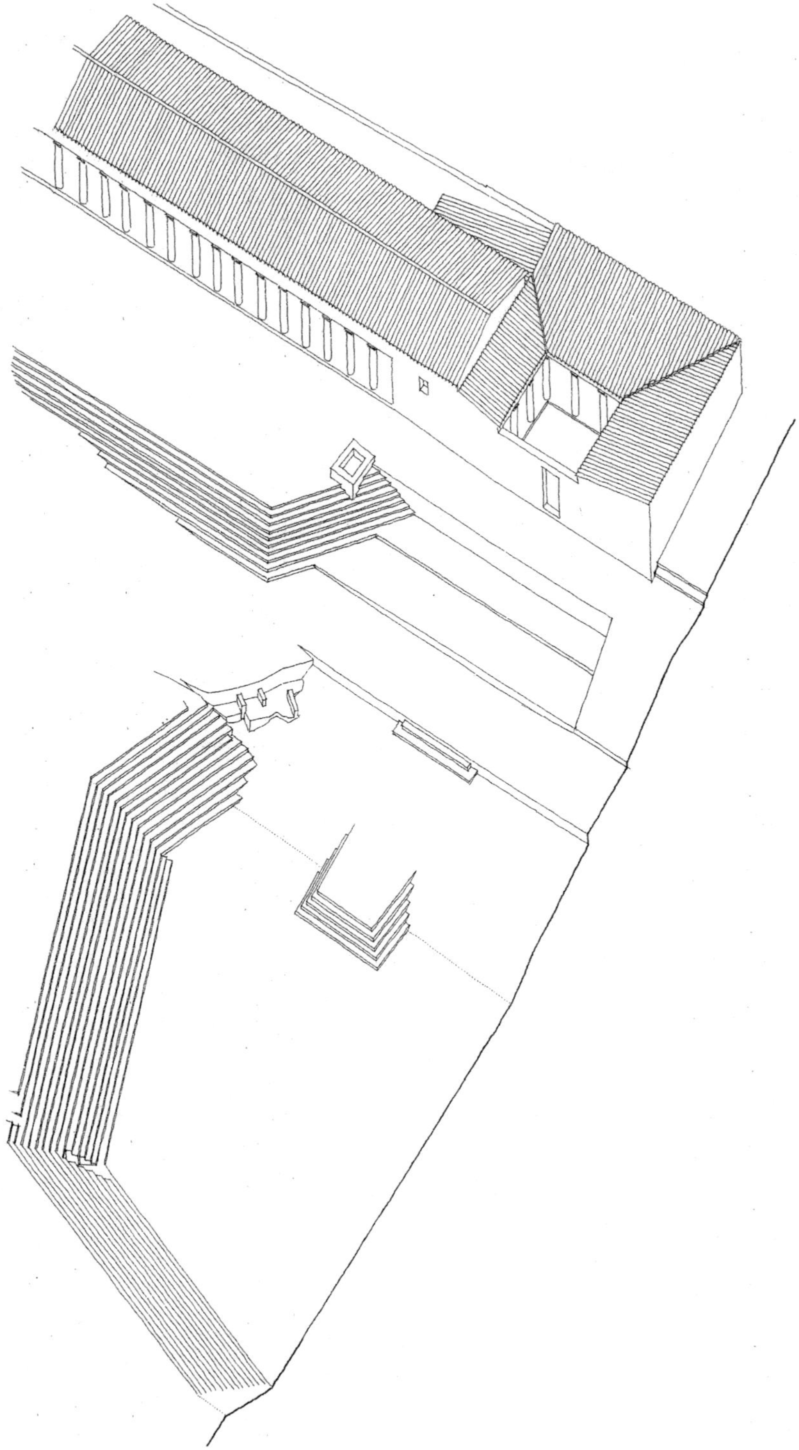

Figure 4. Axonometric reconstruction of the Public Office and *Ekklesiasterion* (drawing by Erik Thorkildsen).

Figure 5. Reconstruction of the façade of room 5, Public Office (drawing by Erik Thorkildsen).

end of the East Stoa; these now opened on the north arm of a peristyle court, with five new rooms occupying the other two arms (see plan, Figure 1, p. 119).

The Public Office is sufficiently well preserved to allow us to propose uses for several of the rooms. The principal evidence consists of large windows giving on the peristyle in rooms D, 2, and 4; and a series of very narrow windows, probably six in number, in room 5 (Figure 5). In all of these rooms the windows appear to have served as counters over which business could be transacted. Most interesting are the narrow windows in room 5, each centred on a round, basin-like cavity within the room, cut into a projecting course of limestone blocks (Figure 6). In the floor of this room are two stone-lined trenches, the side walls of which are offset at the top to allow for a cover of flat stone slabs or heavy boards. The narrow windows (w. 0.17-0.18 m) show that whatever passed through them was small in size and that there was evidently a need for security. The three surviving 'basins' are all cut at the joins of the limestone blocks and so can hardly have been used to contain liquids, although terracotta bowls could have been placed within them. The projection of this course on the interior suggests that functionaries could have sat on stools at each window, their knees conveniently placed beneath the 'basins'.

I have recently argued that this public building within the agora should be identified as a bank, operated either by the city as a *demosia trapeza*, or by the kingdom itself as a *basilike trapeza*.[41] Although no written source confirms the existence of a royal Hieronian bank, I favour that hypothesis for the following reasons: 1) the complex Hieronian tax law is likely to have created a need for an institution to deal with deposits, loans, and exchange; 2) the circulation throughout the kingdom of the Hieronian gold, silver, and bronze coinage argues for the existence of a central financial institution;[42] 3) a *basilike trapeza* is attested for Egypt,

41 Bell (2004a). For similar installations in private houses of the second century BC: Bell (2004b).

42 The Hieronian coinage is the subject of a recent general study: Caccamo Caltabiano (1995).

Figure 6. Room 5 of the Public Office, from the south.

where papyrus records have survived.[43] There is no comparable paper trail in Sicily, but the absence of evidence is hardly proof of non-existence. Rostovtzeff suggested that such a bank might have existed in early Hellenistic Pergamum, and there seems no *a priori* reason to exclude one in Sicily, especially given what we know of the Hieronian law.[44] Moreover, Hieron's commercial, political, and cultural relations with Egypt are well known.[45] We can also note that branches of the Ptolemaic bank are attested in quite distant subject cities.[46] Finally, 4) a curious architectural detail: the front door of the building giving on to the agora was intentionally placed off-centre by more than a metre, making it coincide precisely with the axis of the *bema* of the *ekklesiasterion* (Figure 4). Through this axial relationship the Public Office thus appears in some sense to 'control' the speaker, a circumstance that may be emblematic of actual royal limitation on the autonomy of the *ekklesia*, as might be expected in a subject city within the kingdom. This relationship may then suggest that the Public Office was the seat of some external authority.

The curious installations in room 5 seem well adapted for financial operations: the narrow windows offered security; the basins can be read as the tills of cashiers engaged in various financial operations; and the trenches in the floor of this room could have served as a kind of safe-deposit vault. Similar features (though not the trenches) recur in second-century BC houses at Soluntum, which I have argued should be identified as residences of *faeneratores* or bankers.[47]

If room 5 of the Public Office served as a bank, could rooms D, 2, and 4 have functioned as offices for the magistrate(s) and scribes engaged in the various operations of the original taxation law? One is tempted to interpret the Public Office as the sort of public structure required for the maintenance and storage of the extensive *litterae publicae* called for by the provisions of Hieron's code.[48] In need of such protection would have been the *subscriptiones aratorum*, the *professiones iugerum*, and the local copies of the *pactiones* drawn up between the farmers and the tax collectors. Cicero shows us that at least some of these records were maintained over time, since he can compare figures from one year to the next.[49] Such documents must have been

43 Rostovtzeff (1941) II 1282-88; Bogaert (1981); Bogaert (1983).

44 Rostovtzeff (1941) II 1287-88.

45 Moschion's description of the *Syrakosia*, Ath. 5.206d-209b. In general Caccamo Caltabiano (1995) esp. 157-79 (E. C. Portale, 'Problemi del mosaico ellenistico in Sicilia, rapporti con Alessandria'); Pantos (1987), for occurrence of the artist's name Sosis in Alexandria and Syracuse. On the relationship of the *lex Hieronica* to the tax law of Ptolemy Philadelphus: Carcopino (1919) 57-70; Rostovtzeff (1941) I 337, 395; de Sensi Sestito (1977) 156-58. Sixty-four Ptolemaic Zeus/eagle bronzes (*c.* 271-246 BC) were found at Morgantina between 1955 and 1981 (Buttrey *et al.* (1989) 118 no. 482); from these we can infer local trade with Egypt during the Hieronian period.

46 Rostovtzeff (1941) III 1418, citing *P. Cairo Zen.* 59036, regarding the Ptolemaic bank in Halicarnassus.

47 Bell (2004b). It may be significant that the demotic Egyptian word for bank/*trapeza* can denote a table with four legs supporting a basin: Vergote (1984) 232.

48 These are the sorts of documents discussed by Jean Andreau, 'Registers, account-books, and written documents in the *de Frumento*', in this volume.

49 Cic. *Ver.* 3.117, 3.120-21.

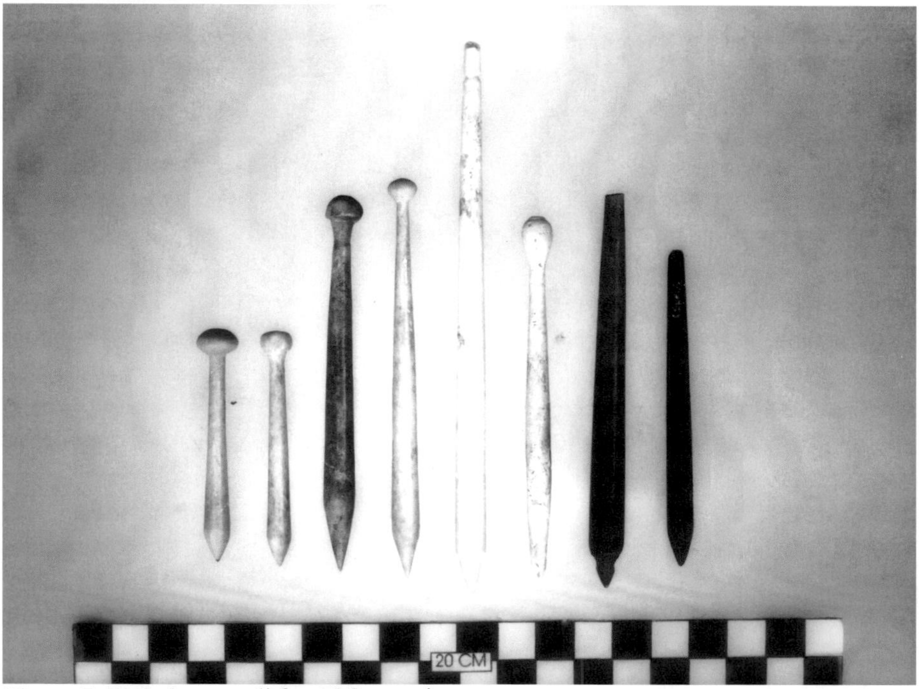

Figure 7. Eight bone styli from Morgantina.

very numerous in the third century BC, when it also seems that there were more small holdings than in the later period.

The *litterae publicae* used for the documentation of the *lex Hieronica* may have taken the form of bulky wooden-leaf tablets or wax tablets, but papyrus records seem equally possible.[50] There is a good deal of evidence at Morgantina for both methods of writing: bone *styli* for writing on wax are very common (Figure 7), and inkwells, which would have been used for writing on wooden-leaf tablets or papyrus, have also been found (Figure 8). One such container dedicated to Demeter and Persephone belonged to a scribe called Antallos, who scratched on its underside his own name as well as the local word for inkwell (μελανόβαφον).[51] The extensive use of papyrus in mid-third-century Sicily is attested by the *c.* 600 clay seal-impressions found in the nineteenth century on the south steps of Temple C at Selinus, which bear the imprint of papyrus on their reverse sides (Figure 9). With two seals per papyrus roll, they indicate the existence of at least 300 documents belonging to an archive that must have been maintained in the temple and that was burned during, or immediately following, the Roman capture of Selinus in 250 BC.[52] Temples often served as banks during the classical and

50 On the public records: Butler (2002) 36-39 and *passim*; Meyer (2004) 21-43, 125-68, and *passim*.

51 The term is a *hapax*; see Sjöqvist (1959) and *IGDS* no. 192. Antallos's inkwell is on the right in figure 8. *Cf.* de Juliis (1984) 494 no. 72 = Graepler (1997) 99 no. 615 (from Tarentum, 175-100 BC); A. M. Bisi, *NSc* (1971) 127 fig. 66 (from Lilybaeum).

52 On the seals from Temple C: *NSc* (1877) 71; *NSc* (1882) 325; A. Salinas, *NSc* (1883) 288; A. Salinas, *NSc* (1898) 224; F. S. Cavallari, *Archivio Storico Siracusano*, n. s. VII (1882) 97-98 (important for the precise provenience); Zoppi (1996).

Figure 8. Two inkwells from Morgantina (left: 58-547; right: 58-536).

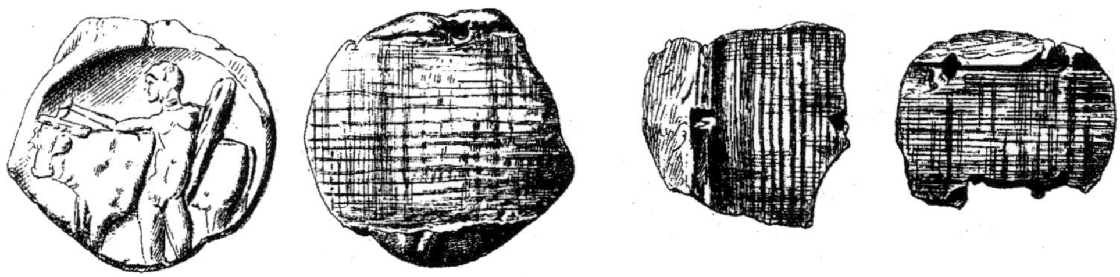

Figure 9. Papyrus impressions on clay seals from Selinus (after *NSc* 1883, tav. VII).

Hellenistic periods, and it seems quite possible that this collection of documents from Temple C was a banking archive. As for the availability of papyrus in Sicily, Hieron's close relations with Egypt may have assured him of the needed supply. Perhaps we should reconsider the old idea that the naturalized papyrus that grows in the Anapos basin south of Syracuse, first attested in the seventeenth century CE, is descended from plants sent to Hieron from Egypt.[53]

The Public Office and East Granary at Morgantina are adjacent contemporary structures which provide possible architectural evidence for the sort of legal and financial system documented in contemporary Egypt in written records on papyrus. It may be significant for our reading of these structures that the Ptolemaic papyri describe an economic system that encompasses both a royal bank and royal granaries, institutions that were parallel and related, yet also autonomous.[54]

53 The first attested observation of *Cyperus papyrus L.* in Sicily is in 972-73 CE at Palermo, by Ibn Haukal, a merchant from Baghdad: Lewis (1974) 18-20; also, Lewis (1989) 12-13 (scepticism regarding an introduction in antiquity). The first record of papyrus growing at Syracuse appears to be by the naturalist Paolo Boccone, *Recherches et observations de Monsieur Boccone touchant* [...] *les plantes qu'on trouve dans la Sicile* [...] (Amsterdam 1674). See also Malerba (1968); Ragab (1980) 91-94 (introduction in Sicily at an uncertain date). It remains to be established whether the plant was introduced at Syracuse in antiquity, by the Arabs in the tenth century or later, or in more recent times.

54 Banks and granaries: Rostovtzeff (1941) I 406-07, with n. 204; II 1283, 1286-87.

Figure 10. *Ekklesiasterion*/assembly place from west; the base for an equestrian statue can be seen at foreground right.

Although the buildings of the agora at Morgantina survived the year 211 BC, thereafter major changes ensue. While the city may not have descended to the vestigial condition of Leontini, by the time of Verres it is evident that maintenance of public buildings had greatly declined. The hall of the East Stoa, or *dikasterion*, had fallen into ruin and was used in part as a stable; the hall of the North Stoa had been taken down. Nine of the fifteen steps of the *ekklesiasterion* were now buried under alluvial earth (Figure 11), as were the Central and South Shops in the lower agora. Commercial activity was centred in the single new public building of the second century BC, a closed market, or *macellum*, placed somewhat incongruously on the terrace above the *ekklesiasterion*. In addition to its political and commercial functions, the agora now became an active industrial centre. Potters' workshops were installed in such public buildings as the North Stoa, the former *dikasterion* or East Stoa, and the late third-century addition to the East Granary; and a fourth, the largest, was added just outside the City Gate (this last also making use of the smaller southern chamber (A) of the East Granary).[55] Still in use in the early first century BC were the Fountain House, theatre, and the diminished *ekklesiasterion*.

Also functioning, and important for the *lex Hieronica*, were the Public Office and probably the large central room of the East Granary. The sills of the narrow windows in room 5 of the Public Office show such extensive wear that we must assume a long period of use. It thus seems likely that the original function of this room continued into the new era. If the *trapeza* in room 5 remained in operation, probably the other adjacent offices did too. There would still

55 For the pottery kilns: Cuomo di Caprio (1993).

have been need for a secure place in which to keep the written records required by the *lex Hieronica*. The survival of this building was thus called for by the Roman adoption of Hieron's code.

The situation of the public granaries is somewhat different. The old West Granary was abandoned immediately after the Roman conquest, and the rooms at either extremity of the East Granary now had new industrial uses. It seems that only the large central room of the East Granary may still have functioned as a warehouse for the tithe. Since cereal production in the *ager Murgentinus* is likely to have remained more or less constant, we must assume the existence of private granaries in the rural farms, and it would have been from those, and not from the urban granaries of the Hieronian period, that the majority of the tithe was exported to the coast in the *deportatio ad aquam* described by Cicero.[56]

If a *decumanus* like Q. Apronius came to Morgantina to collect the tithe – let us say in 71 BC – and set up *triclinia* in the agora, it seems likely that he would have done so in the area of the *ekklesiasterion*, below the Public Office and near the East Granary. The city's magistrate(s) and *litterae publicae* were probably close by. From here he could look back over, and perhaps intimidate, the civic assembly. Such a tax collector – let us imagine he was Apronius – will also have observed across the broad space the bronze statue that stood on a high rectangular base facing the assembly (Figures 10-12).[57] The base rests on foundations laid over the seventh and eighth steps of the *ekklesiasterion*, thus rising from the new level of the early first century BC. The rubble packing of the core of the base contained two bronze coins of the late second or early first century: one an issue of the Hispani of Morgantina, the other an Apollo/Isis of Catina (the most common coin at Morgantina in the later period).[58] This numismatic evidence confirms the dating of the base to the period around or after 100 BC.

As the proportions of the shaft of the statue base are those for an equestrian sculpture, we may wonder what mounted figure our *decumanus* saw there, dominating the assembly?[59] It is, of course, tempting to propose that it was C. Verres, who, as Cicero tells us in the second oration of the *Actio secunda*, forced the Sicilian cities, even poor and inconsequential places like Leontini, to erect portrait sculptures of himself.[60] Most, if not all, of these sculptures are likely to have been of bronze, and some were mounted. Cicero specifically mentions equestrian

56 A granary-like structure, similar in design to the buildings at Morgantina, has recently been excavated at the Roman imperial farm site of Casalgismondo, in the valley east of Morgantina.

57 On bronze as the preferred material for equestrian sculptures: Bergemann (1990) 20-23; Luni (2001) 22-24.

58 The latest coins from the base are find no. 85-79, obv.: head of Apollo facing left / rev.: standing Isis (Catina, second-century BC; Buttrey *et al.* (1989) no. 141); and no. 85-82, obv.: head of Minerva left / rev.: horseman (Morgantina, *Hispanorum*, later second-century BC; Buttrey *et al.* (1989) no. 249).

59 The large Morgantina base (shaft 1.26 m by 3.05 m, proportions roughly 2:5) has parallels at Gortyn (Bergemann (1990) E115: 2.1 m by 3.40 m, first-century CE), at Kaunos (Bergemann (1990) E116: plinth 1.04 m by 2.34 m, first-century BC), and at Veleia (Bergemann (1990) E50: shaft *c.* 0.96 m by 2.16 m, first-century CE). It is uncertain whether the plinth of the Morgantina statue would have been larger or smaller than the shaft, which is constructed of rubble masonry and was originally plastered.

60 Cic. *Ver.* 2.141-65.

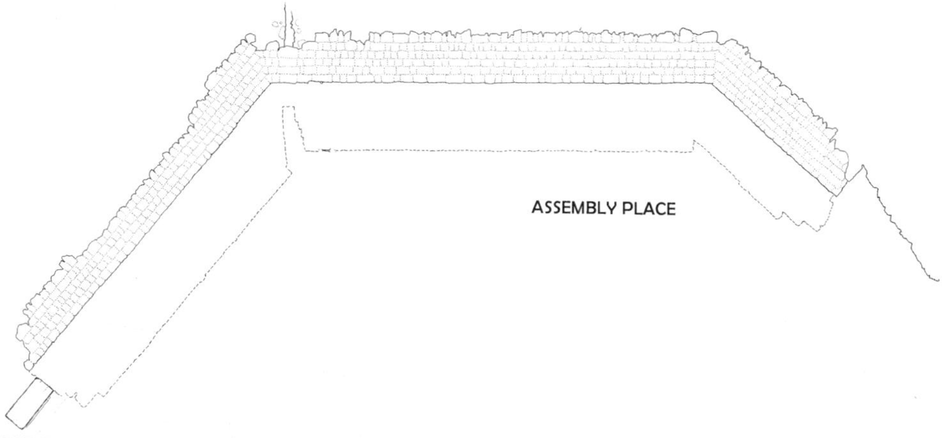

Figure 11. Plan of the assembly place at Morgantina, first century BC.

Figure 12. Base for equestrian statue in the assembly place, *c.* 100 BC or later.

statues of Verres in the agoras of Tyndaris and Syracuse.[61] The placement of the base at Morgantina suggests that the sculpture was intended to dominate the assembly. If it indeed depicted the praetor C. Verres, it may have been short-lived. We cannot say whether the Hispani of Morgantina were impetuous enough to participate in the widespread iconoclasm that followed upon the governor's departure at the end of 71 BC, or whether the sculpture was

61 Cic. *Ver*. 2.154 (Syracuse); 2.160 (Tyndaris).

destroyed when the city was abandoned some forty years later.[62] All that we know is that the base itself survived for several decades, down until the time of Sextus Pompey's duel with Octavian, after which it and the remaining steps of the assembly place were rapidly buried in rain-borne alluvial earth carried down through the abandoned city.

While the visit to Morgantina by Apronius is hypothetical, the base for an equestrian sculpture is real, and the dating evidence does not exclude Verres. A statue of the praetor in the agora of a Sicilian city (at Tyndaris, at Syracuse, perhaps at Morgantina) would be in some way analogous to the performative aspects of Apronius's visits to Aetna and the other cities.[63] Through his permanent sculptural 'presence' in the city centre the governor could claim legitimacy for his administration. Viewed in this light, the extraordinary pair of gilt bronze equestrian statues of the governor near the temple of Vulcan in Rome, paid for under duress by the Sicilian *aratores* and bearing the inscription 'A COMMVNI SICILIAE DATAE', is brazenly consistent.[64]

University of Virginia

62 In 70 BC Cicero saw some of Verres' portrait sculptures lying about where they had recently been thrown down; at Tauromenium the base of one was intentionally left standing in the agora (Cic. *Ver.* 2.158-60).

63 Wilson (2000) 146 has suggested that one of the statue bases in the agora of Halaesa could have borne a portrait of Verres.

64 Cicero refers repeatedly to Verres' gilt statues in Rome (Cic. *Ver.* 2.114, 2.145, 2.150, 2.154), which were set up 'propter aedem Volcani' (2.150). This passage has been taken to refer to the temple of Vulcan that stood either in the Campus Martius or the Circus Flaminius; but recently Shane Butler has suggested that the statues may instead have stood near the Volcanal in the Roman Forum, and so would have been visible to Cicero's audience at the trial (Butler (2002) 130 n. 90); on Verres' Roman sculptures: Bergemann (1990) 35; L15, L41, L43.

LA LOI DE HIÉRON ET LES ROMAINS DE JÉRÔME CARCOPINO: *ALTERTUMSWISSENSCHAFT* ET HISTOIRE ÉCONOMIQUE EN FRANCE AU DÉBUT DU 20E SIÈCLE[1]

JÉRÔME FRANCE

L'histoire du *de frumento* de Cicéron est étroitement liée au livre que Jérôme Carcopino lui consacra, il y aura bientôt un siècle, et il demeure à vrai dire impossible aujourd'hui d'entreprendre un travail sur le troisième discours de la seconde action des *Verrines* sans cet indispensable compagnon qu'est *La loi de Hiéron et les Romains*. On a pu présenter cet ouvrage comme un livre à part dans la production de Carcopino,[2] mais c'est en partie inexact. En effet, ce livre doit plutôt être défini comme un aboutissement précoce, celui des recherches entreprises par le jeune et brillant historien, formé à toutes les disciplines des sciences de l'Antiquité, sur le thème de la fiscalité et de l'histoire agraire. Ces recherches s'étalent sur une quinzaine d'années, entrecoupées par la guerre,[3] entre 1905, date de ses premiers articles consacrés à la Sicile dans les *Mélanges d'archéologie et d'histoire*, et 1922, avec son article 'Fermier général ou sociétés publicaines'. C'est là sa dernière publication spécifique sur ce thème dont il s'éloigna ensuite, sans toutefois l'abandonner totalement. Le livre *La loi de Hiéron et les Romains* est lui-même issu de son mémoire de l'École française de Rome,

1 Je remercie Claude Nicolet dont les conseils ont été déterminants pour la réalisation de ce travail et Jean-Louis Ferrary qui a accepté de le relire et dont les suggestions m'ont été très utiles. Un premier état en a été présenté lors d'une séance du programme 'Notions et comportements économiques' dirigé par Jean Andreau, dans le cadre du Centre Gustave Glotz, et il a bénéficié des remarques et des observations de Jean Andreau, Véronique Chankowski, Monique Dondin-Payre, Sylvie Pittia, Jean-Manuel Roubineau et Nicolas Tran. Il a également fait l'objet d'une communication au colloque *Sicilia nutrix plebis Romanae*, organisé en février 2004 par Jonathan Prag à l'Institute of Classical Studies de Londres, bénéficiant cette fois des suggestions de Michael Crawford. Je remercie mesdames Mireille Pastoureau, Fabienne Queyroux et Mireille Lamarque de leur accueil et de leur aide dans mes recherches à la bibliothèque et aux archives de l'Institut de France.

2 Corcy-Debray (2001) 455. Le livre de Stéphanie Corcy-Debray est issu d'une thèse de doctorat consacrée à Jérôme Carcopino. Je suis extrêmement redevable à ce travail qui est nourri d'une information abondante et sûre, mais qui présente, pour la partie concernant la formation, la carrière et l'oeuvre de l'historien, des faiblesses de méthode et des interprétations que je ne partage pas.

3 Carcopino fut mobilisé dès les premiers jours et servit durant toute la durée de la guerre, principalement sur le front d'Orient.

déposé à l'Institut en 1907,[4] et il a été soutenu en Sorbonne comme thèse complémentaire le 12 décembre 1919. Cependant, il était à cette date achevé depuis longtemps. En effet, il avait reçu le permis d'imprimer du recteur Louis Liard dès le 12 décembre 1912 et il le fut effectivement en 1914. Sa publication n'intervint toutefois qu'en 1919.[5] Le temps réel que Jérôme Carcopino consacra à ces questions couvre donc moins d'une dizaine d'années, et ce sont des années de jeunesse puisque *La loi de Hiéron* a été conçu et écrit alors qu'il avait entre 24 et 31 ans, et publié alors qu'il en avait 39.

L'enquête de Carcopino sur la loi d'Hiéron et les dîmes de Sicile prend place dans un contexte historiographique marqué, dans le domaine de l'histoire ancienne, par un élargissement vers le domaine des faits économiques et sociaux. On connaît bien sûr les débats à travers lesquels certains historiens et économistes allemands, à la fin du XIXe siècle, se sont opposés sur la question de la nature de l'économie antique. Cette démarche théorique a profondément influencé les études économiques sur l'Antiquité tout au long du XXe siècle. Toutefois, elle ne doit pas faire négliger l'émergence parallèle, dans les années 1890 et 1900 et en particulier en France, de tendances nouvelles qui, tout en restant liées à l'approche institutionnelle et juridique qui avait été celle des grands maîtres de la génération précédente, commençaient à aborder des sujets sous un angle plus spécifiquement économique. D'autre part, Carcopino entre dans la carrière au moment où la prééminence allemande dans les études anciennes est à son zénith. Dans une ambiance encore fortement marquée par la compétition entre les établissements et les savants français et allemands, les choix qu'a pu faire le jeune historien en matière de recherche et de publication n'ont certainement pas été étrangers au souci qu'il avait de se mesurer avec les maîtres de l'*Altertumswissenschaft*.

A travers une présentation de ce contexte scientifique et académique, je voudrais établir ici ce qui a amené Jérôme Carcopino à travailler sur la loi d'Hiéron et le texte de Cicéron. Plus précisément, il s'agit d'essayer de remonter à l'origine de ce sujet et d'identifier le ou les maîtres duquel ou desquels il l'a reçu. D'autre part, je voudrais aussi mesurer la place que tint cette enquête durant ses premières années de travail et de carrière, et définir celle qu'elle occupe dans la production historiographique du début du XXe siècle.

I. L'histoire ancienne et les études économiques et sociales au début du XXe siècle

Il est inutile de revenir ici sur le développement épistémologique et scientifique de l'histoire économique de l'Antiquité. Les étapes en ont été retracées, depuis les érudits des XVIe-XVIIIe siècles qui ont forgé les outils de la critique historique tout en abordant sans recul les réalités de l'économie antique, et les doutes, finalement surmontés, des précurseurs de la science économique et des premiers économistes, jusqu'aux livres d'Auguste Boeckh et d'Adolphe Dureau de La Malle, publiés respectivement en 1817 et 1840.[6] Claude Nicolet a estimé que ces deux livres avaient permis à l'histoire économique de l'Antiquité de conquérir sa

4 Sous le titre *La lex Hieronica et son application par les Romains*; *cf.* École française de Rome (1987) 24.

5 C'est pour cette raison que la première édition de 1914 porte la date de 1919 sur la couverture. Le livre a fait l'objet d'une réimpression anastatique en 1965.

6 Boeckh (1817); Dureau de La Malle (1840). Je me réfère ici au bilan réalisé par Nicolet (1988) 13 *sq.* qui donne l'essentiel de la bibliographie sur cette question.

légitimité. On ne saurait en douter, mais on ne peut pas ignorer pourtant que cette légitimité a été longue à s'imposer. En effet, dans le grand essor des études anciennes qui marque la deuxième moitié du XIXe siècle, et que sanctionne le Prix Nobel reçu par Theodor Mommsen en 1903, l'histoire de l'économie et de la société demeure un parent pauvre. Par rapport aux avancées décisives réalisées dans l'histoire des institutions et des faits politiques, elle a souffert d'un certain désintérêt et d'un scepticisme dont les causes tenaient bien sûr à une surévaluation de l'histoire politique et à une vision hypercritique convaincue de la définitive insuffisance des sources en ce domaine mais aussi, certainement, à un manque de connaissances et de concepts appropriés.

En 1904, au moment où Jérôme Carcopino vient d'être reçu premier à l'agrégation d'histoire et d'entrer à l'École française de Rome, les choses ont cependant commencé à changer. Depuis les années 1890, les questions économiques et sociales font l'objet de recherches et provoquent des débats animés, notamment en Allemagne. On ne s'étendra pas sur la querelle qui, en opposant l'économiste Karl Bücher et sa théorie des trois stades de l'évolution économique à l'historien Eduard Meyer, relançait le débat déjà ancien entre 'primitivistes' et 'modernistes',[7] car l'écho de ces débats ne parvint que très assourdi en France, et n'y pénétra pas le milieu des antiquisants.[8] Il est logique que Carcopino, malgré son excellente maîtrise de l'allemand, n'en ait pas eu connaissance, et qu'il ne l'évoque pas dans ses souvenirs, pas plus qu'il ne cite les noms de ses protagonistes dans la bibliographie ni dans les notes de son livre. S'il n'a pas perçu la portée des débats engagés en Allemagne sur la nature de l'économie antique, il connaissait en revanche les ouvrages d'une nouvelle école d'histoire administrative et agraire qui appartient à ce qu'on peut appeler la troisième génération de l'*Altertumswissenschaft*. Max Weber, au début de sa carrière,[9] avait inauguré ce mouvement avec sa *Römische Agrargeschichte*.[10] Carcopino la cite dans son livre, mais à

7 Nicolet (1988) 18 *sq.* et 30 *sq.*, a bien montré que ce débat remontait en fait aux origines mêmes de l''économie politique', et il en a retracé les étapes et le contenu. Sur son développement à la fin du XIXe et au XXe siècle, voir en particulier 32 et 33, nn. 34 et 35; les textes de la querelle entre Bücher et Meyer ont été rassemblés par Finley (1979); voir aussi Austin & Vidal-Naquet (1972) 11 *sq.* et Christ (1979) 286 *sq.*

8 Will (1954) 8 *sq.*; Austin & Vidal-Naquet (1972) 12 *sq.*; Andreau & Étienne (1984) 57 *sq.* soulignent la durée de ce phénomène, particulièrement en France.

9 Voir Käsler (1996) 15 *sq.*, sur la formation et les maîtres de Weber. Ses liens avec Mommsen ont souvent été soulignés, surtout à cause de la fameuse phrase prononcée par ce dernier lors de la *disputatio* du doctorat de Weber en août 1889. Pourtant, et même s'il avait suivi le cours de droit public romain de Mommsen à Berlin, il ne fut pas à proprement parler son élève et était avant tout un juriste et un économiste, voir sur ce point les remarques de Bruhns (1998) 19 *sq.*

10 Weber (1891). Ce livre a été soutenu comme thèse d'habilitation en février 1892, *cf.* Käsler (1996) 20, et 45 *sq.* pour une analyse de ce travail dans la perspective de l'oeuvre du sociologue. On sait qu'il s'agit du seul des ouvrages que Max Weber consacra à l'Antiquité, et particulièrement à l'économie antique, à avoir été rapidement reçu et régulièrement lu par les antiquisants. Une traduction italienne en fut d'ailleurs publiée dès 1907 par Ettore Ciccoti dans la prestigieuse *Biblioteca di storia economica* dirigée par Vilfredo Pareto, *cf.* Weber (1907). Les autres travaux d'histoire ancienne du grand sociologue allemand, surtout les *Agrarverhältnisse im Altertum*, dont la première version date de 1897 et la version définitive et considérablement augmentée de 1909 (voir Bruhns (1998) 24 *sq.*; bibliographie complète de Max Weber dans Käsler (1996) 239 *sq.*) ne furent guère connus des spécialistes, toutes nationalités confondues, et l'importance comme la portée de la contribution de Max

vrai dire très incidemment, à propos du statut fiscal des terres en Sicile.[11] D'autres historiens avaient suivi, entreprenant de renouveler et d'étendre les méthodes comme les thèmes des maîtres des générations précédentes, celle de Theodor Mommsen (1817-1903) et de Joachim Marquardt (1812-1882), et celle d'Otto Hirschfeld (1843-1922) et des premiers collaborateurs de Mommsen. Ils ne remettaient nullement en cause les apports de leurs prédécesseurs, ni d'ailleurs leur conception de l'histoire. Simplement, ils élargissaient et complétaient leurs perspectives.[12] Sur le plan des méthodes, ils promouvaient une discipline neuve, la papyrologie, qui ouvrait l'accès à des milliers de documents renseignant sur le fonctionnement concret et quotidien de l'administration et de l'économie. Sur le fond, ils déplaçaient l'étude de l'Empire romain vers ses périphéries provinciales. C'est ainsi que des savants tels que Ulrich Wilcken (1862-1944) et Ludwig Mitteis (1859-1921) se penchèrent sur l'histoire administrative de l'Égypte romaine. Ils montrèrent comment le droit romain avait reçu le droit local et comment les structures économiques, sociales et administratives du royaume hellénistique antérieur avaient survécu dans le système romain. D'autres historiens participaient à ce mouvement comme Adolf Schulten (1870-1960) pour l'histoire des structures agraires et domaniales, notamment en Afrique,[13] Ferdinand Kniep (1830-1921) pour les sociétés de publicains,[14] Wilhelm Liebenam (1859-1918) avec son livre sur l'administration des cités mais aussi ses articles sur des sujets économiques et fiscaux[15] et bien sûr Michel Rostovtzeff (1870-1952). Professeur à l'université de Saint-Pétersbourg depuis 1898, ce dernier avait acquis très tôt une renommée internationale. Il était en effet connu aussi bien en Italie, où il avait participé au *Dizionario epigrafico* d'Ettore De Ruggiero,[16] qu'auprès des plus grands savants allemands avec lesquels il avait travaillé et correspondu.[17] D'après Momigliano, Rostovtzeff était d'ailleurs l'un des rares étrangers que ceux-ci respectaient.[18] Il avait aussi séjourné en Angleterre et en France durant les années 1896-1898, rencontrant

Weber à l'étude de l'économie antique furent largement et durablement négligées. Voir sur cette question la mise au point de Bruhns (1996) 1273 *sq.* et (1998) 33 *sq.*, spécialement 37 nn. 77 et 78 sur la réception de la *Römische Agrargeschichte*. L'exemple de Rostovtzeff est ici très significatif, *cf.* Andreau (1988) xlv et Bruhns (1998) 32 et surtout 36 n. 74; il souligne d'autre part et *a contrario* l'exception de 'l'approche wébérienne' de Hasebroek.

11 Carcopino (1919) 235 n. 2; il se trompe d'ailleurs sur la date et le lieu de publication du livre de Weber: 1881, Iéna, au lieu de 1891, Stuttgart.

12 Voir Momigliano (1955).

13 Schulten (1894) et (1897). On trouvera une bibliographie détaillée des oeuvres de Schulten, en particulier en ce qui concerne l'arpentage et les cadastres, dans Chouquer et Favory (2001) 478.

14 Kniep (1896).

15 Liebenam (1900), (1901) et (1905).

16 Rostovtzeff (1900a). Sur la formation et les débuts de la carrière de Rostovtzeff, voir Andreau (1988) viii *sq.* et Marcone (1999).

17 Andreau (1988) xii *sq.* mentionne sa correspondance avec O. Hirschfeld et U. Wilcken, à partir de 1896 ou 1897, et rappelle que c'est E. Bormann, à Vienne, qui l'engagea à travailler sur la ferme d'État. Un fait significatif montre le renom de Rostovtzeff à ce moment: c'est à lui qu'Hirschfeld demanda de lire les épreuves de sa deuxième édition des *Kaiserlichen Verwaltungsbeamten* (Hirschfeld (1905)).

18 Momigliano (1955) 344.

à Londres Bernard Grenfell et John Mahaffy, les éditeurs du *Papyrus des revenus*, document dont nous verrons tout à l'heure qu'il eut un rôle sans doute déterminant dans l'origine des travaux de Carcopino sur la loi d'Hiéron. Rostovtzeff travailla aussi à Paris sur les tessères et les plombs de commerce avec Maurice Prou et Ernest Babelon.[19] Par ses orientations scientifiques et ses travaux des années 1890 et 1900,[20] Rostovtzeff s'affirme bien comme une des figures principales de la seconde *Altertumswissenschaft*. Rappelons d'ailleurs que c'est à lui que fut confié l'article 'Frumentum' de la *Realencyclopädie*, ainsi que celui sur le colonat du *Handwörterbuch der Staatswissenschaften* de Conrad, après que Max Weber eut finalement renoncé à l'écrire.[21] Surtout, Wilcken publia son livre sur l'histoire du colonat romain dans le premier volume de la collection de l'*Archiv für Papyrusforschung*.[22] Carcopino connaissait bien les travaux du savant russe qu'il mentionne dans sa bibliographie et cite abondamment dans ses notes.

Comme je l'ai dit plus haut, l'écho des débats entre Bücher et Meyer n'était pas parvenu jusqu'en France. Toutefois, cette lacune théorique n'empêchait pas les historiens français de disposer d'outils et de notions pour aborder l'histoire des faits économiques et sociaux, et ils pouvaient notamment revendiquer l'héritage de Dureau de La Malle[23] et surtout de Fustel de Coulanges.[24] Elle ne signifiait pas non plus que l'intérêt pour l'histoire économique ne se

19 *Cf.* Andreau (1988) xii *sq*. En 1900, Rostovtzeff fut invité en France pour une conférence sur les dons de blé des empereurs aux cités d'Asie mineure, devant la Société nationale des Antiquaires, voir Rostovtzeff (1900b).

20 Andreau (1988) x.

21 Rostovtzeff (1910a); sur cet épisode voir Bruhns (1998) 19 *sq*. et 32 *sq*.

22 Momigliano (1955) 347 *sq*. remarque que l'intérêt de Rostovtzeff pour les questions agraires ne doit pas laisser penser qu'il ne faisait que rallier un mouvement allemand; en effet, l'histoire agraire était aussi une spécialité des historiens russes; dans la Russie de la fin du XIXe siècle, cela s'expliquait bien sûr par des raisons sociales et politiques, mais il faut savoir aussi que les travaux de Fustel sur le colonat romain (Fustel de Coulanges (1885)) avaient été introduits en Russie dès 1886 et y avaient connu une grande faveur. D'autre part, Michael Khostov, de deux ans l'aîné de Rostovtzeff, travailla également sur ces questions dans le cadre de l'Égypte et influença ce dernier, *cf.* Momigliano (1955) 347. Sur l'importance de l'histoire socio-économique dans l'historiographie russe d'avant 1914, voir les remarques de Raskolnikoff (1975) 20 *sq*.

23 Dureau de La Malle (1840); traduit dans la *Biblioteca di storia economica* de Pareto (Dureau de La Malle (1905)); réimprimé avec une introduction et des notes par B. Hemmerdinger (Dureau de La Malle (1986)); sur Dureau, voir Nicolet (1988) 26.

24 Sans vouloir introduire de dichotomie dans l'oeuvre de Fustel, je pense ici plus particulièrement à ses ouvrages sur la question de la propriété foncière (qui était déjà essentielle dans *La cité antique*, publiée en 1864), *cf.* Fustel de Coulanges (1880), (1885) et (1889). La bibliographie sur Fustel est encore assez réduite, on en trouvera l'essentiel mentionné par Momigliano (1975) 163 n. 1, et Nicolet (2003) 304 n. 1. Pour expliquer l'influence de Fustel, on doit rappeler qu'il fut maître de conférences à l'École normale supérieure (1870-1875), puis directeur de cet établissement (1880-1883) après être passé par une chaire à la Sorbonne (1875-1880), *cf.* Charle (1985) 76 *sq*. Il a donc contribué à former la génération des maîtres de Carcopino. Pour citer quelques ouvrages importants sur Fustel, on rappellera d'abord sa biographie par un de ses élèves, Guiraud (1896); plus récemment Hartog (1988) a insisté sur les questions de méthode historique. Sur l'importance de Fustel pour la génération des historiens formés après 1870, voir Momigliano (1975) et Mucchielli (1995) 80 *sq*.; voir aussi la mise en perspective réalisée par Nicolet (1989) et (2003) 208 *sq*.

manifestait pas dans l'université française, et plusieurs éléments montrent même qu'il fut assez vif durant cette période de la fin du XIXe et du début du XXe siècle. En effet, et sans abandonner complètement la conception fustélienne d'une histoire marquée par le caractère déterminant des institutions,[25] ses élèves Gustave Glotz et Paul Guiraud s'orientèrent vers l'étude de questions plus spécifiquement économiques comme le travail, l'activité financière et les échanges commerciaux.[26] Dans l'avant-propos de sa thèse sur Pouzzoles antique (Puteoli), Charles Dubois rappelle que Paul Guiraud encourageait lui-même beaucoup ses élèves à l'étude des questions d'histoire économique.[27] A l'instar de ce sujet sur Pouzzoles, orienté à l'origine vers l'étude du commerce et de l'industrie,[28] beaucoup de ceux dont on peut retrouver la trace, en particulier parmi les condisciples de Carcopino à Rome et à Athènes, portent sur les échanges et les questions annonaires. Ainsi Louis Gernet publie en 1909 un article sur l'approvisionnement d'Athènes en blé, que Carcopino cite dans *La loi de Hiéron*.[29] Dans la même veine, René Cagnat, alors professeur au Collège de France, suggéra vainement à Carcopino avant son départ pour l'École française de Rome un sujet sur la culture de l'olivier et le commerce de l'huile dans l'Empire romain.[30] Par la suite il travailla d'ailleurs lui-même sur l'annone d'Afrique.[31] Le sujet de Jean Hatzfeld sur les trafiquants italiens en Orient envisage l'histoire des échanges sous un angle plus social,[32] tandis que Robert Laurent-Vibert travailla sur les sociétés de publicains, un sujet voisin de celui de Carcopino, pour sa contribution aux *Mélanges* et consacra son mémoire à l'industrie à Rome.[33] Enfin, les

25 Sur l'importance des institutions chez Fustel, voir Nicolet (1993) et (2003) 218 *sq.*

26 Paul Guiraud fut chargé de cours puis professeur d'histoire grecque à la Faculté des lettres de Paris de 1888 à sa mort en 1907, *cf.* Charle (1985) 91 *sq.*; après des premiers travaux axés sur l'histoire des institutions, notamment Guiraud (1887), il passa à des recherches qui lui valent aujourd'hui une réputation d''historien de l'économie' (Nicolet). Notons d'ailleurs que son livre sur la propriété en Grèce (Guiraud (1894)) fut intégré dans la *Biblioteca di storia economica* de Pareto (Guiraud (1907)). Également élève de Fustel de Coulanges, Gustave Glotz fut chargé de cours puis professeur d'histoire grecque à la Faculté des lettres de Paris de 1907 à 1935, *cf.* Charle (1986) 92; voir en particulier Glotz (1906). Sur le rôle et l'influence de ces deux historiens, dont l'étude reste encore à faire, voir Mucchielli (1995) 76 et Corcy-Debray (2001) 440 *sq.* et 452 *sq.*

27 Dubois (1907) ix.

28 Dans le compte-rendu du livre de Dubois qu'il réalisa pour la *Revue de synthèse historique*, Carcopino (1909a) 198 déplore toutefois qu'il soit à cet égard si décevant.

29 Gernet (1909), cité par Carcopino (1919) 29 n. 3, et publié dans le même volume que Carcopino (1909b); on notera que Louis Gernet fut l'un des seuls en France à prendre part au débat sur l'économie antique, en approuvant les thèses d'Hasebroek, *cf.* Austin & Vidal-Naquet (1972) 16 n. 3; Andreau & Étienne (1984) 57 *sq.*

30 Carcopino (1968a) 73; à ce moment, le cours de Cagnat au Collège de France portait sur la vie municipale dans le monde romain, considérée dans ses aspects privés (*cf. Annuaire du Collège de France* 1901-1905).

31 Cagnat (1916).

32 Hatzfeld (1908), (1909) et aussi (1919); voir le rapport de Haussoulier (1910).

33 Laurent-Vibert (1908) et (1909); le rapport de Haussoulier (1910) 602 montre qu'il s'agit surtout d'un travail sur la production domestique, les prix et les transports d'après Caton, Varron et Cicéron. Carcopino (1968a) 162 et 194 évoque Hatzfeld et Laurent-Vibert sans faire de rapprochement d'ordre

questions foncières sont au centre du mémoire de Maurice Pernot sur le colonat partiaire ou de celui de Félix de Pachtère sur la table de Veleia.[34] On notera au total que parmi les vingt-quatre sujets de mémoires de l'École française de Rome déposés entre 1895 et 1914 par des antiquisants, la place de l'histoire économique et sociale est loin d'être négligeable. En effet, on peut lui attribuer six sujets,[35] pour trois qui concernent l'histoire religieuse, cinq qui relèvent de la philologie et dix qui se rattachent d'une manière ou d'une autre à l'archéologie.[36]

Pour compléter cette évocation de l'horizon dans lequel prend place l'enquête de Carcopino, il faut mentionner aussi les travaux de certains historiens qui apparaissent dans la bibliographie de *La loi de Hiéron*, tel celui d'Antonin Deloume sur les manieurs d'argent ou ceux des orientalistes et spécialistes des Lagides comme Auguste Bouché-Leclercq.[37] Concernant l'Égypte, ces derniers accordaient bien sûr une grande place aux questions financières et fiscales, auxquelles Cagnat pour le *portorium* et les impôts indirects de l'Empire romain[38] et Paul Guiraud pour l'impôt sur le capital en Grèce et à Rome s'étaient aussi intéressés.[39] Dans l'étude de ces questions, les antiquisants français trouvaient par ailleurs un puissant renfort dans l'existence déjà ancienne d'une école de juristes et de fiscalistes, formés eux aussi aux disciplines classiques et spécialisés dans l'étude du droit romain, en raison de l'organisation des études de droit qui accordait alors une place importante à cette discipline. Parmi eux s'impose d'abord la haute figure de Gustave Humbert, professeur de droit romain à Toulouse puis procureur général près la Cour des comptes, garde des Sceaux et vice-président du Sénat. Il dirigea la traduction française du *Handbuch der römischen Alterthümer* de Mommsen et Marquardt, et consacra un ouvrage aux finances publiques des Romains.[40] Des travaux de moindre importance, tirés de thèses de droit, furent consacrés aux questions fiscales, parmi lesquels on citera ceux de Naquet, Vigié et Thibault.[41] Toujours dans le domaine juridique, mais d'une tout autre portée, s'avèrent les travaux de Huvelin et, en

historiographique avec ses travaux de l'époque. Une lettre de Laurent-Vibert à Carcopino (MS 7153; correspondance de J. Carcopino, voir *infra* n. 44), datée du 28 novembre 1908, témoigne de liens entre les deux hommes et contient une discussion à propos d'un passage de Cicéron concernant les publicains (*Att.* 5.15 (= SB 108) et 11.10 (= SB 221)).

34 De Pachtère (1909), voir Haussoulier (1910) 603-04.

35 A ceux qui ont été mentionnés, on ajoutera celui d'E. Albertini, *Les travaux publics sous le règne de Claude* (1906).

36 Dépouillement réalisé à partir de l'annuaire des membres de l'EFR (École française de Rome (1987)).

37 Deloume (1892); Maspero (1905); Bouché-Leclercq (1903-1907).

38 Cagnat (1880) et (1882).

39 Guiraud (1905). Ce volume rassemble plusieurs articles parus dans diverses revues, parmi lesquels deux grosses études sur l'impôt sur le capital à Rome et à Athènes et un article sur l'impérialisme romain envisageant notamment ses aspects économiques, financiers et fiscaux.

40 Humbert (1886) et aussi (1867). Humbert s'occupa encore d'une grande partie des articles de droit public, de droit criminel et de finances publiques pour le dictionnaire de Daremberg et Saglio.

41 Naquet (1875), Vigié (1882-1883) et Thibault (1888).

Belgique, de Waltzing sur des aspects normatifs de la vie économique et sociale.[42] D'une manière générale, ce domaine de l'histoire progressa aussi à travers le rôle de l'économie politique dans les facultés de droit, qui s'illustra avec la fondation en 1908, par Auguste Deschamps et Auguste Dubois, tous deux professeurs d'économie politique, de la *Revue d'histoire des doctrines économiques et sociales*, qui devint en 1913 la *Revue d'histoire économique et sociale*.[43]

II. La lex Hieronica *et les débuts de la carrière de Jérôme Carcopino*

Je n'ai découvert aucun élément mentionnant les raisons directes qui ont amené Jérôme Carcopino à travailler sur le *de Frumento* et la loi d'Hiéron. Dans ses *Souvenirs romains*, parus en 1968, il demeure muet sur ce point alors qu'il s'étend longuement sur ses recherches à Ostie ou sur son séjour en Afrique. Il est possible que lorsqu'il écrivit ce volume de souvenirs, à plus de cinquante ans de distance, cet aspect de son travail à Rome ne lui ait pas semblé être le plus significatif ou le plus important. Peut-être aussi jugeait-il ces questions trop arides pour être évoquées dans un livre destiné à un public cultivé certes, mais pas spécialiste. Cherchant des informations plus précises, j'avais pensé pouvoir trouver des éléments dans la correspondance de Jérôme Carcopino conservée à l'Institut de France.[44] Elle ne comporte, en-dehors de quelques exceptions, que des lettres reçues, et sa communication est réservée jusqu'en 2010. Toutefois, la famille de l'historien a laissé au service des archives de l'Institut la liberté d'accorder l'accès à des lettres antérieures à 1939, et j'ai pu consulter celles qui furent envoyées à Carcopino (et à quelques autres personnes dont l'identité n'est pas précisée) par un certain nombre de correspondants entre 1906 et le milieu des années trente, parmi lesquels ses maîtres René Cagnat, Gustave Bloch et Auguste Bouché-Leclercq et quelques uns de ses camarades et collègues. Si cette recherche n'a pas donné les résultats explicites et probants que j'avais espérés, elle a tout de même fourni quelques indices qui sont venus préciser l'idée que je m'étais faite de l'origine de ce sujet. J'y reviendrai tout à l'heure.

Pour commencer, peut-on savoir à quel moment ce sujet a été déterminé? Il est certain en tout cas qu'il l'a été rapidement. En effet, après son succès à l'agrégation en juillet 1904, Carcopino arrive à l'École française de Rome au mois de novembre,[45] et ses deux premiers articles sur cette question paraissent dans le volume de 1905 des *Mélanges d'archéologie et d'histoire*. Pour essayer d'aller plus loin, on ne dispose guère que d'un passage bref et malheureusement assez imprécis des *Souvenirs romains*. Il vaut la peine de le citer en entier.

> Pour ma part, j'avais écarté le projet qu'à son cours du Collège de France mon maître René Cagnat m'avait recommandé et qui eût consisté dans l'étude de la culture de l'olivier et du commerce de l'huile dans l'Empire romain. Je lui avais préféré un dessein apparemment

42 Huvelin (1897) et aussi (1904) (vaste revue historiographique des questions de droit commercial, citée par Laurent-Vibert (1908) 171 n. 8); Waltzing (1895-1900).

43 Mucchielli (1995) 79.

44 Elle tient dans 39 cartons cotés de 7133 à 7171 (1 carton supplémentaire est coté 7678); elle est classée par ordre alphabétique des noms de correspondants. Monique Dondin-Payre me signale par ailleurs que Carcopino a légué des papiers à la Corse.

45 Carcopino (1968a) chap. 3.

> plus modeste, en fait, comme on le verra, trop ambitieux: celui d'entreprendre une histoire de la ville et du port d'Ostie dont les fouilles avaient été suspendues depuis plusieurs années. J'étais résolu à ne point m'en laisser distraire et, par précaution, j'avais emporté de Paris les manuscrits et les fiches où je comptais puiser les éléments de ma collaboration éventuelle aux *Mélanges* et de l'élaboration de mon mémoire final; et comme il n'était pas question pendant l'hiver de m'en aller prendre sur le terrain d'Ostie des notes que le vent du large aurait fait s'envoler de mes mains, j'employais mes premiers mois, non seulement à me mettre en règle avec les *Mélanges*, mais à parcourir en tout sens les antiquités de la Ville Éternelle suivant le conseil de Mgr Duchesne.[46]

Carcopino avait donc emmené de Paris des dossiers comprenant des éléments sur lesquels il comptait continuer à travailler à Rome. Ils avaient vraisemblablement été constitués durant ses études à l'École normale et plus particulièrement sans doute pendant son année de licence, à partir des conseils de ses maîtres.[47] Il ne dit rien de leur contenu précis, mais les deux allusions aux *Mélanges* indiquent implicitement qu'il s'agit de matériaux utilisés pour les deux articles sur le *de Frumento* et permettent par conséquent de penser que ce sujet a été élaboré à Paris avant son départ. Y avait-il aussi dans ces dossiers parisiens des choses destinées au sujet sur Ostie? Cela paraît peu probable car il semble bien que la formation de ce sujet soit postérieure à celle du *de Frumento*, et postérieure aussi, ou au moins concomitante, à son arrivée à Rome. Dans l'avant-propos de sa thèse sur Ostie, il écrit en effet:

> Dès mon arrivée à l'École de Rome, il y a quatorze ans, j'avais jeté mon dévolu sur Ostie, port de Rome, espérant par ce choix, accorder pratiquement mes propres intentions avec les conseils qu'à mon départ de France j'avais sollicités et reçus de mes maîtres.[48]

D'après ce texte, dont la rédaction peut être placée, suivant ce que dit Carcopino, en 1918, le choix proprement dit du sujet ne semble pas antérieur à l'arrivée au Farnèse. Peut-être avait-il toutefois commencé à y réfléchir durant le bref laps de temps qui sépara l'agrégation de son départ, moment de vacances qui fut en partie consacré à une croisière sur la Méditerranée offerte au cacique du concours par la *Revue générale des sciences*.[49] Dans le texte des *Souvenirs romains* cité plus haut, il sous-entend d'ailleurs qu'il a engagé, au début de son séjour romain, deux recherches de front. D'une part Ostie, qui semble constituer son sujet principal, celui qu'il réserve peut-être à son futur mémoire. D'autre part les dossiers (sur le *de Frumento*?) apportés de Paris, qui fournissent la matière des articles qu'il destine aux *Mélanges* et à partir desquels il peut travailler durant l'hiver 1904-1905. Pourquoi ce sujet sur Ostie, et quels rapports entretient-il éventuellement avec le *de Frumento* et la loi d'Hiéron? Ce sont des questions qu'il faut, bien entendu, se poser. On le sait, Carcopino n'avait pas

46 Carcopino (1968a) 73.

47 N'oublions pas d'autre part son travail sur l'ostracisme athénien, engagé dès 1901-1902 pour un mémoire de licence, et qui fut publié dans le même volume que le mémoire de Gernet sur l'approvisionnement d'Athènes (Gernet (1909) et Carcopino (1909b)).

48 Carcopino (1968b) ix.

49 Carcopino (1968a) 23 et 24 *sq*.

retenu le sujet que lui avait suggéré René Cagnat, mais il avait du moins entendu ses conseils et ceux de son autre maître Gustave Bloch.[50] Ici encore, il faut citer l'avant-propos de sa thèse:

> M. Cagnat, qui n'aime point 'l'archéologie en chambre', m'avait, avec raison, détourné d'entreprendre un travail que j'aurais pu tout aussi bien élaborer à Paris, dans les bibliothèques. Mais, de son côté, M. G. Bloch, dont la critique exemplaire apprend à reconstruire solidement le passé sur le difficile terrain des textes, m'avait à juste titre, mis en garde contre les recherches trop exclusivement topographiques, d'où l'intérêt humain finit par disparaître, contre des sujets qui ne tiennent que du dehors, sans autre unité que celle de 'lieu'.[51]

C'est visiblement pour suivre le conseil de René Cagnat que Carcopino n'avait pas voulu consacrer entièrement son séjour à un travail à partir du texte de Cicéron. Il s'était donc mis en quête d'un sujet plus archéologique et s'était décidé pour une monographie locale. Ce type de sujet n'était pas nouveau à l'École française, puisque trois des premiers pensionnaires du Farnèse, Théophile Homolle (1874-1875), Emmanuel Fernique (1876-1878) et René de La Blanchère (1878-1881) avaient consacré leur mémoire et/ou leur thèse respectivement à (déjà) Ostie, Préneste et Terracine.[52] Par la suite, ces monographies étaient devenues plus rares[53] avant de connaître un renouveau à la fin du XIXe siècle, notamment avec le mémoire puis la thèse de Charles Dubois sur Pouzzoles.[54] Le sujet sur Ostie se rattachait donc à cette tradition,[55] mais Carcopino avait aussi, en le choisissant, tenu compte des avertissements de Gustave Bloch. Des sources littéraires abondantes et un imposant corpus épigraphique constituaient de solides garanties contre une approche trop matérielle du site et, surtout, l'histoire même de la ville et du port était suffisamment dense et importante pour rattacher cette monographie à celle de Rome des origines à l'époque impériale.[56] Toujours dans cet avant-propos, Carcopino établit aussi un lien entre 'le développement des institutions annonaires' à Ostie et 'ses études antérieures', c'est-à-dire celles sur la loi de Hiéron et la dîme de Sicile. Sans doute ce lien s'est-il distendu lorsque les travaux de Carcopino à Ostie

50 Gustave Bloch avait été le maître de Carcopino à l'École normale supérieure; il fut nommé professeur à la Sorbonne en 1904, au moment où son jeune élève partait à Rome; voir sa notice dans Charle (1985) 29 *sq*.

51 Carcopino (1968b) ix; une lettre de Cagnat (M 7139, s. d.) confirme cette préoccupation et l'exprime dans des termes similaires.

52 Voir leurs notices dans École française de Rome (1987) 51 *sq*., 71 et 75. Il est intéressant de signaler que dans la préface de son livre, Fernique écrit que son sujet sur Préneste faisait partie de ceux qui avaient été suggérés à l'École par l'Académie des Inscriptions et belles-lettres (Fernique (1880) 3).

53 On ne peut citer que le mémoire d'Etienne Michon sur Aléria en 1889 et la thèse d'Auguste Audollent sur Carthage romaine, publiée en 1901.

54 Dubois (1907).

55 Carcopino (1909a) 194 souligne l'existence de cette tradition et y rattache également les thèses de Maurice Besnier sur l'Île Tibérine en 1902 et d'Alfred Merlin sur l'Aventin, en 1906. On y ajoutera aussi les deux monographies urbaines réalisées peu après par Louis Chatelain sur Mactar, en 1911, et de Dominique Anziani sur Caere, en 1912.

56 Carcopino (1968b) ix.

ont pris une autre orientation que celle qu'il avait d'abord envisagée, mais il n'empêche qu'il a existé au départ et qu'il plaçait l'ensemble de ses recherches dans une perspective commune.

Les articles des *Mélanges d'archéologie et d'histoire* ont donc été rédigés à la bibliothèque de l'École française entre la fin 1904 et la fin 1905.[57] Ils portent respectivement sur le statut et la hiérarchie des cités siciliennes devant les dîmes et sur la condition des *decumani*.[58] Un troisième article parut encore cette même année dans les *Vierteljahrschrift für Social- und Wirtschaftsgeschichte*, qui livrait une synthèse sur l'organisation agricole de la Sicile à l'époque romaine.[59] On sait que son travail sur les *decumani* lui valut une sévère attaque de Rostovtzeff. Dans l'article 'Frumentum' qu'il avait rédigé pour la *Realencyclopädie*,[60] l'historien russe l'accusa d'avoir reproduit une opinion émise dans un article publié quelques années auparavant par son compatriote et ami Thaddeus Zielinski, et cela sans le citer.[61] Or, l'idée avancée par Carcopino allait en fait dans un sens exactement contraire à celle de Zielinski. Piqué au vif et sûr de son bon droit, le Français écrivit une lettre de protestation à Wilhelm Kroll, alors directeur de la *Realencyclopädie*, et obtint une *retractatio* de Rostovtzeff qui figura dans le volume VII de la collection.[62]

L'année suivante, le travail de Carcopino se vit favorisé par un de ces coups heureux que le hasard réserve parfois à ceux qui sont le mieux à même d'en tirer profit. En avril 1906, il fut envoyé en Tunisie par le directeur de l'École française de Rome, Mgr Duchesne, pour se mettre à la disposition du service des Antiquités de la Régence, dirigé par Alfred Merlin et Louis Poinssot qui lui confièrent le chantier de fouilles d'Aïn Tounga. Là, il fut bientôt informé de la découverte d'une pierre inscrite dans le lit de l'Oued Khalled, à Aïn El Djemala. Il saisit immédiatement l'importance du document qui venait s'agréger au dossier des inscriptions domaniales africaines,[63] et il le publia sans tarder dans les *Mélanges d'archéologie*

57 Les deux articles sont datés: Carcopino (1905a) 53: 15 février 1905; et (1905b) 442: 8 décembre 1905.

58 Carcopino (1905a), (1905b); sur ces deux articles voir l'analyse et les remarques de Grimal *et al.* (1981) 161 *sq.*

59 Carcopino (1906a).

60 Rostovtzeff (1910b) col. 152.

61 Zielinski (1894). Celui-ci était en réalité Polonais. Professeur à l'Université de Saint-Pétersbourg, il regagna son pays, devenu indépendant, en 1922; sur les relations entre Zielinski et Rostovtzeff, voir Andreau (1988) vi *sq.* La réaction de Rostovtzeff s'explique aussi sans doute par le souci qu'il avait de défendre la science russe et les intérêts des institutions auxquelles il appartenait à l'étranger, *cf.* là aussi Andreau (1988) xv.

62 Voir le récit de cet épisode par Carcopino lui-même (1968a) 74 *sq.*, et aussi Carcopino (1919) 100 n. 4.

63 Dossier constitué par les trois grandes inscriptions domaniales découvertes entre 1879 et 1896 en Tunisie, notamment dans la vallée du *Bagradas* (Medjerda). Il s'agit des inscriptions de Souk El Khmis (*Saltus Burunitanus*): *CIL* VIII 10570 et 14424; *ILS* 6870 (180-83 p.C.); Ain Ouassel: *CIL* VIII 26416 (198-212 p.C.); Henchir Mettich (*Villa Magna Variana*): *CIL* VIII 25902 (116-17 p.C.). Pour l'inscription d'Aïn El Djemala: *CIL* VIII 25943 (117-38 p.C.). Ces textes sont relatifs à de grands domaines, sans doute impériaux. Ils apportent de précieux renseignements sur l'organisation et le régime d'exploitation des terres, lié à une *lex Manciana* dont la nature, la date et l'objet posent toujours problème; voir la bibliographie et les remarques de François Burdeau dans Giuffrè (1977) 561 *sq.*; une

et d'histoire de 1906 avec un commentaire approfondi.[64] Grâce à ses travaux précédents sur la Sicile, il se montra parfaitement à même de montrer la portée du texte et il put effectuer un certain nombre de rapprochements entre la *lex Manciana* et la *lex Hieronica*.[65] Qui plus est, cette publication lui donna l'occasion de remporter un nouveau succès en se voyant accorder par Kornemann un droit de réponse dans *Klio* pour répliquer aux critiques qu'Adolf Schulten lui avait adressées dans le volume de 1907 de cette revue.[66]

Tout cela permet à Carcopino de se faire connaître au niveau international et, lorsqu'il quitte le Palais Farnèse, à l'âge de 26 ans, il apparaît comme un archéologue et un épigraphiste de premier plan et comme un historien reconnu des questions économiques et fiscales.[67] De retour en France, il est nommé au lycée du Havre (1907-1912), mais obtient deux congés sans solde, en 1910-1911 et 1911-1912, afin de poursuivre ses travaux sur Ostie. En 1912, il accède à l'enseignement supérieur: il est chargé d'un cours d'Antiquités de l'Afrique à l'Université d'Alger et se voit dans le même temps nommé inspecteur adjoint des Antiquités algériennes.[68]

C'est aussi en 1912, le 12 décembre précisément, que le manuscrit de *La loi de Hiéron et les Romains* reçoit le permis d'imprimer. S'il est par conséquent certain que le livre était achevé à cette date, on peut se demander quand Carcopino a terminé son enquête. En effet, il semble bien qu'entre 1907 et 1912, il ait assez peu travaillé sur la Sicile et se soit consacré avant tout à Ostie et, à partir de 1912, à l'Afrique. Pour en être sûr, il faudrait pouvoir comparer le texte de son livre avec celui du mémoire déposé à l'Institut en 1907. Malheureusement, il n'y en a aucune trace dans les archives de cet établissement, ce qui d'après Mme Mireille Lamarque, conservateur en chef de ce service, s'explique vraisemblablement par le fait que Carcopino a dû l'y reprendre peu après, sans doute dans la perspective de sa publication. C'était selon elle une pratique courante. Il y a cependant un autre moyen de se faire une idée sur cette question, en comparant le texte du livre de 1912 avec celui des deux articles parus dans les *Mélanges d'archéologie et d'histoire* en 1905 et qui, selon les propres mots de Carcopino devaient préparer le mémoire.[69] Le rapprochement du premier article sur le statut fiscal des cités de Sicile avec le chapitre correspondant du

rapide synthèse récente dans Whittaker (2000) 531 *sq.*

64 Carcopino (1906b). Sur cet épisode voir Carcopino (1968a) chap. 7.

65 En particulier sur la question de la *pactio*, voir Carcopino (1919) 14 *sq.* et les remarques de Marrou (1977) 211 et de Grimal *et al.* (1981) 163.

66 Schulten (1907); Carcopino (1908); voir le récit de Carcopino (1968a) 128 *sq.* et Marrou (1977) 211. Avant de se consacrer aux fouilles de Numance (Numantia), Schulten avait travaillé sur les textes africains et la *lex Manciana*, *cf.* Schulten (1897).

67 Marrou (1977) 211; Grimal *et al.* (1981) 162; Corcy-Debray (2001) 417 *sq.*

68 Charle (1986) 47; Corcy-Debray (2001) 418 *sq.*, avec d'autres références, analyse cette partie de la carrière de Carcopino et la situe dans le contexte de la démographie universitaire de l'époque. A ce propos elle qualifie Jérôme Carcopino d''outsider sur le marché universitaire' (p. 423), ce qui me semble être un contresens total sur son parcours et son profil académiques.

69 Carcopino (1968a) 73.

livre[70] révèle des changements dans l'appareil des titres ou de sous-titres,[71] ainsi que quelques ajouts[72] et des rectifications d'erreurs.[73] Mais dans l'ensemble les deux textes sont quasiment identiques. L'article sur les *decumani* a pour sa part fait l'objet d'un travail de réécriture plus important. Plusieurs passages ont été remaniés et ce qui concernait les *societates publicanorum*, romaines, extérieures à la Sicile et par conséquent au sujet du livre, en a été enlevé.[74] En dehors de cela, la matière de son argumentation se trouve déjà dans l'article, et d'une manière générale, cette comparaison laisse supposer que le mémoire de 1907 contenait l'essentiel du livre terminé en 1912. Par la correspondance de Jérôme Carcopino, nous savons qu'Auguste Bouché-Leclercq fut le rapporteur du manuscrit déposé en Sorbonne pour obtenir l'autorisation d'imprimer.[75] Une lettre du 27 juillet 1912 montre le souci qu'avait Carcopino de voir son manuscrit enregistré le plus rapidement possible, sans doute à cause de son départ prochain pour Alger.[76] Bouché-Leclercq souligne le caractère tardif de la démarche par rapport à la date de fermeture des bureaux de la Sorbonne pour les vacances, et estime que Carcopino n'a pas intérêt à brusquer ainsi les choses, compte tenu du peu qui lui reste à faire pour que le manuscrit soit au point. Finalement, c'est au début du mois de décembre qu'il est déposé et enregistré. A ce moment, et d'après la façon dont Bouché-Leclercq présente les choses, il est clair que *La loi de Hiéron* est destinée à être soutenue en tant que thèse complémentaire.[77]

Deux ans plus tard, en 1914, la guerre interrompt la rédaction de sa thèse principale sur Ostie. Toutefois, un premier manuscrit de trois cents pages est prêt dès 1917. Gustave Bloch, qui dirige son travail, et René Durand[78] qui en corrige le manuscrit sont d'accord pour reconnaître la valeur de ce travail. Ils lui proposent deux solutions. La première est de soutenir rapidement, en faisant de *La loi d'Hiéron*, qui présente 'toute l'ampleur et [...] toute la portée nécessaire' sa thèse principale, et d'Ostie sa thèse complémentaire. La seconde est d'attendre, en étoffant son travail sur Ostie pour le présenter comme thèse principale.[79] Leur préférence va clairement à la première de ces deux solutions, mais Carcopino hésite et finalement décide

70 Carcopino (1905a) et (1919) section II chap. 5.

71 Comparer par exemple Carcopino (1905a) 15 et 21 avec (1919) 216 et 225, et *passim*.

72 Par exemple le tableau de Carcopino (1919) 218-22.

73 Ainsi dans Carcopino (1919) 208, à propos de Liv. 26.40 (l'expédition de Laevinus au lieu de Marcellus).

74 Comparer Carcopino (1905b) et (1919) pour les pages 402 *sq.* et 89 *sq.*, 419-23 et 100-02; la dernière partie de (1905b) 428 *sq.* ne se retrouve pas dans (1919).

75 Lettres d'Auguste Bouché-Leclercq (MS 7137, folios 257-69).

76 MS 7137, folio 267.

77 Lettre du 4 décembre 1912 (MS 7137, folio 268).

78 Comme Gustave Bloch, René Durand avait été auparavant le maître de Carcopino à l'École normale supérieure.

79 Lettre de Gustave Bloch à Carcopino du 3 novembre 1917 (MS 7137, folio 35), dans laquelle il dit qu'il a eu un entretien préalable avec Durand et qu'il exprime leur position commune; ceci est confirmé par une lettre de René Durand à Carcopino du 28 janvier 1918 (MS 7143, folios 292-300). Voir Corcy-Debray (2001) 421 *sq.* pour un récit détaillé de cet épisode.

de ne pas déposer une thèse qu'il considère vraisemblablement comme inachevée. Peut-être souhaitait-il aussi soutenir une thèse principale portant sur un autre sujet que celui de son mémoire de l'École française. En effet, celui-ci avait été critiqué à l'Institut par son rapporteur, non pas pour sa valeur scientifique mais pour une question de principe: alors que Carcopino avait choisi Ostie comme sujet d'étude à Rome, il avait déposé à l'Institut un travail qui aurait pu être réalisé dans une bibliothèque de Paris.[80] Certes, le choix de consacrer son mémoire à la loi d'Hiéron s'expliquait sans doute par les difficultés et les déceptions que Carcopino avait rencontrées à Ostie,[81] et par le concours de circonstances qui lui avait permis de devenir un spécialiste reconnu des questions juridiques et agraires. Mais il est possible qu'il ait voulu ensuite montrer qu'il avait en quelque sorte compris la leçon, en donnant toute son importance au sujet qui avait justifié son séjour à Rome puis ses années de congé.[82] Quoi qu'il en soit, c'est deux ans plus tard, le vendredi 12 décembre 1919 à 13 heures, qu'il soutient ses deux thèses, la principale: *Virgile et les origines d'Ostie*, et la complémentaire: *La loi de Hiéron et les Romains*.[83] Cette soutenance lui ouvre les portes de la Sorbonne. Le 14 janvier 1920 il est élu pour succéder à Gustave Bloch, contre Maurice Besnier et Jules Toutain,[84] et il est nommé maître de conférences d'histoire romaine le 23 janvier 1920.

III. La loi de Hiéron*: aux origines d'un sujet*

Durant ses études à l'École normale supérieure et à la Sorbonne, Carcopino fut formé et encadré par des maîtres qui étaient presque tous des élèves et des héritiers de Fustel de Coulanges. Dans l'université française du début du XXe siècle, il se trouva en contact avec un milieu historien marqué par l'étude des faits institutionnels et sociaux, mais aussi par le développement des études statistiques[85] et celui de l'école sociologique de Durkheim, un autre élève de Fustel,[86] engagée dans une démarche d'affirmation de ses concepts et de ses méthodes, qui tentait de concurrencer et de remettre en question la discipline historique et les positions académiques des historiens.[87] Dans ce milieu, et durant les années 1890-1900, l'histoire économique et sociale connaît un mouvement d'expansion auquel les antiquisants

80 Chapelain (1908) 301-02.

81 Carcopino (1968a) 130 *sq*; (1968b) x; Grimal *et al.* (1981) 138 *sq*.

82 *Cf.* la remarque de Carcopino (1968a) 94: '[...] j'ai entrevu le moment où, démentant enfin le reproche qui devait, en 1907, m'être lancé sous la Coupole, à la séance publique annuelle de l'Académie des Inscriptions, de trop aimer "l'archéologie en chambre", je pourrais enrichir ma documentation livresque et compléter mon exploration au sol par des sondages exécutés à six lieues de Rome.'

83 Corcy-Debray (2001) 425: le jury, présidé par Jules Martha, était composé de Gustave Bloch, Gustave Glotz, Plessis, Lafarge et Émile Bourgeois.

84 Sur cette élection, voir Corcy-Debray (2001) 425 *sq*.

85 Mucchielli (1995) 63 *sq*.

86 Sur les rapports entre Fustel de Coulanges et Durkheim, voir Momigliano (1975) 175 *sq*.

87 Sur l'émergence et l'offensive de l'école durkheimienne voir Mucchielli (1995) 64 *sq*. et Prost (1996) 37.

participent pleinement.[88] Les sujets de mémoire et de thèse proposés aux jeunes chercheurs constituent un des domaine d'exercice du pouvoir universitaire, et l'on a vu qu'en histoire ancienne ils traduisaient bien cette nouvelle tendance. En ce qui concerne Carcopino, j'ai insisté plus haut sur les liens qui unissaient, au départ au moins, ses deux sujets dans la perspective commune des études annonaires, et il semble bien que celles-ci connurent alors, notamment autour de Cagnat et de Glotz, une faveur certaine. Les premières recherches de Carcopino se placent clairement dans ce contexte de développement et de renouvellement de l'historiographie française. Mais, dans le même temps, la façon dont il aborde les sources et mène leur explication, dans le domaine de la fiscalité et de l'histoire agraire, le rattache aussi à l'*Altertumswissenschaft*. L'influence de l'érudition allemande imprime profondément sa formation d'historien, et la marque de Mommsen se retrouve dans son intérêt pour le droit, l'analyse des institutions et de la législation, et le fonctionnement de l'administration. A la différence de Camille Jullian, son aîné de vingt ans, lui aussi marqué par l'enseignement de Mommsen, mais dans le contexte des années qui suivirent la défaite,[89] il est plus proche de ce dernier que de Fustel, et sa vision des institutions est plus liée à l'histoire de l'administration à la façon d'un Hirschfeld, qu'à celle des faits sociaux défendue par l'auteur de *La cité antique*.[90]

Dans les années 1900, la science française a surmonté le choc de 1870 et rattrapé le retard que ses savants estimaient être une des causes de la défaite.[91] Loin de provoquer chez le jeune Carcopino un complexe d'infériorité, les travaux de Mommsen, comme ceux de ses collègues, et de ses élèves et successeurs, semblent constituer pour lui un puissant modèle en même temps qu'un appel à rivaliser avec eux. Ce souci est très présent dans les souvenirs et la correspondance de Carcopino.[92] Dans cette perspective, la querelle avec Rostovtzeff puis la réplique apportée à Schulten prennent une dimension tout à fait significative et montrent bien la particularité de sa position. Héritier et en même temps émule de l'*Altertumswissenschaft*, il s'agissait pour lui de prouver ses capacités dans les disciplines qui en relevaient en tentant

88 Voir le tableau dressé par Mucchielli (1995) 75 *sq*. Dans cet article très riche, l'auteur montre que la dénonciation par l'École des *Annales* du poids de l'histoire événementielle dans l'université d'avant 1914 a été excessive, et il étudie les conditions intellectuelles et institutionnelles de l'expansion de l'histoire économique et sociale dans les années 1870-1930. Sur cette question, on se reportera aussi aux auteurs qu'il cite 56 n. 4 et à Prost (1996) 37 *sq*.

89 Camille Jullian était né en 1859. En 1883, à l'issue de son séjour à l'École française de Rome, il se rendit en Allemagne, dans le cadre d'une mission d'études, pour suivre le séminaire de Mommsen à Berlin; voir Motte (1980) et (1990); sur le rôle de Jullian et ses rapports avec l'Allemagne, voir aussi Nicolet (2003) 226 *sq*.

90 Même si l'oeuvre de Fustel et celle de Mommsen ne sont pas de ce point de vue sans rapports, comme le souligne Nicolet (2003) 218 *sq*.

91 Voir Mucchielli (1995) 59 *sq*. avec l'ensemble des références sur cette question; voir aussi le chapitre de Nicolet (2003) intitulé 'La bataille de l'érudition'.

92 On citera par exemple l'anecdote concernant Albert Grenier et Wolfgang Helbig, rapportée par Carcopino (1968a). La lettre envoyée par Gustave Bloch à Carcopino le 3 novembre 1917 (MS 7137, folio 35) montre bien la réalité de cette concurrence. Lui montrant les avantages d'une soutenance rapide (voir *supra*), il insiste sur l'importance de ne pas se laisser devancer par les Allemands, en précisant 'Nous ne savons pas ce qu'ils ont fait ou ce qu'ils préparent depuis la guerre'.

de la battre sur son propre terrain. On insistera d'ailleurs sur l'admiration que Carcopino nourrissait visiblement pour Rostovtzeff, dont l'exemple montrait que l'on pouvait assimiler la science allemande et en égaler les savants,[93] sans pour autant perdre son caractère national.[94]

Mais on doit aller plus loin, car ce qui rattache Carcopino à la science allemande ne tient pas seulement aux méthodes mais aussi au sujet de ses recherches. J'ai évoqué plus haut la seconde génération de l'*Altertumswissenschaft* et l'ouverture qui s'était opérée à travers elle vers une histoire administrative, agraire et régionale. Il me semble que le Carcopino de *La loi de Hiéron* se rattache aussi à cette nouvelle tendance historiographique et que le sujet de son livre trouve ici une autre origine. Rappelons en effet que son enquête s'inscrit dans un horizon documentaire enrichi par la découverte et la publication de plusieurs sources relatives à la fiscalité et à l'organisation agraire dans l'Antiquité. J'ai déjà évoqué les inscriptions domaniales africaines, et il faut aussi souligner l'importance des documents papyrologiques et tout particulièrement du *Papyrus des revenus* (*Revenue Law*). Apparu sur le marché des antiquités en 1893-1895 et publié par Grenfell et Mahaffy en 1896,[95] il fut repris et amélioré pour les passages les plus importants dans le recueil de Mitteis et Wilcken.[96] On sait qu'il s'agit d'une loi financière de Ptolémée II Philadelphe, datant de 264-263 a.C. et instituée pour subvenir au culte de sa femme défunte Arsinoé.[97] Or, Wilcken et Rostovtzeff avaient souligné dès 1897-1899 les analogies entre ce règlement et la *lex Hieronica*, qui lui est très légèrement

93 Sur l'influence de la science allemande sur Rostovtzeff, Andreau (1988) xi *sq.*; sans nier son importance, Marcone (1999) insiste aussi sur le rôle de l'Italie et des savants italiens.

94 Voici la présentation qu'en donne Carcopino (1968a) 74: 'La renommée de Rostovtzeff avait déjà débordé les frontières de sa Russie natale et son autorité devait grandir d'année en année jusqu'au moment où, émigré aux Etats-Unis après la révolution bolchevique, il allait, de sa chaire de Yale, susciter une renaissance éclatante des études classiques en Amérique et imposer la moindre de ses productions à l'attention des érudits dans le monde entier.' Par la suite, Rostovtzeff et Carcopino entretinrent une correspondance assez suivie jusque vers le milieu des années 1930. Ces lettres sont instructives sur l'estime qu'ils se portaient, et deux exemples suffiront à l'illustrer. Tout d'abord le projet formé par Carcopino de traduire la *Social and economic history of the Roman Empire*. Il fut fortement soutenu par Rostovtzeff auprès de l'éditeur anglais mais échoua, apparemment pour des raisons financières (lettres du 18 juillet 1928 (folio 202) et du 2 août 1928 (folio 203)). Ensuite, en 1929, Rostovtzeff souhaita que Carcopino vienne à Doura Europos comme délégué de l'Académie des Inscriptions et belles lettres, pour conseiller les fouilles et renforcer de son autorité la position de Rostovtzeff vis-à-vis de la Fondation Rockfeller qui finançait le chantier (lettre du 29 novembre 1929, (folio 210); la lettre n'est pas adressée à Carcopino mais à un correspondant dont l'identité n'est pas précisée; il s'agit à l'évidence d'un membre de l'Institut, dont Carcopino ne faisait alors pas encore partie).

95 Grenfell & Mahaffy (1896).

96 Mitteis & Wilcken (1912) I no. 181, 249, 258 et 299.

97 Bouché-Leclercq (1903-1907) II 193 *sq.*

postérieure,[98] et que l'on connaît par le texte du *de Frumento*.[99] Il y avait là un sujet à traiter, à condition de posséder une solide formation classique, et Carcopino l'a saisi.

Si l'on suppose comme je l'ai fait plus haut que les sujets de recherche étaient en premier lieu suggérés par les maîtres, il faut tenter, pour terminer, de se prononcer sur celui qui pourrait être le candidat le plus probable pour avoir orienté ou conforté Carcopino dans cette direction. Sans négliger le rôle de Gustave Bloch, dont il fut très proche, j'hésite pour *La loi de Hiéron* entre deux noms. D'abord celui de René Cagnat, dont Carcopino avait suivi les cours au Collège de France. Il avait sollicité ses conseils, et pour s'être intéressé aux questions fiscales à Rome, Cagnat ne devait pas ignorer les progrès récents des connaissances en ce domaine. A côté de lui, Auguste Bouché-Leclercq pourrait aussi avoir joué un rôle déterminant. Avec Maspero, il était certainement le meilleur connaisseur en France de l'Égypte hellénistique et de son système financier et fiscal dont on commençait à entrevoir la complexité. Son *Histoire des Lagides* avait commencé à paraître en 1903, et il était professeur à la Sorbonne depuis 1887.[100] Nous savons qu'il fut en relation avec Carcopino, qui le tint dès 1906 informé de ses travaux par des envois réguliers.[101] Nous savons aussi qu'il fut le rapporteur du manuscrit de *La loi de Hiéron*.[102] Son rôle est d'ailleurs implicitement souligné par Gustave Bloch qui peu de temps avant la soutenance de sa thèse annonça à Carcopino l'absence dans son jury de Bouché-Leclercq, en précisant qu'elle serait d'autant plus regrettable qu'il était 'le seul qui ait pris connaissance de [sa] *Loi d'Hiéron*'.[103]

Conclusion: Carcopino et l'histoire économique

Les premiers travaux de Jérôme Carcopino s'inscrivent tout à fait dans le contexte de l'historiographie au début du XXe siècle et participent même aux renouvellements de la discipline historique, dans ses méthodes comme dans ses objets, et cela tant en France qu'en Allemagne, ou parmi les historiens qui sans être Allemands, comme Rostovtzeff, se rattachaient à l'école allemande. Avec *La loi de Hiéron*, qui levait le voile sur la manière dont

98 La *lex Hieronica* n'a pu être mise en place qu'à partir du moment où Hiéron a établi fermement son pouvoir et procédé à la réorganisation intérieure du royaume, soit à partir de 261 a.C; Carcopino (1919) 65 *sq.*; de Sensi Sestito (1977) 233.

99 Carcopino (1919) xv n. 1 a fait état de l'incertitude concernant la paternité du rapprochement entre la loi de Ptolémée II Philadelphe et la *lex Hieronica*. Selon lui, 'la priorité serait en faveur de M. Wilcken' dans son compte-rendu de l'édition Grenfell et Mahaffy (Wilcken (1897)) et dans son volume sur les *ostraka* (Wilcken (1899) 513). Cependant, Rostovtzeff (1910c) 233 affirme que Wilcken et lui-même sont arrivés indépendamment l'un de l'autre à des conclusions identiques sur cette question. La publication en russe de sa thèse de magistère consacrée à la ferme d'État date précisément de 1899. Quant à la traduction allemande de 1902, elle contient une analyse détaillée des analogies entre les deux documents, mais cite aussi et discute les publications de Wilcken mentionnées plus haut.

100 Charle (1985) 31 *sq.*

101 Lettre du 2 juillet 1906 (MS 7137, folio 261).

102 Lettres du 27 juillet et du 4 décembre 1912 (MS 7137, folios 267 et 268).

103 Lettre du 13 novembre 1919 (M 7137, folio 57); Bouché-Leclercq avait pris sa retraite en 1918 et semble d'après ses dernières lettres à Carcopino avoir eu ensuite une activité scientifique réduite; il mourut en 1923.

le système fiscal d'un État hellénistique avait été conservé et aménagé par le droit de Rome et montrait un aspect de 'l'économie royale' de la Sicile d'Hiéron, et avec la publication de l'inscription d'Aïn El Djemala, qui enrichissait la connaissance de la législation domaniale de l'Afrique, il prenait place parmi les spécialistes des études juridiques, administratives et agraires qui dominaient alors l'histoire ancienne. On a dit souvent que Carcopino s'était ensuite détourné de l'histoire économique, pour s'orienter vers ce que l'on présente tantôt comme une 'histoire politique événementielle et religieuse', au contenu 'généraliste' et à la forme 'narrative traditionnelle' et 'sans aucune innovation méthodologique',[104] tantôt comme une histoire davantage tournée vers les individus, et s'inscrivant dans une perspective à la fois humaniste et empreinte d'une dimension spirituelle.[105] Je ne prendrai pas part à ce débat dont les termes ne me semblent pas bien posés, et je me limiterai donc à quelques remarques pour essayer de nuancer une présentation du parcours scientifique de Jérôme Carcopino durant cette période que je trouve par trop tranchée. D'abord, on ne doit pas négliger le fait qu'il n'oublia pas ses premières recherches et qu'il y revint même, quelques années plus tard, avec ses travaux sur les Gracques et la question agraire, y compris pour le manuel qu'il rédigea en partie avec Gustave Bloch pour la collection Glotz.[106] Ensuite, il ne paraît pas exact ni approprié de parler d''abandon' de l'histoire économique à propos de Carcopino, et de réorientation vers un autre domaine de l'histoire, parce qu'il est peu probable qu'il se serait lui-même défini à ce moment-là comme un historien de l'économie. Ses travaux sur la Sicile et l'Afrique se rattachent à la fois à l'héritage fustélien et à celui de l'*Altertumswissenschaft*, c'est-à-dire à une histoire dont l'angle d'attaque était d'abord institutionnel,[107] ce qui correspond d'ailleurs à la nature et au contenu des sources écrites qui constituaient alors l'essentiel de la documentation disponible. Dans le domaine économique, cette histoire s'attachait donc en priorité à l'administration de l'économie, au prélèvement d'État, à l'approvisionnement et aux cadres juridiques et fiscaux de l'activité agraire. Enfin, les savants

104 Corcy-Debray (2001) 450 *sq.*; elle n'approfondit pas les raisons de l'évolution qu'elle décrit, ce qui est regrettable, y compris dans l'optique adoptée dans ce livre. Le grand reproche qui lui est fait ici est bien sûr d'être passé 'à côté de l'étude des structures, de l'histoire économique et sociale défendue par les Annales et par Marc Bloch' (p. 462) et d'être resté 'imperméable aux nouveaux territoires et aux nouvelles méthodes impulsées par l'école des Annales' (p. 466). Carcopino n'a cependant pas été complètement étranger aux mouvements qui ont préparé les Annales, puisqu'il a été en contact avec Henri Berr et a donné des comptes-rendus à la *Revue de synthèse historique* (on en trouvera la liste dans les Tables de cette revue pour 1900-1910, 7); sa collaboration s'est cependant estompée dès avant 1914, plus pour des raisons professionnelles et éditoriales que scientifiques, voir Corcy-Debray (2001) 452 *sq.* Sur Henri Berr, voir Mucchielli (1995) 71 *sq.*, avec d'autres références; pour une approche générale des rapports entre les antiquisants et les Annales, voir Frézouls (1983); Hartog (1983); et Corcy-Debray (2001) 459 pour le cas de Piganiol.

105 Grimal *et al.* (1981) 346 *sq.*, qui motive l'abandon de l'histoire économique par l'insuffisance des sources et le rôle très secondaire qu'y joue 'l'initiative des hommes'; ces lignes font toutefois peut-être allusion à des positions exprimées plus tard par Carcopino, et il n'est pas sûr qu'elles ne reflètent pas, en partie au moins, les idées de Grimal lui-même.

106 Carcopino (1928) et (1929). Dans Bloch & Carcopino (1932), le chapitre 7 consacré à la crise agraire a été rédigé par Carcopino.

107 Il est significatif que la *Revue de synthèse historique* dans son 'Bulletin critique' présente ainsi, en 1910, la rubrique consacrée à l'histoire économique: 'Histoire économique (faits et institutions)' (vol. 19 (1910) 390), ou 'Histoire des institutions politiques et économiques' (vol. 20 (1910) 383).

de cette époque n'étaient pas aussi spécialisés que nous le sommes devenus. Tout le champ de l'histoire ancienne s'ouvrait devant eux et ils l'exploraient de la manière la plus large et avec toute la voracité d'une science encore nouvelle. On ne peut pas se mettre dans la tête du Carcopino de 1912 ou de 1919, et je ne crois pas qu'il se soit expliqué sur ce point, mais il ne me semble pas qu'il ait vu les choses de cette manière. Dans la suite immédiate de sa carrière et l'évolution de sa production scientifique, on doit admettre que l'Afrique, Ostie, puis des orientations éditoriales plus larges, eurent un rôle beaucoup plus déterminant qu'un choix thématique de spécialité.

On trouverait certainement un grand profit à poursuivre l'étude de l'oeuvre de Carcopino, particulièrement en la mettant en parallèle avec celle de Rostovtzeff dans la même période. La ressemblance de leurs parcours et leurs profils scientifiques avant 1914 est en effet frappante et fait d'autant mieux ressortir les différences qui les éloignent après 1919. Engagés au départ sur des pistes communes, leurs travaux empruntèrent alors des directions divergentes, en même temps que leurs conceptions du questionnement historique tendirent aussi à s'éloigner l'une de l'autre. Il me semble qu'une comparaison comme celle-là ne pourrait faire l'impasse sur une réflexion plus large sur la disparition dans les études anciennes en France, après la Première guerre mondiale et jusque vers 1960, du courant d'histoire économique et sociale dont nous avons vu l'émergence et le dynamisme dans les années 1890-1900. Tout se passe comme si la génération des héritiers de Fustel de Coulanges, celle de Glotz, Guiraud, Cagnat et Bloch, n'avait pas eu, dans ce domaine, de successeurs immédiats. Sans nullement remettre en cause l'orientation ni la valeur de sa production ultérieure, le fait que Carcopino n'ait pas orienté ses travaux dans cette direction, pour devenir ce qui aurait pu être une sorte de Rostovtzeff français, a peut-être à voir avec ce mouvement de repli des études anciennes du champ de l'histoire économique et sociale dans la France de l'entre-deux-guerres. Les causes de ce repli sont certainement complexes et doivent, selon moi, être recherchées dans deux directions. Il faut naturellement faire la part des tendances et des inerties propres à la discipline et à son organisation institutionnelle et académique. A côté de cela, il faut aussi, je crois, essayer de mesurer l'impact du conflit, tant sur le plan humain qu'intellectuel. D'une manière générale, étudier les effets de la Première guerre mondiale sur le monde universitaire et la vie scientifique serait d'ailleurs une tâche à la fois indispensable et passionnante, à la condition d'y intégrer les spécialistes qui en ont récemment renouvelé l'histoire.[108]

Université de Bordeaux – Institut Ausonius

108 Je pense à l'équipe internationale qui gravite autour de l'Historial de Péronne, et je citerai simplement l'ouvrage qui me semble le plus significatif de ce renouvellement, Audoin-Rouzeau & Becker (2000). Le 10 novembre 2003, Stéphane Audoin-Rouzeau, a prononcé, devant les étudiants de l'Université de Bordeaux, une conférence sur les jeunes et la mort des jeunes durant la Première guerre mondiale, en particulier les étudiants. Cette évocation de l'impact du conflit dans le monde universitaire m'a semblé aller dans la direction de ce que pourrait être un projet pluridisciplinaire sur ce thème.

BIBLIOGRAPHY

Adriani, A. *et al.* 1971. *Odeon ed altri 'monumenti' archeologici* (Palermo)

Alexander, M. C. 1976. 'Hortensius' speech in defence of Verres', *Phoenix* 30: 46-53

—— 1985. '*Praemia* in the *Quaestiones* in the late Republic', *CPh* 80: 20-32

—— 2002. *The case for the prosecution in the Ciceronian era* (Ann Arbor)

Allen, R. E. 1983. *The Attalid kingdom: a constitutional history* (Oxford)

Ampolo, C., A. Magnetto & L. Porciani. 2001. 'Note per una nuova edizione delle tavole di Entella', *ASNP*, ser. IV, 6: 1-10

Ampolo, C. *et al.* 2001. *Da un'antica città di Sicilia: i decreti di Entella e Nakone* (Pisa)

Ampolo, C. & M. C. Parra. 2005. 'L'agora di Segesta', in P. Minà (ed.), *Urbanistica e architettura nella Sicilia greca* (Palermo), 167-70

Andreau, J. 1988. 'Antique, moderne et temps présent: la carrière et l'oeuvre de M. I. Rostovtzeff (1870-1952)', in M. I. Rostovtzeff, *Histoire économique et sociale de l'Empire romain*, transl. O. Demange (Paris), i-lxxxiv

—— 2001. *Banques et affaires dans le monde romain IVe av. J.-C.–IIIe apr. J.-C.* (Paris) (original English edn *Banking and business in the Roman world* (Cambridge 1999))

Andreau, J. & R. Étienne. 1984. 'Vingt ans de recherches sur l'archaïsme et la modernité des sociétés antiques', *REA* 86.1-4: 55-83

Andreau, J. & C. Virlouvet (eds). 2002. *L'Information et la mer dans le monde antique* (Rome)

Audoin-Rouzeau, S. & A. Becker. 2000. *14-18 Retrouver la guerre* (Paris)

Austin, M. & P. Vidal-Naquet. 1972. *Économie et sociétés en Grèce ancienne* (Paris)

Badian, E. 1962. 'Waiting for Sulla', *JRS* 52: 47-61

—— 1964. 'Notes on provincial governors from the Social War down to Sulla's victories', in *Studies in Greek and Roman history* (Oxford), 71-104

—— 1984. 'Three non-trials in Cicero', *Klio* 66: 291-309

Bell, M., III. 1981. *Morgantina studies*, I, *the terracottas* (Princeton)

—— 1986-87. 'La fontana ellenistica di Morgantina', *Quaderni dell'Istituto di Archeologia della Facoltà di Lettere e Filosofia della Università di Messina* 2: 111-24

—— 1988. 'Excavations at Morgantina 1980-1985, preliminary report XII, with a note by R. R. Holloway', *AJA* 92: 313-42

—— 1993. 'Observations on Western Greek stoas', in R. T. Scott & A. R. Scott (eds), *Eius virtutis studiosi: classical and postclassical studies in memory of Frank Edward Brown (1908-1988)*, Studies in the History of Art 43 (Washington), 327-41

—— 1999. 'Centro e periferia nel regno siracusano di Ierone II', in *La colonisation grecque en Méditerranée occidentale, Actes de la rencontre scientifique en homage à Georges Vallet*, Coll. EFR 251 (Paris, Rome), 257-77

—— 2000. 'La provenienza ritrovata, cercando il contesto di antichità trafugate', in *Antichità senza provenienza*, II, supplement to *BA* 101-02 (Rome), 31-41

—— 2004a. 'Una banca pubblica sull'agora di Morgantina?', in M. Caccamo Caltabiano, L. Campagna & A. Pinzone (eds), *Nuove prospettive della ricerca sulla Sicilia del III sec. a.C., archeologia, numismatica, storia*, Pelorias 11 (Messina), 135-49

—— 2004b. 'Bankers' houses at Soluntum and Agrigentum', in S. T. A. M. Mols & E. M. Moorman (eds), *Omni pedum stare, saggi architettonici e circumvesuviani in memoriam Jos de Waele* (Naples), 99-106

—— 2005. 'L'agora di Morgantina', in P. Minà (ed.), *Urbanistica e architettura nella Sicilia greca* (Palermo), 166

—— In press. 'Rapporti urbanistici fra Camarina e Morgantina', in L. de Lachenal (ed.), *Camarina 2600 anni dopo la fondazione, nuovi studi sulla città e sul territorio*

Bergemann, J. 1990. *Römische Reiterstatuen, Ehrendenkmäler im öffentlichen Bereich* (Mainz)

Bernabò Brea, L. 1956. *Akrai* (Catania)

Bloch, G. & J. Carcopino. 1932. *La République romaine de 133 avant J.–C. à la mort de César*, I, *des Gracques à Sulla* (Paris)

Boeckh, A. 1817. *Die Staatshaushaltung der Athener* (Berlin)

Bogaert, R. 1981. 'Le statut des banques en Égypte ptolémaïque', *AC* 50: 86-99 (repr. in R. Bogaert, *Trapezitica Aegyptiaca, recueil de recherches sur la banque en Égypte gréco-romaine* (Florence 1994), 47-57)

—— 1983. 'Les modèles des banques ptolémaïques', in *Egypt and the Hellenistic world, proceedings of the international colloquium (Leuven, 24-26 May 1982)*, Studia Hellenistica 27 (Louvain), 13-29 (repr. in R. Bogaert, *Trapezitica Aegyptiaca, recueil de recherches sur la banque en Égypte gréco-romaine* (Florence 1994), 33-45)

Bongert, Y. 1952. 'Recherches sur les récupérateurs', in *Varia. Études de droit romain*, Publications de l'Institut de Droit romain de l'Université de Paris 9 (Paris), 99-266

Bouché-Leclercq, A. 1903-07. *Histoire des Lagides*, 4 vols (Paris)

Bruhns, H. 1996. 'Max Weber, l'économie et l'histoire', *Annales* (*HSS*) 6: 1259-87

—— 1998. 'A propos de l'histoire ancienne et de l'économie politique chez Max Weber', in M. Weber, *Économie et société dans l'Antiquité; précédé de Les causes sociales du déclin de la civilisation antique*, trans. Cl. Colliot-Thélène & F. Laroche (Paris)

Brunt, P. A. 1980. 'Patronage and politics in the *Verrines*', *Chiron* 10: 273-89

—— 1987 (revised edn). *Italian manpower* (Oxford)

Bülow-Jacobsen, A., H. Cuvigny & K. A. Worp. 2000. '*Litura:* ἀλειφάς not ἄλειφαρ, and other words for "erasure"', *ZPE* 130: 175-82

Burkhalter, F. 1990. 'Archives locales et archives centrales en Egypte romaine', *Chiron* 20: 191-216

Butler, S. 2002. *The hand of Cicero* (London)

Buttrey, T. V., K. T. Erim, T. D. Groves & R. Ross Holloway. 1989. *Morgantina studies*, II, *the coins* (Princeton)

Caccamo Caltabiano, M. (ed.). 1995. *La Sicilia tra l'Egitto e Roma, la monetazione siracusana dell'età di Ierone II*, Atti Accademia Peloritana dei Pericolanti Suppl. 1 (Messina)

Cagnat, R. 1880. *Le 'portorium' (douanes, péages, octrois) chez les Romains* (Paris)

—— 1882. *Étude historique sur les impôts indirects chez les Romains jusqu'aux invasions des barbares d'après les documents littéraires et épigraphiques* (Paris)

—— 1916. 'L'annone d'Afrique', *MAI*, 247-77

Cahill, N. 2002. *Household and city organization at Olynthus* (New Haven)

Calderone, S. 1964-65. 'Problemi dell'organizzazione della provincia di Sicilia', *Kokalos* 10-11: 63-98

Camodeca, G. 1999. *Tabulae Pompeianae Sulpiciorum*, 2 vols (Rome)

Campagna, L. 2003. 'La Sicilia di età repubblicana nella storiografia degli ultimi cinquant'anni', *Ostraka* 12.1: 7-31

—— 2004. 'Architettura e ideologia della basileia a Siracusa nell'età di Ierone II', in M. Caccamo Caltabiano, L. Campagna & A. Pinzone (eds), *Nuove prospettive della ricerca sulla Sicilia del III sec. a.C., archeologia, numismatica, storia*, Pelorias 11 (Messina), 151-89

Carandini, A. 1983. 'Columella's vineyard and the rationality of the Roman economy', *Opus* 2.1: 177-204

Carcopino, J. 1905a. 'Les cités de Sicile devant l'impôt romain, *Ager decumanus* et *ager censorius*', *MEFR* 25: 3-53

—— 1905b. '*Decumani.* Notes sur l'organisation des sociétés publicaines sous la République', *MEFR* 25: 401-42

—— 1906a. 'La Sicile agricole au dernier siècle de la République romaine', *Vierteljahrschrift für Social- und Wirtschaftsgeschichte*, 128-85

—— 1906b. 'L'inscription d'Aïn-el-Djemala. Contribution à l'histoire des *saltus* africains et du colonat partiaire', *MEFR* 26: 365-481

—— 1908. 'Encore l'inscription d'Aïn-el-Djemala', *Klio* 8.2: 154-85

—— 1909a. 'Les monographies locales dans les études d'histoire ancienne. A propos d'une thèse récente' (review of Dubois 1907), *Revue de synthèse historique* 19: 194-202

—— 1909b. 'Histoire de l'ostracisme athénien', in F. Alcan (ed.), *Mélanges d'histoire ancienne*, Université de Paris, Bibliothèque de la Faculté des Lettres 25 (Paris), 87-266

—— 1919. *La loi de Hiéron et les Romains* (Paris)

—— 1928. 'Les triumvirs de la *lex Sempronia* et l'histoire des Gracques', in *Autour des Gracques* (Paris), 125-290

—— 1929. 'Les lois agraires des Gracques et la guerre sociale', *BAGB* 22: 3-23

—— 1968a. *Souvenirs romains* (Paris)

—— 1968b (2nd edn). *Virgile et les origines d'Ostie* (Paris) (1st edn 1919)

Carettoni, G. 1961. 'Tusa (Messina). Scavi di Halaesa (seconda relazione)', *NSc*, ser. 8, 15: 266-321

Carey, C. 1994. 'Legal space in classical Athens', *G&R* 41: 172-86

Ceserani, G. 2000. 'The charm of the siren: the place of classical Sicily in historiography', in C. Smith and J. Serrati (eds), *Sicily from Aeneas to Augustus* (Edinburgh), 174-93

Chapelain, E. 1908. 'Rapport sur les travaux des Écoles d'Athènes et de Rome pendant les années 1906-1907', *CRAI*, 288-305

Charle, C. 1985. *Les professeurs de la faculté des lettres de Paris. Dictionnaire biographique*, I, *1809-1908* (Paris)

—— 1986. *Les professeurs de la faculté des lettres de Paris. Dictionnaire biographique*, II, *1909-1939* (Paris)
Chouquer, G. & F. Favory. 2001. *L'Arpentage romain. Histoire des textes. Droit. Techniques* (Paris)
Christ, K. 1979. *Von Gibbon zu Rostovtzeff* (Darmstadt)
Classen, C. J. 1985. *Recht, Rhetorik, Politik* (Darmstadt)
Coarelli, F. 1981. 'La Sicilia tra la fine della guerra annibalica e Cicerone', in A. Giardina & A. Schiavone (eds), *Società romana e produzione schiavistica*, I, *l'Italia: insediamenti e forme economiche* (Rome, Bari), 3-18
Constans, L.-A. 1934. *Cicéron, correspondance*, I, Collection des Universtiés de France (Paris)
Corbeill, A. 1996. *Controlling laughter: political humor in the late Roman Republic* (Princeton)
Corcy-Debray, St. 2001. *Jérôme Carcopino, un historien à Vichy* (Paris)
Cordano, F. 1999. 'Le istituzioni delle città greche di Sicilia nelle fonti epigrafiche', in M. I. Gulletta (ed.), *Sicilia epigrafica, atti del convegno internazionale di Erice, 15-18 ottobre 1998*, 2 vols (Pisa), I, 149-58
Costa, E. 1928 (2nd edn). *Cicerone giureconsulto*, 2 vols (Bologna)
Coudry, M. 1994. 'Sénatus-consultes et *acta senatus*: rédaction, conservation et archivage des documents émanant du Sénat, de l'époque de César à celle des Sévères', in S. Demougin (ed.), *La mémoire perdue. À la recherche des archives oubliées, publiques et privées, de la Rome antique* (Paris), 65-102
Cowles, F. H. 1917. *Gaius Verres, an historical biography* (Ithaca)
Crawford, J. W. 1994. *M. Tullius Cicero: the fragmentary speeches* (Atlanta)
Crawford, M. H. 1977. 'Rome and the Greek world: economic relationships', *Economic History Review* 30: 42-52
—— 1990. 'Origini e sviluppi del sistema provinciale romano', in G. Clemente, F. Coarelli & E. Gabba (eds), *Storia di Roma*, II, *l'impero mediterraneo*, i, *la repubblica imperiale* (Turin), 91-121
Crook, J. A. 1976. '"Sponsione prouocare": its place in Roman litigation', *JRS* 66: 132-38
—— 1995. *Legal advocacy in the Roman world* (London)
Cuomo di Caprio, N. 1993. *Morgantina studies*, III, *le fornaci* (Princeton)
Daehn, H.-S. 1991. *Studia Ietina*, III, *die Gebäude an der Westseite der Agora von Iaitas* (Zürich)
David, J.-M. 1992. *Le patronat judiciaire au dernier siècle de la République romaine*, Bibliothèque des Écoles françaises d'Athènes et de Rome 277 (Rome)
de Angelis, F. 1998. 'Ancient past, imperial present: the British Empire in T. J. Dunbabin's "The western Greeks"', *Antiquity* 72: 539-49
—— 2000. 'Estimating the agricultural base of Greek Sicily', *PBSR* 58: 111-48
Degenkolb, H. 1861. *Die Lex Hieronica und das Pfändungsrecht der Steuerpächter. Beitrag zur Erklärung der Verrinen* (Berlin) (repr. Amsterdam 1968)
de Juliis, E. M. 1984. *Gli ori di Taranto in età ellenistica* (Milan)
Deloume, A. 1892 (2nd edn). *Les manieurs d'argent à Rome jusqu'à l'Empire* (Paris)
de Martino, F. 1993. 'La storia dei pubblicani e gli scritti dei giuristi', *Labeo* 39: 5-41

Demougin, S. (ed.). 1994. *La mémoire perdue. À la recherche des archives oubliées, publiques et privées, de la Rome antique* (Paris)

de Pachtère, F. G. 1909. *La propriété foncière dans l'Apennin de Plaisance d'après la table de Veleia*, Mémoire de l'École française de Rome (unpubl. MS)

de Ste Croix, G. E. M. 1956. 'Greek and Roman accounting', in A. C. Littleton & B. S. Yamey (eds), *Studies in the history of accounting* (London), 14-74

de Sensi Sestito, G. 1977. *Gerone II. Un monarca ellenistico in Sicilia* (Palermo)

Deussen, P. W. 1994. 'The granaries of Morgantina and the Lex Hieronica', in *Le ravitaillement en blé de Rome et des centres urbains des débuts de la république jusqu'au haut empire* (Naples, Rome), 231-35

de Visscher, F. 1964. 'La justice romaine en Cyrénaïque', *RIDA* 11: 321-33

—— 1965. *Les édits d'Auguste découverts à Cyrène* (Osnabrück)

Dickison, S. K. 1992. *Cicero's Verrine Oration II.4* (Detroit MI)

Dilke, O. A. 1980. 'Divided loyalties in eastern Sicily under Verres', in *Atti del IV colloquium Tullianum, Palermo 28 settembre-2 ottobre 1979*, Ciceroniana 4 (Rome), 43-51

Dubois, C. 1907. *Pouzzoles antique. Histoire et topographie* (Paris)

Duncan Jones, R. 1982 (2nd edn). *The economy of the Roman empire: quantitative studies* (Cambridge)

—— 1990. *Structure and scale of the Roman economy* (Cambridge)

Dunkle, J. R. 1967. 'The Greek tyrant and Roman political invective of the late Republic', *TAPhA* 98: 151-71

Dureau de La Malle, A. 1840. *Économie politique des Romains* (Paris)

—— 1905. *L'economia politica dei Romani*, in V. Pareto (ed.), *Biblioteca di storia economica* (Milan 1903-1929), I, 2, 5-515

—— 1986. *Économie politique des Romains*, anastatic repr. with intro. and notes by B. Hemmerdinger (Milan)

École française de Rome. 1987. *Annuaire des membres (1873-1986)* (Rome)

Erskine, A. 1991. 'Hellenistic monarchy and Roman political invective', *CQ* 41: 106-20

Fantasia, U. 1999. 'I *sitophylakes* e i *sitônia* di Tauromenio', in M. I. Gulletta (ed.), *Sicilia epigrafica, atti del convegno internazionale Erice, 15-18 ottobre 1998*, 2 vols (Pisa), I, 251-79

Fernique, E. 1880. *Étude sur Préneste, ville du Latium*, BEFAR 17 (Paris)

Ferrary, J.-L. 1975. 'Cicéron et la loi judiciaire de Cotta (70 av. J.-C.)', *MEFR(A)* 87: 321-48

Ferruti, F. 2004. 'L'attività di Ierone II a favore dei ginnasi', in M. Caccamo Caltabiano, L. Campagna & A. Pinzone (eds), *Nuove prospettive della ricerca sulla Sicilia del III sec. a.C., archeologia, numismatica, storia*, Pelorias 11 (Messina), 191-206

Fezzi, L. 2003. *Falsificazione di documenti pubblici nella Roma tardorepubblicana (133-31 a.C.)* (Florence)

Finley, M. I. 1974. *L'Économie antique* (Paris) (first publ. as *The ancient economy* (London 1973))

—— (ed.). 1979. *The Bücher-Meyer controversy* (New York)

—— 1982. 'Le document et l'histoire économique antique', *Annales* (*ESC*) 37.5-6: 697-713 (repr. in *Sur l'histoire ancienne* (Paris 2001) 68-96; English edn in *Ancient history: evidence and models* (London 1985) 27-46)

Fiorentini, G. (ed.). 1990. *Gli edifici pubblici civili di Agrigento antica* (Agrigento)

—— 2005. 'Le *agorai* e gli edifici civili di Agrigento', in P. Minà (ed.), *Urbanistica e architettura nella Sicilia greca* (Palermo), 61-63

Fisher, N. 1992. *Hybris* (Warminster)

—— 2001. *Aeschines: against Timarchos* (Oxford)

Frank, T. 1933-40. *An economic survey of ancient Rome*, 6 vols (Baltimore)

Fraschetti, A. 1981. Per una prosopografia dello sfruttamento in Sicilia', in A. Giardina & A. Schiavone (eds), *Società romana e produzione schiavistica*, I, *l'Italia: insediamenti e forme economiche* (Rome, Bari), 51-77

Frazel, T. D. 2004. 'The composition and circulation of Cicero's *In Verrem*', *CQ* 54: 128-42

Frézouls, É. 1983. 'Les sciences de l'Antiquité à l'Université de Strasbourg au lendemain de 1919', in Ch.-O. Carbonell & G. Livet (eds), *Au berceau des Annales. Le milieu strasbourgeois. L'histoire en France au début du XXe siècle* (Toulouse), 39-41

Fuhrmann, M. 1980. 'Tecniche narrative nella seconda orazione contro Verre', *Ciceroniana. Rivista di studi ciceroniani* 4: 27-42

Fustel de Coulanges, N. D. 1880. *Étude sur la propriété à Sparte* (Paris)

—— 1885. 'Le colonat romain' and 'Les Germains connaissaient-ils la propriété des terres?', in *Recherches sur quelques problèmes d'histoire* (Paris) 3-186, 188-315

—— 1889. 'Le problème des origines de la propriété foncière', in *Questions historiques*, revised and completed following the author's notes by C. Jullian (Paris), 19-117

Gagarin, M. & D. MacDowell (trans.). 1998. *Antiphon and Andocides*, The Oratory of Classical Greece 1 (Texas)

Gallant, T. W. 1991. *Risk and survival in ancient Greece: reconstructing the rural domestic economy* (Stanford)

Garnsey, P. & R. Saller. 1987. *L'Empire romain, economie, société, culture* (Paris) (English edn, *The Roman empire: economy, society and culture* (London 1987))

Gelzer, M. 1962-64. *Kleine Schriften*, 3 vols (Wiesbaden)

Genovese, M. 1999. *Gli interventi edittali di Verre in materia di decime sicule*, Pubblicazioni della Facoltà di Giurisprudenza di Catania 162 (Milan)

Gernet, L. 1909. 'L'approvisionnement d'Athènes en blé aux Ve et IVe siècles', in F. Alcan (ed.), *Mélanges d'histoire ancienne*, Université de Paris, Bibliothèque de la Faculté des Lettres 25 (Paris) 269-391

Giammellaro, P. 2005. 'Il problema della presenza fenicia in Sicilia nella storiografia europea alla fine del XIX secolo: Adolf Holm ed Edward Freeman', in *Atti del V congresso internazionale di studi fenici e punici, Marsala-Palermo, 2-8 ottobre 2000*, 3 vols (Palermo), II, 567-74

Giuffrè, V. (ed.). 1977. *Les lois des Romains, 7e édition par un groupe de romanistes des 'Textes de droit romain', Tome II de Paul Frédéric Girard et Félix Senn*, Pubblicazioni della Facoltà di Giurisprudenza dell'Università di Camerino 12 (Naples)

Glotz, G. 1906. *Études sociales et juridiques sur l'antiquité grecque* (Paris)

Gotoff, H. C. 1986. 'Cicero's analysis of the prosecution speeches in the *Pro Caelio*: an exercise in practical criticism', *CPh* 81: 122-32

Graepler, D. 1997. *Tonfiguren im Grab: Fundkontexte hellenistischer Terrakotten aus der Nekropole von Tarant* (Munich)

Grenfell, B. P. & J. P. Mahaffy. 1896. *Revenue laws of Ptolemy Philadelphus. Edited from a Greek papyrus in the Bodleian Library, with a translation, commentary and appendices* (Oxford)

Grimal, P., Cl. Carcopino & P. Ourliac. 1981. *Jérôme Carcopino. Un historien au service de l'humanisme* (Paris)

Gros, P. & D.Theodorescu. 1985. 'Le mur nord du "forum" d'Assise, ornementation pariétale e spécialisation des espaces', *MEFR(A)* 97: 879-97

Gröschler, P. 1997. 'Die *tabellae* – Urkunden aus den pompejanischen und herkulanensischen Urkundenfunden', *Freiburger rechtsgeschichtliche Abhandlungen* 26: 199-245

Gruen, E.S. 1968. *Roman politics and the criminal courts, 149-78 B.C.* (Cambridge MA)

—— 1995 (2nd edn). *The last generation of the Roman Republic* (Berkeley)

Guiraud, P. 1887. *Les assemblées provinciales dans l'Empire romain* (Paris)

—— 1894. *La propriété foncière en Grèce jusqu'à la conquête romaine* (Paris)

—— 1896. *Fustel de Coulanges* (Paris)

—— 1905. *Études économiques sur l'Antiquité* (Paris)

—— 1907. *La proprieta fondiaria in Grecia sino alla conquista romana*, in V. Pareto (ed.), *Biblioteca di storia economica* (Milan 1903-1929), II, 2, 3-454

Haensch, R. 1992. 'Das Statthalterarchiv', *ZRG* 106: 209-317

Hansen, M. H. 1976. *Apagoge, endeixis and ephegesis against kakourgoi, atimoi, and pheugontes*, Odense University Classical Studies 8 (Odense)

Hartog, F. 1983. 'Strasbourg et l'histoire ancienne en 1919', in Ch.-O. Carbonell & G. Livet (eds), *Au berceau des Annales. Le milieu strasbourgeois. L'histoire en France au début du XXe siècle* (Toulouse), 41-44

—— 1988. *Le XIXe siècle et l'histoire, le cas Fustel de Coulanges* (Paris)

Hatzfeld, J. 1908. *Sur la date de l'agora des Italiens à Délos*, Mémoire de seconde année à l'École française d'Athènes

—— 1909. *Remarques sur les Italiens établis à Délos*, Mémoire de seconde année à l'École française d'Athènes (= 'Les Italiens résidant à Délos', *BCH* 36 (1912), 1-208)

—— 1919. *Les trafiquants italiens dans l'Orient hellénique* (Paris)

Haussoulier, B. 1910. 'Rapport sur les travaux des Écoles d'Athènes et de Rome en 1909', *CRAI*, 592-608

Heuss, A. 1963 (2nd edn). *Stadt und Herrscher des Hellenismus in ihren staats- und völkerrechtlichen Beziehungen*, Klio, Beiträge zur alten Geschichte, Beiheft 39 (Aalen)

Hinard, F. 1985. *Les proscriptions de la Rome républicaine*, CEFR 83 (Paris)

Hirschfeld, O. 1905 (2nd edn). *Die kaiserlichen Verwaltungsbeamten bis auf Diocletian* (Berlin)

Hoepfner, W. & E.-L. Schwandner. 1986. *Haus und Stadt im klassischen Griechenland* (Munich)

Holm, A. 1898. *Geschichte Siziliens im Alterthum*, III (Leipzig)

Hultsch, F. 1882 (2nd edn). *Griechische und römische Metrologie* (Berlin).

Humbert, G. 1867. 'Les douanes chez les Romains', *Recueil de l'Académie de législation de Toulouse* 16: 67-133

—— 1886. *Essai sur les finances et la comptabilité publique chez les Romains*, 2 vols (Paris)

Huvelin, P. 1897. *Essai historique sur le droit des marchés et des foires* (Paris)

—— 1904. 'Histoire économique: droit commercial (histoire interne et histoire externe)', *Revue de synthèse historique* 8: 198-243

Innocenti, B. 1994. 'Towards a theory of vivid description as practised in Cicero's Verrine Orations', *Rhetorica* 12: 355-81

Isler, H. P. 1994. 'Grabungen auf dem Monte Iato 1993', *AK* 37: 31-42

—— 2002. 'Grabungen auf dem Monte Iato 2001', *AK* 45: 112-23

—— 2004. 'Monte Iato: la trentatreesima campagna di scavo', *Sicilia Archeologica* 37(102): 5-33

—— 2005. 'L'agora di Iaitas', in P. Minà (ed.), *Urbanistica e architettura nella Sicilia greca* (Palermo), 165

Jacques, F. 1990. *Les cités de l'Occident romain, du Ier au VIe s. ap. J.-C.* (Paris)

Johnston, D. 1987. 'Three thoughts on Roman private law and the *Lex Irnitana*', *JRS* 77: 62-77

Jones, A. H. M. 1948. *Ancient economic history: an inaugural lecture delivered at University College London* (London)

Jouanique, P. 1968. 'Le "codex accepti et expensi" chez Cicéron: étude d'histoire de la comptabilité', *RD* 46: 5-31

Karlsson, L. 1993. 'Did the Romans allow the Sicilian Greeks to fortify their cities in the third century BC?', in P. G. Bilde, I. Nielsen & M. Nielsen (eds), *Aspects of Hellenism in Italy: towards a cultural unity?*, Acta Hyperborea 5 (Copenhagen), 31-51

Käsler, D. 1996. *Max Weber. Sa vie, son oeuvre, son influence*, trans. P. Fritsch (Paris)

Kelly, J. M. 1976. *Studies in the civil judicature in the Roman Republic* (Oxford)

Kennedy, G. 1968. 'The rhetoric of advocacy in Greece and Rome', *AJPh* 89: 419-36

Kennedy, G. 1972. *The art of rhetoric in the Roman world* (Princeton)

Kniep, F. 1896. *Societas publicanorum* (Iéna)

—— 1972. *The art of rhetoric in the ancient world* (Princeton)

Laffi, U. 1988. 'I limiti della competenza giurisdizionale dei magistrati locali', in *Estudios sobre la Tabula Siarensis*, Anejos de Archivo español de Arqueologia 9 (Madrid), 141-56

Lamberti, F. 1993. "*Tabulae Irnitanae*". *Municipalità e "ius Romanorum*", Pubblicazioni del Dipartimento di Diritto romano e Storia della Scienza romanistica dell'Università degli Studi di Napoli 'Federico II' 6 (Naples)

La Rosa, V. 1987. '"Archaiologhia" e storiografia: quale Sicilia?', in M. Aymard & G. Giarrizzo (eds), *Storia d'Italia. Le regioni dall'Unità a oggi. La Sicilia* (Turin), 699-731

Laurent-Vibert, R. 1908. 'Les publicains d'Asie en 51 av. J.-C. d'après la correspondance de Cicéron en Cilicie', *MEFR* 28: 171-84

—— 1909. *Études sur l'industrie à la fin de la République romaine,* Mémoire de l'École française de Rome (unpubl. MS)

Lazzeretti, A. 2006. *M. Tulli Ciceronis, In C. Verrem actionis secundae liber quartus (De signis): commento storico e archeologico* (Pisa)

Lemosse, M. 1998. 'Le procès provincial classique', in M. Humbert & Y. Thomas (eds), *Mélanges de droit romain et d'histoire ancienne. Hommage à la mémoire de A. Magdelain* (Paris), 239-46

Le Roux, P. 1991. 'Le juge et le citoyen dans le municipe d'Irni', *CCG* 2: 99-124
Levens, R. C. G. 1946. *Cicero. The Fifth Verrine Oration* (London)
Lewis, N. 1974. *Papyrus in classical antiquity* (Oxford)
—— 1989. *Papyrus in classical antiquity: a supplement*, Papyrologica Bruxellensia 23 (Brussels)
Liebenam, K. 1900. *Städteverwaltung im römischen Kaiserreiche* (Leipzig)
—— 1901. *s.v.* 'Decuma', in *RE* IV, 2, cols 2306-14
—— 1905. *s.v.* 'Dispensator', in *RE* V, 1, cols 1189-98
Lintott, A. 1976. 'The procedure under the *leges Calpurnia* and *Iunia de repetundis* and the *actio per sponsionem*', *ZPE* 22: 207-14
—— 1981. 'The *leges de repetundis* and associate measures under the Republic', *ZRG* 98: 162-212
—— 1990. 'Le procès devant les *recuperatores* d'après les données épigraphiques jusqu'au règne d'Auguste', *RD* 68: 1-11
—— 1992. *Judicial reform and land reform in the Roman Republic* (Cambridge)
Long, G. 1862 (2nd edn). *M. Tulli Ciceronis Orationes,* I, Bibliotheca Classica (London)
Luni, M. 2001. *Statue di bronzo a Forum Sempronii e in città del versante medioadriatico* (Urbino)
MacDowell, D. M. 1978. *The law in classical Athens* (London)
Macve, R. H. 1985. 'Some glosses on "Greek and Roman Accounting"', in P. A. Cartledge & F. D. Harvey (eds), *Crux. Essays presented to G. E. M. de Ste Croix on his 75th birthday* (Exeter), 233-64
Maggio, L. 1993. 'Processo criminale e giudici locali nella Sicilia dell'età ciceroniana', *Labeo* 39: 238-56
Malerba, L. 1968. *Storia della pianta del papiro in Sicilia e la produzione della carta in Siracusa* (Bologna)
Mancuso, G. 1997. '*Decretum praetoris*', *SDHI* 63: 343-400
Manganaro, G. 1963. 'Tre tavole di bronzo con decreti di "prossenia" del Museo di Napoli e il problema dei proagori in Sicilia', *Kokalos* 9: 205-20
—— 1972. 'Per una storia della Sicilia romana', *ANRW*, I.1 (Berlin), 442-61
—— 1980. 'La provincia romana', in E. Gabba & G. Vallet (eds), *La Sicilia antica*, 5 vols (Naples), II.2, 415-61
—— 1988. 'Le tavole finanziarie di Tauromenion', in D. Knoepfler (ed.), *Comptes et inventaires dans la cité grecque, actes du colloque de Neuchâtel en l'honneur de Jacques Tréheux* (Neuchâtel, Geneva), 155-90
—— 1989. 'Iscrizioni latine nuove e vecchie della Sicilia', *Epigraphica* 51: 161-96
—— 1999. *Sikelika: studi di antichità e di epigrafia della Sicilia antica*, Biblioteca di Quaderni Urbinati di Cultura Classica 8 (Pisa, Rome)
Maniscalco, L. & B. E. McConnell. 2003. 'The sanctuary of the divine Palikoi (Rocchichella di Mineo, Sicily): fieldwork from 1995-2001', *AJA* 107: 145-80
Mantovani, D. 2000. 'Aspetti documentali del processo criminale nella Repubblica: le *tabulae publicae*', *MEFR(A)* 112: 651-91

Marcone, A. 1997. *Storia dell'agricoltura romana. Dal mondo arcaico all'età imperiale* (Rome)

—— 1999. 'Introduzione', in A. Marcone (ed.), *Rostovtzeff e l'Italia* (Naples), 11-22

Marinone, N. 1949. *Cicerone. Il processo di Verre*, Collana di testi latini e greci (Verona)

—— 1950. *Quaestiones Verrinae. Cronologia del processo di Verre*, Università di Torino, Pubblicazioni della Facoltà di Lettere e Filosofia 2.3 (Turin)

Marrou, H.-I. 1977. 'Notice sur la vie et les travaux de M. Jérôme Carcopino', in *Hommage a la mémoire de Jérôme Carcopino* (Paris), 205-16

Martini, R. 1969. *Ricerche in tema di editto provinciale*, Università di Genova Fondazione Nobile Agostino Poggi 7 (Milan)

Maspero, H. 1905. *Les finances de l'Égypte sous les Lagides* (Paris)

Mazza, M. 1980. 'Recente prospettive sull'economia agraria siciliana in età ciceroniana', in *Atti del IV colloquium Tullianum, Palermo 28 settembre-2 ottobre 1979*, Ciceroniana 4 (Rome), 223-38

—— 1980-81. 'Economia e società nella Sicilia romana', *Kokalos* 26-27: 292-358

—— 1981. 'Terra e lavoratori nella Sicilia tardorepubblicana', in A. Giardina & A. Schiavone (eds), *Società romana e produzione schiavistica*, I, *l'Italia: insediamenti e forme economiche* (Rome, Bari), 19-49

Mazzarino, S. 1961. 'In margine alle "Verrine" per un giudizio storico sull'orazione "De Frumento"', in *Atti del primo congresso internazionale di studi ciceroniani* (Rome), II, 99-118

McDermott, W. C. 1977. 'TheVerrine jury', *RhM* 120: 64-75

Mellano, L. D. 1977. *Sui rapporti tra governatore provinciale e giudici locali alla luce delle Verrine*, Università di Genova Fondazione Nobile Agostino Poggi 13 (Milan)

Metzger, E. 1997. *A new outline of the Roman civil trial* (Oxford)

Meyer, E. A. 2004. *Legitimacy and law in the Roman world: tabulae in Roman belief and practice* (Cambridge)

Miller, S. G. 1978. *The prytaneion: its function and architectural form* (Berkeley)

Mitchell, T. N. 1986. *Cicero Verrines II.i* (Warminster)

Mitteis, L. & U. Wilcken. 1912. *Grundzüge und Chrestomathie des Papyruskunde*, 2 vols (Leipzig, Berlin)

Momigliano, A. 1955. 'M. I. Rostovtzeff', in *Contributo alla storia degli studi classici* (Rome), 341-54 (first publ. in *The Cambridge Journal* 7 (1954), 334-46)

—— 1975. 'La città antica di Fustel de Coulanges', in *Quinto contributo alla storia degli studi classici e del mondo antico*, 2 vols (Rome), I, 159-78 (first publ. in *Rivista storica italiana* 82.1 (1970), 81-98)

—— 1984. 'The rediscovery of Greek history in the eighteenth century: the case of Sicily', in *Settimo contributo alla storia degli studi classici e del mondo antico* (Rome), 133-53 (first publ. in R. Runte (ed.), *Studies in eighteenth-century culture* (Wisconsin 1979), IX, 167-87)

Mommsen, Th. 1892. *Droit public romain*, trans. P.-F. Girard, Manuel des Antiquités romaines 1-9, 9 vols (Paris)

—— 1899. *Römisches Strafrecht* (Leipzig)

—— 1907. *Droit pénal romain*, trans. J. Duquesne, Manuel des Antiquités romaines 17-19, 3 vols (Paris)

—— 1909a. 'Quinquagenta milia', *Gesammelte Schriften* VII. *Philologische Schriften* (Berlin), 788-91 (first publ. in *Hermes* 3 (1869), 467-68; 7 (1873), 366; 10 (1876), 472; 20 (1885), 317)

—— 1909b. 'Zahl- und Bruchzeichen', *Gesammelte Schriften* VII. *Philologische Schriften* (Berlin) 765-87 (first publ. in *Hermes*, 22 (1887), 596-614; 23 (1888), 152-56)

—— 1985. *Histoire romaine*, trans. C. Alexandre *et al.*, 2 vols (Paris)

Moreau, P. 1994. 'La mémoire fragile: falsification et destruction des documents publics au Ier siècle av. J.-C.', in S. Demougin (ed.), *La mémoire perdue, à la recherche des archives oubliées, publiques et privées, de la Rome antique* (Paris), 121-47

—— 2000. 'Quelques aspects documentaires de l'organisation du procès pénal républicain', *MEFR(A)* 112: 693-721

Motte, O. 1980. 'Camille Jullian, élève de Mommsen à l'Université de Berlin', *Ius commune* 9: 315-453

—— 1990. *Camille Jullian, les années de formation*, CEFR 124 (Rome)

Mucchielli, L. 1995. 'Aux origines de la nouvelle histoire en France: l'évolution intellectuelle et la formation du champ des sciences sociales (1880-1930)', *Revue de synthèse*, ser. 4, 1: 55-98

Naquet, H. 1875. *Des impôts indirects chez les Romains sous la République et sous l'Empire* (Paris)

Nenci, G. 1989. 'L'etnico *elumoi* e il ruolo del panico nell'alimentazione antica', *ASNP*, ser. 3, 19: 1255-65

Nicolet, C. 1988. *Rendre à César. Économie et société dans la Rome antique* (Paris)

—— 1989. '1889. Réflexions sur Fustel de Coulanges', *CRAI*, 721-26

—— 1993. 'Rome et les conceptions de l'État en France et en Allemagne au XIXe siècle', in W. Blockmans & J.-Ph. Genet (eds), *Visions sur le développement des États européens: théories et historiographies de l'État moderne*, CEFR 171 (Rome), 17-44

—— 2000a. 'Dîmes de Sicile, d'Asie et d'ailleurs', in *Censeurs et publicains* (Paris), 277-93 (first publ. in *L'Italie méridionale et le ravitaillement en blé de Rome et des centres urbains des debuts de la République romaine jusqu'au Haut-Empire*, Colloque du centre J. Bérard–Naples 1991 (Rome 1994) 215-27)

—— 2000b. 'Documents fiscaux et géographie dans la Rome ancienne', in *Censeurs et publicains* (Paris), 247-64 (first publ. in S. Demougin (ed.), *La mémoire perdue. À la recherche des archives oubliées, publiques et privées, de la Rome antique* (Paris 1994) 149-72)

—— 2003. *La fabrique d'une nation. La France entre Rome et les Germains* (Paris)

Nicolet, C. & C. Moatti (eds). 1998. *La mémoire perdue, recherches sur l'administration romaine* (Rome)

Nisbet, R. G. M. 1992. 'The orator and the reader: manipulation and response in Cicero's Fifth Verrine', in T. Woodman & J. G. F. Powell (eds), *Author and audience in Latin literature* (Cambridge), 1-17

Ochs, D. J. 1982. 'Rhetorical detailing in Cicero's Verrine Orations', *Central Studies Speech Journal* 33: 313-18

Omitowoju, R. 1997. 'Regulating rape: soap operas and self interest in the Athenian courts', in S. Deavy & K.F. Pierce (eds), *Rape in antiquity* (London), 1-24

Pantos, P. A. 1987. 'Sos[is?]', *Horos* 5: 155-61

Parker, V. 1998. 'τύραννος: the semantics of a political concept from Archilochus to Aristotle', *Hermes* 126: 145-72

Pearson, L. 1968. 'Cicero's debt to Demosthenes: the *Verrines*', *Pacific Coast Philology* 3: 49-54

—— 1976. *The art of Demosthenes* (Meisenheim am Glan)

Pelagatti, P. 1976. 'Sul parco archeologico di Camarina: le fase edilizie dell'abitato greco', *BA*, ser. 5, 61.1-2: 122-32

Pinzone, A. 1999. '*Civitates sine foedere immunes ac liberae*: a proposito di Cic. II *Verr.* III 6,13', *Mediterraneo antico. Economie, società, culture* 2.2: 463-95

—— 2000. 'Adolf Holm nel contesto della cultura siciliana', *Mediterraneo antico. Economie, società, culture* 3.1: 113-40

Platschek, J. 2001. 'Das *ius Verrinum* im Fall des Heraclius von Syrakus', *ZRG* 118: 234-63

Pritchard, R. T. 1969. 'Land tenure in Sicily in the first century BC', *Historia* 18: 545-56

—— 1970. 'Cicero and the *lex Hieronica*', *Historia* 19: 352-68

—— 1971. 'Gaius Verres and the Sicilian farmers', *Historia* 20: 224-38

—— 1972. 'Some aspects of first-century Sicilian agriculture', *Historia* 21: 646-60

—— 1975. '*Perpaucae Siciliae civitates*: notes on *Verr.* 2.3.6.13', *Historia* 24: 33-47

Prost, A. 1996. *Douze leçons sur l'histoire* (Paris)

Pugliese, G. 1947-49. *Il processo formulare,* 2 vols (Gènes)

—— 1948. 'Figure processuali ai confini tra *iudicia priuata* e *iudicia publica*', in *Studi in onore di Siro Solazzi* (Naples), 391-417

Ragab, H. 1980. *Contributions à l'étude du papyrus (Cyperus papyrus L.) et à sa transformation en support de l'écriture (papyrus des Anciens)* (Cairo)

Raskolnikoff, M. 1975. *La recherche soviétique et l'histoire économique et sociale du monde hellénistique et romain* (Strasbourg)

Rawson, E. 1985. *Intellectual life in the late Roman Republic* (Baltimore)

Reynolds, L. D. (ed.). 1983. *Texts and transmission, a survey of the Latin classics* (Oxford)

Rickman, G. 1980. *The corn supply of ancient Rome* (Oxford)

Riggsby, A. M. 1997. 'Did the Romans believe in their verdicts?', *Rhetorica* 15.3: 235-52

—— 2004. 'The rhetoric of character in the Roman courts', in J. G. F. Powell & J. J. Paterson (eds), *Cicero the advocate* (Oxford), 165-85

Rodger, A. 1996. 'Postponed business at Irni', *JRS* 86: 61-74

Rostovtzeff, M. I. 1900a. *s.v.* 'Conductor', in E. De Ruggiero, *Dizionario epigrafico di antichità romane* (Rome 1886-), II, 1, 578-97

—— 1900b. 'Dons de blé faits par les empereurs des IIe et IIIe siècles aux cités d'Asie Mineure', *BSAF*, 226-27.

—— 1910a. *s.v.* 'Kolonat', in J. Conrad (ed.), *Handworterbuch der Staatswissenschaften* (3rd edn, Iéna) 913-21

—— 1910b. *s.v.* 'Frumentum', in *RE* VII, 1, cols 126-87

—— 1910c. *Studien zur Geschichte des römischen Kolonates*, Archiv für Papyrusforschung, Beiheft 1 (Leipzig, Berlin)

—— 1941. *The social and economic history of the Hellenistic world*, 3 vols (Oxford)

Rotondi, G. 1912. *Leges publicae populi Romani* (Milan)

Russell, H. E. 1950. *Advancements in rank under the Roman Republic as a reward for the soldier and the public prosecutor* (unpublished dissertation, Bryn Mawr)

Salmeri, G. 1992. 'Ettore Pais e la Sicilia antica', in G. Salmeri, *Sicilia romana, storia e storiografia* (Catania), 97-123

Schmidlin, B. 1964. '"*Si uter uolet recuperatores dabo.*" Cicero *in Verrem* II, III, 35', *ZRG* 81: 191-211

Schulten, A. 1894. 'Die Landgemeinden im römischen Reich', *Philologus* 52: 630-70

—— 1897. 'Die *lex Manciana*, eine Afrikanische Domänenordnung', *Abhandlungen der königlichen Gesellschaft der Wissenschaften zu Göttingen*, Phil.-hist Klasse, n. F., 2, 3, 1-51

—— 1907. 'Die *lex Hadriana de rudibus agris* nach einer neue Inschrift', *Klio* 7: 188-212

Scramuzza, V. M. 1937. 'Roman Sicily', in T. Frank (ed.), *An economic survey of ancient Rome*, 6 vols (Baltimore 1933-40), III, 225-377

Scuderi, R. 1994. 'Il comportamento di Verre nell'orazione ciceroniana *De Suppliciis*. Oratoria politica e realtà storica', *RAL* 9.5: 119-43

—— 1996. 'La raffigurazione ciceroniana della Sicilia e dei suoi abitanti: un fattore ambientale per la condanna di Verre', in C. Stella & A. Valvo (eds), *Studi in onore di Albino Garzetti* (Brescia), 409-30

Shackleton Bailey, D. R. 1987. *M. Tulli Ciceronis, epistulae ad Atticum*, Bibliotheca scriptorum Graecorum et Romanorum Teubneriana, 2 vols (Stuttgart)

Shatzman, I. 1975. *Senatorial wealth and Roman politics*, Collection Latomus 142 (Brussels)

Sjöqvist, E. 1959. 'Morgantina: Hellenistic inkstands', *AJA* 63: 275-77

—— 1960. 'Excavations at Morgantina (Serra Orlando) 1959: preliminary report IV', *AJA* 64: 125-35

Soraci, C. 2003. '*Sicilia frumentaria*: contributi allo studio della Sicilia in epoca repubblicana', *Quaderni Catanesi di studi antichi e medievali*, n. s. 2: 289-401

Steel, C. E. W. 2001. *Cicero, rhetoric and empire* (Oxford)

—— 2004. 'Being economical with the truth: what really happened at Lampsacus', in J. G. F. Powell & J. J. Paterson (eds), *Cicero the advocate* (Oxford), 233-251

Stone, S. C., III. 2002. 'Sextus Pompeius, Octavianus, and Sicily', in A. Powell & K. Welch (eds), *Sextus Pompeius* (Swansea), 135-65

Stroh, W. 1975. *Taxis und Taktik. Die advokatische Dispositionskunst in Ciceros Gerichtsreden* (Stuttgart)

Sumner, G. V. 1973. *The orators in Cicero's 'Brutus': prosopography and chronology*, Phoenix Supp. 11 (Toronto)

Taylor, L. R. 1949. *Party politics in the age of Caesar* (Berkeley)

Thibault, F. 1888. *Les douanes chez les Romains* (Paris)

Thilo, R. M. 1980. *Der Codex accepti et expensi im römischen Recht* (Göttingen)

Thompson, L. A. 1962. 'The relation between provincial quaestors and their commanders-in-chief', *Historia* 11: 339-55

Thompson, S. M. 1999. *A central Sicilian landscape: settlement and society in the territory of ancient Morgantina (5000 BC–AD 50)* (diss. University of Virginia)

Vaggioli, M. A. 1997. 'Ricerche archeologiche e topografiche sull'*agora* di Segesta', in *Seconde giornate internazionali di studi sull'area elima*, 3 vols (Pisa, Gibellina), III, 1329-54

Vasaly, A. 1993. *Representations: images of the world in Ciceronian oratory* (Berkeley)

—— 2002. 'Cicero's early speeches', in J. M. May (ed.), *Brill's companion to Cicero: oratory and rhetoric* (Leiden), 71-111

Verbrugghe, G. P. 1972. 'Sicily 210-70 B.C.: Livy, Cicero and Diodorus', *TAPhA* 103: 535-59

Vergote, J. 1984. 'Dém. *shn*: *trapeza* "Banque"', *Mélanges Adolphe Gutbub* (Montpellier), 231-32

Vigié, A. 1882-83. 'Des douanes dans l'Empire romain', *Bulletin de la Société languedocienne de géographie* (Montpellier), 5 (1882), 465-503; 6 (1883), 5-57, 181-216, 527-574

von Sydow, W. 1984. 'Die hellenistischen Gebälke in Sizilien', *MDAI(R)* 91.2: 239-358

Waltzing, J.–P. 1895-1900. *Étude historique sur les corporations professionnelles chez les Romains depuis les origines jusqu'à la chute de l'Empire d'Occident*, 4 vols (Louvain)

Watson, A. 1965. *The law of obligations in the late Roman Republic* (Oxford)

Weber, M. 1891. *Die römische Agrargeschichte in ihrer Bedeutung für das Staats- und Privatrecht* (Stuttgart)

—— 1907. *La storia agraria romana in rapporto al diritto publico e privato*, in V. Pareto (ed.), *Biblioteca di storia economica* (Milan 1903-1929), II, 2, 509-705

Weische, A. 1972. *Ciceros Nachahmung der attischen Redner* (Heidelberg)

White, D. 1964. 'Demeter's Sicilian cult as a political instrument', *GRBS* 5: 261-79

Whittaker, C. R. 2000. 'Africa', in A. K. Bowman, P. Garnsey & D. Rathbone (eds), *The Cambridge Ancient History*, XI, *The High Empire A.D. 70-192* (Cambridge), 514-46

Wilcken, U. 1897. Review of Grenfell & Mahaffy (1896). *Deutsche Literaturzeitung*, col. 1015

—— 1899. *Griechische Ostraka aus Aegypten und Nubien*, 2 vols (Leipzig, Berlin)

Will, E. 1954. 'Trois quarts de siècle de recherche sur l'économie grecque antique', *Annales (ESC)* 9: 7-22

Wilson, P. J. 1991. 'Demosthenes 21 (*Against Meidias*): democratic abuse', *PCPhS* 37: 164-95

Wilson, R. J. A. 1990. *Sicily under the Roman Empire: the archaeology of a Roman province, 36 B.C.–A.D. 535* (Warminster)

—— 2000. 'Ciceronian Sicily: an archaeological perspective', in C. Smith & J. Serrati (eds), *Sicily from Aeneas to Augustus* (Edinburgh), 134-60

Wlassak, M. 1891. *Die römische Prozessgesetze, ein Beitrag zur Geschichte des Formularverfahrens* (Leipzig)

—— 1919. *Zum römischen Provinzialprozess*, Akademie der Wissenschaften in Wien, Philosophisch-historische Klasse, Sitzungsberichte 190, Band 4, Abhandlung (Vienna)

—— 1921. *Der Judicationsbefehl der römischen Prozesse, mit Beiträgen zur Scheidung des privaten und öffentlichen Rechtes*, Akademie der Wissenschaften in Wien, Philosophisch-historische Klasse, Sitzungsberichte 197, Band 4, Abhandlung (Vienna)

Wolff, J. G. 1997. '"Intertium", und keine Ende?', *BIDR* 100: 1-36

Wooten, C. W. 1977. 'Cicero's reactions to Demosthenes: a clarification', *CJ* 73: 37-43

—— 1983. *Cicero's Philippics and their Demosthenic model* (North Carolina)

Wörrle, M. 1975. 'Zwei neue griechische Inschriften aus Myra zur Verwaltung Lykiens in der Kaiserzeit', in J. Borchhardt (ed.), *Myra, ein lykische Metropole in antiker und byzantinischer Zeit* (Berlin), 254-86

Zangsmeisters, K. 1887. 'Enstehung der römischen Zahlzeichen', *Sitzungsberichte der königlich-preussischen Akademie der Wissenschaften zu Berlin* 2: 1011-28

Zielinski, Th. 1894. 'Verrina', *Philologus* 52: 248-94

Zoppi, C. 1996. 'Le cretule di Selinunte', in M.-F. Boussac & A. Invernizzi (eds), *Archives et sceaux du monde hellénistique*, BCH suppl. 29 (Paris), 327-40

GENERAL INDEX

by M. Leach

Page numbers in *italics* denote diagrams/illustrations. *n* = footnote. The number of the *RE* entry for individual Romans is included in order to identify individuals; Romans are listed by *nomen*.

INDEX LOCORUM

As a rule, ancient texts which are cited simply by name and without more specific reference are not listed in this index (but see General Index). Reference here to the note where the citation occurs does not preclude discussion in the main text, but is intended to facilitate location of the exact place on the page.

Literary texts

Papyrological texts